THE PRINCIPLES

OF THE

LAW OF CRIMES

IN

BRITISH INDIA

THE PRINCIPLES

OF THE

LAW OF CRIMES

IN

BRITISH INDIA

NAWAAB SYED SHAMSUL HUDA

GYAN

Published by

GYAN

Gyan Publishing House
5, Ansari Road
Daryaganj, New Delhi-110002
Phone: 011-47034999, 9811692060
E-mail: books@gyanbooks.com

Distribution Network
gyanbooks.com
India, USA, Canada, UK, Australia

ISBN: 978-93-7169-376-9 (PB)

First Published, 1919

2nd Impression 2025

Printed at: Gyan Press, Delhi.

THE PRINCIPLES OF THE LAW OF CRIMES IN BRITISH INDIA
Author: NAWAAB SYED SHAMSUL HUDA

THE PRINCIPLES

THE PRINCIPLES

OF THE

LAW OF CRIMES

IN

BRITISH INDIA

BY

SYED SHAMSUL HUDA

TABLE OF CONTENTS.

INDEX OF CASES CITED.

K

L

M

T

U

V

W

Z

LECTURE I.

INTRODUCTION.

THE subject of these lectures is the Principles of the Law of Crimes in British India. I shall first endeavour to explain to you what Crimes are. In common parlance we apply the word to acts that we consider worthy of serious condemnation. In legal phraseology Crime means any act which the law of the country visits with punishment, and in this sense it is synonymous with the word 'Offence.' In other words it is an act committed or omitted in violation of public law forbidding or commanding it. Crime defined

According to Bentham, 'if the question relates to a system of laws already established, offences are whatever the legislature has prohibited for good or for bad reasons. If the question relates to a theoretical research for the discovery of the best possible laws according to the principles of utility, we give the name of offence to every act which we think ought to be prohibited by reason of some evil which it produces or tends to produce.'

In British India, where the whole criminal law is codified, Crime means an act punishable by the Indian Penal Code or other penal statutes. This, though a simple and perfectly accurate definition, is of very little help in bringing home to you a true conception of the essential attributes of a Crime. I shall, therefore, endeavour to explain to you the elementary ideas involved in the word and enumerate the peculiarities that distinguish it from Civil injuries.

Wrongs.

There are certain acts which the large majority of civilised people look upon with disapprobation, as tending to reduce the sum total of human happiness, which is the ultimate aim of all laws. These we call Wrongs, such, for instance, as lying, gambling, cheating, stealing, homicide, etc. The evil tendencies of these acts widely differ in degree. Some of them are not considered sufficiently serious for law's notice. These we only disapprove. We call them mere moral Wrongs. Moral Wrongs are checked to a great extent by social laws and laws of religion. There are other more serious wrongs which the law takes notice of, either—

(*a*) for punishment, *i.e.*, infliction of pain upon the wrong-doer, or,

(*b*) for indemnification, *i.e.*, for making good the loss to the person injured by the Wrong.

Crimes and Civil injuries distinguished

Wrongs dealt with under the first head are called Crimes, those under the second head are called Civil injuries.

According to Blackstone, Crimes are public wrongs and affect the whole community; Civil injuries are private wrongs and concern individuals. Public and private wrongs are, however, not exclusive of one another, for what concerns individuals must necessarily concern the community of which the individual is a unit, and similarly everything that affects or concerns the community, must also concern and affect the individuals that form that community.

According to Austin, an offence which is pursued at the discretion of the injured party and his representatives, is a Civil injury; an offence which is pursued by the Sovereign and his subordinates is a Crime. This is a distinction not of substance but of procedure, and so far as the Indian Criminal Law is concerned, there are a number of offences which cannot be pursued except by the injured party. These lie on the border-line between Crimes and Civil injuries. For the true basic distinction between Crimes and Civil injuries we must look to the principles upon which civilised communities have selected some wrongs for retributive and others for remedial justice. I do not think in any country any principles were definitely laid down before making the selection, but this itself does not negative the existence of the principles. We often act in accordance with principles without being conscious that we are so acting. The general agreement of civilised countries, as shown by the result of the selection, strongly points to the existence of common principles leading to common results. It is only by a process of analytical reasoning that we can get at these principles.

In this world the interests of individuals often clash. Every right vested in one imposes a corresponding obligation on others. These others sometimes comprise the rest of the world and sometimes particular individuals only. Every obligation is a fetter and a restraint. Human mind is ordinarily so constituted as to be impatient of all such fetters. It is not, therefore, enough for the legislature only to define rights and lay down bounds within which they are to be confined, but it is also necessary to provide checks on this tendency to transgress. This tendency is sometimes weak and sometimes strong, and accordingly the checks provided by the legislature vary in their strength also.

The strongest check is the infliction of pain or punishment as it is generally called. This again varies in severity according to the value of the right to be protected and the amount of misery that the violation of the right involves, as also according to the strength of the tendency to be counteracted, which again varies according to the advantage to be gained by the transgression, and according to the nature and temperament of the people against whom the law is directed.

In Civil cases the punishment—I am using the word in its widest sense—is of the mildest nature and the law is satisfied with restitution or compensation in full and only penalises the wrongdoer by mulcting him in costs. Punishment in its true sense and as understood in Criminal Law is, however reserved for the more serious transgressions, specially those the effect of which goes beyond the individual and extends to society at large. In these cases full restitution to the wronged individual and to society is often impossible and the law instead of proceeding on remedial lines punishes the offender partly as a measure of prevention and partly of retribution. Punishment, however, to be effective as a measure of prevention deals with deliberate acts directed by an evil mind, and thereby aims at the eradication of the evil will. Where there is no evil will, the act, injurious though it be, does not evoke the feeling of resentment nor calls for vengeance from society or individual. In such cases society feels no concern and the individual is more anxious for restitution than retribution.

From what I have said above it follows that Crimes are comparatively graver wrongs than Civil injuries. They are graver because they constitute greater interference with the happiness of others, and affect the well-being not only of particular individuals but of the whole community considered in its social aggregate capacity. They are graver because the impulse to commit them is often very strong, or because the advantage to be gained by the wrongful act and the facility with which it can be accomplished are often so great or the risk of detection so small, that human nature inclined to take the shortest cut to happiness is likely to be tempted often to commit such wrongs. They are graver also because they are ordinarily deliberate acts directed by an evil mind and hurtful to society by the bad example they set. Being graver wrongs they are singled out for punishment with the object partly of making an example of the criminal, partly of deterring him from repeating the same act, partly of reforming him by eradicating the evil will, and partly of satisfying society's feeling of vengeance which the act is supposed to evoke. Civil injuries, on the other hand, are the less serious wrongs, the effect of which is supposed to be confined mainly to individuals, and in which none of the graver elements which mark out a criminal act are present. Sometimes a criminal act, which is essentially a personal wrong, is selected for punishment, not because of its gravity or of its effect on society, but because the injury to individual is of a nature that damage cannot be assessed on any reasonable basis or the pain caused to the individual wronged is wholly disproportionate to any pecuniary loss suffered by him. Once the selection of wrongful acts for punishment is made, or in other words once an act is labelled as a Crime certain subsidiary distinctions follow. In Criminal cases having regard to the severity of the sanction the defendant is treated with greater indulgence than in Civil cases. The procedure as well as the rules of evidence are modified in order to reduce to a minimum the risk of an innocent person being punished. The accused in a criminal case is not called upon to prove anything. He is not bound to make any statement to the Court, he is not compellable to answer any question or to give any explanation. It is left to the prosecution to prove the existence of all the facts necessary to constitute the offence charged, and lastly, if there is any reasonable doubt regarding the guilt of a person charged with a Crime, the benefit of it is always given to the accused. It is said that it is better that ten guilty men should escape than that one innocent man should suffer. The continental law is slightly less indulgent to the accused than the English law, in so far as it allows an accused person to be interrogated but the general principle holds good. Crimes and Civil injuries are generally dealt with in different tribunals.

As I have said before, in the case of a Civil injury, the only object aimed at is to indemnify the individual wronged and to put him as far as practicable in the position he was, before the wrong was done. Consequently in all civil suits the injured party alone or his successors can pursue the wrong-doer and parties may always by mutual consent settle their differences, whereas in criminal cases generally the State alone, as the protector of the rights of its subjects, pursues the offender and often does so in spite of the injured party. There are exceptions to the rule, but what I have said is correct with regard to a large majority of cases.

Malice.

I have already told you that an act to be criminal must ordinarily be an act done with malice or criminal intent. This is called the condition of criminality, or according to some jurists, the state of imputability, and it includes both positive and negative states of the mind, such as intention, will, knowledge, negligence, rashness, heedlessness, etc. It may be said generally that there is no Crime without an evil intent. The same act is either a Crime or a Civil injury according as it is done with or without such an evil intent.

The following illustration taken from Section 378 of the Indian Penal Code will bring out the distinction more clearly. *A* finds a ring belonging to *Z* on a table in the house which *Z* occupies. Here the ring is in *Z's* possession, and if *A* removes it dishonestly, *i.e.*, with the intention of causing wrongful gain to himself or wrongful loss to the owner, he commits theft and may be sentenced under Section 379, Indian Penal Code, to imprisonment for three years. But if *A* does the same act in good faith believing that the ring belonging to *Z* is his own and takes it out of *Z's* possession, *A* not taking dishonestly commits no Crime, but commits a Civil wrong for which he may be compelled to make restitution. It is the existence of the criminal intent in the one case and its absence in the other that makes one an offence and the other a mere Civil wrong. In a Civil suit for the recovery of his property *Z* will be entitled to relief irrespective of any question of intention on the part of *A*. But without proof of criminal intent a Criminal Court cannot punish the wrong-doer. There must be a mind at fault before there can be a Crime. This is the doctrine of *mens rea* which forms, as it were, the corner-stone of the whole Criminal Jurisprudence. I shall revert to this subject later on.

A crime, though it involves in most cases an injury to one or more individuals, is noticed by law not for the purpose of setting right such individual injury, but to protect Society from its evil consequences. I have criticised the somewhat broad statement that Crimes are public wrongs and affect the whole community, whilst Civil injuries are private wrongs and affect individuals. In a case of theft, for instance, no one suffers more than the individual whose property is stolen, and it is hardly correct to say that the community suffers more than the individual wronged, and yet when a case of theft is brought before a Criminal Court, the injury to the individual is merged in the injury to Society and the gravity of the wrong is judged not so much by the extent of loss caused to the individual, but among others by considerations of the age, experience and previous conduct of the accused, the circumstances under which he committed the act, the temptations that were in his way, and the frequency of such offences in the locality.

When again upon the same facts the injured party asks for relief in a Civil action, the facts being established, almost the sole consideration that arises in passing the decree is the amount of loss sustained by the plaintiff. It will perhaps be generally correct to say that so far as consequences are concerned a wrongful act, whether amounting to a Crime or a mere Civil injury, is a wrong both against the individual and Society, and it is a Civil injury or a Crime, according as it is viewed with reference to its consequence upon the individual directly affected thereby, or with reference to its consequences upon Society. I do not mean to say that all wrongful acts are both Civil injuries and Crimes, although this is so in a large majority of cases. There are cases in which there is very slight injury to any individual and the wrong is a wrong mainly against Society. Suicide is one such instance. Bigamy by one married party with the consent of the other may be taken as another such instance. If *A* allows *B* his wife to go through a ceremony of marriage with *C*, who is fully cognisant of *B* being a married woman, *A* can hardly complain of an injury to himself but Society is scandalised and *A's* consent or connivance will not justify the act. All cases of mere attempts must, from their very nature, be outside the scope of Civil law and can only come under the purview of the law of Crimes. The classification of wrongs into Crimes and Civil injuries often *leads* to a difference in the view we take of their consequences as affecting Society or individuals, instead of the classification being based and determined by them.

Essentials of a Crime.

When an act constitutes a serious menace to the peace and happiness of Society and at the same time causes an infringement of individual rights, not altogether light or trivial, it affords grounds for Civil action and is also punishable as a Crime. When, however, its effect upon Society is inappreciable in comparison to the loss it entails upon a particular individual, it is merely treated as a Civil injury. When, on the other hand, the effect of such an act upon Society is great and upon individuals inappreciable, it is treated merely as a Crime.

Even when a wrong is treated as one against Society and is pursued with the object of *punishing* the wrong-doer the injury to the individual is not always ignored, and we have in Sections 517, 545 and 546 of the Criminal Procedure Code a recognition of the individual wrong even in Crimes. Section 545 provides that a Criminal Court may, when passing judgment, order the whole or any part of a fine recovered from an accused person to be applied—

(*a*) in defraying expenses properly incurred in the prosecution;

(*b*) in compensation for the injury caused by the offence committed where substantial compensation is, in the opinion of the Court, recoverable by Civil suit.

Section 517 provides for making restitution to any person deprived of any property by means of a Criminal offence. Section 546 provides that any compensation so awarded is to be taken into account in assessing damages in a Civil suit. These represent attempts to combine retributive with remedial justice and are founded on sound reason and common sense.

A case of defamation is a good example of an act which is both a Civil injury and a Crime. Such an act is not only a serious menace to the peace and well being of Society, but is a serious wrong to the person defamed. The Criminal Court will, to protect Society, punish the offender and the Civil Court with equal readiness will decree money compensation. In a Civil Court the amount of damage will be assessed with reference to the position of the party defamed and the amount of loss which he has suffered in consequence of the libel. These considerations will, however, play a very unimportant part in determining the amount of imprisonment or fine to be inflicted on the accused by a Criminal Court. There the more important consideration would be the intelligence of the accused person, the extent of his appreciation of the gravity of the wrongful act, the motive for the act and other considerations connected more intimately with the accused and his mental condition than with the complainant.

As an example of an act in which the wrong to an individual plays a very minor part and the really serious wrong is the injury to Society, I may refer to offences against public tranquillity. It is almost impossible in those cases to reduce to pounds shillings and pence the injury to individual, and justice proceeding on remedial lines will be wholly unsuited to meet cases of this nature.

On the other hand as an example of a Civil injury, pure and simple, we may take an ordinary case of a breach of contract. *A* borrows money from *B* promising to pay within a year. *A* fails to keep his promise. This gives rise to a Civil injury for which *B* can obtain adequate compensation in a Civil action. Although it may be said that *A's* action is also injurious to Society at large as setting a bad example, which, if generally followed, may become a matter of public concern, but in vast majority of such cases the breach of promise by the debtor would be found to be due to his inability to pay and would not be attributable to any evil intent. It would be wrong to treat such an act as a crime, because, in the first place, money compensation is an adequate remedy which will fully indemnify the individual wronged, and the costs generally allowed against the unsuccessful party in a Civil action will cause sufficient pain to deter *A* from making such a breach in the future if he can help it. There may, however, be cases of mere Civil injury, which it may be necessary to punish as a Crime, either because the inconvenience caused is so great that money compensation is not adequate, or if adequate is obtainable under conditions so harassing as to be prohibitive, or because the chances of detection are so small that unless punished as a Crime great many others may be tempted to act in the same way and take the risk, or because the evil has become so widespread as to become a matter of public concern. You will find in Sections 490, 491 and 492 of the Indian Penal Code, examples of Crimes which in reality are mere instances of breach of contract. The principles, which I have tried to deduce from the usual classification of wrongs into Crimes and Civil injuries, are not, however, of universal application and exceptions will perhaps readily occur to you.

It may also be pointed out that " the penal law of ancient communities is not the law of Crimes ; it is the law of Wrongs. The person injured proceeds against the wrong-doer by an ordinary Civil action and recovers compensation in the shape of money damages if he succeeds." (In the passage I have quoted the word ' wrong ' is used in its technical legal sense in which it is equivalent with tort, but I have, in these lectures, used the expression in a broader sense.) In support of this view we may cite the ancient practice of compounding murder by payment of " blood-money " to the heirs of the person killed. In Muhammadan countries in which the Muhammadan law is strictly followed even now a homicide may be purged by payment of ' blood-money ' to the relations of the deceased provided they agree.

The idea that all Crimes are wrongs against the State or aggregate community, and that it is the proper function of the State to pursue Crimes without reference to the person wronged, is a conception of comparatively modern growth and with reference to modern criminal jurisprudence, it would be perfectly correct to say that in all serious offences it is the State that prosecutes the offender irrespective of the wishes of the individual injured and is also entitled to drop the prosecution at its will. Upon an examination of the Code of Criminal Procedure, you will observe that the proportion of compoundable offences, to those that are non-compoundable, is very small, and the right of ' compounding ' is limited to comparatively minor offences in which individual injury is more largely involved. (S. 345 Cr. P. C.)

Essentials of a Crime.

Essentials of Crime.

Having tried to explain the principal points of difference between a Civil injury and a Crime, I shall now proceed to deal with the elements necessary to constitute a Crime. The following elements must be present in every Crime :—

(1) A human being under a legal obligation to act in a particular way and a fit subject for the infliction of appropriate punishment ;
(2) An evil intent on the part of such a human being ;
(3) An act committed or omitted in furtherance of such an intent ;
(4) An injury to another human being or to Society at large by such act.

Examples are not wanting in old legal institutions of punishment inflicted on animals for injury done. This is by no means to be wondered. Criminal law in its earlier stages was largely dominated by the idea of retribution. This was in accordance with human nature. When a child falls on the ground and hurts itself, you often kick the ground to console it. Its sentiments of vengeance is thereby satisfied. The feeling is not wholly confined to children. The story of Llewelyn and his dog is an instance in point. In that stage of development when Society has not taken away from the individual the right to punish injuries done to himself, punishment will not be, from the very nature of things, always confined to human beings. There will also be a stage when Society has just stepped into the place of the individual, when it will do for the individual what the individual was doing for himself, and we read of laws for the punishment of animals and even of inanimate things.

We read of Jewish laws in which Moses gave the command "If an ox gore a man or a woman that they die, then the ox shall be surely stoned and his flesh shall not be eaten; but the owner of the ox shall be quit." The mediæval lawgivers of Europe carried these commands into laws and administered them with all the ceremonials of a modern Law Court. The following few instances taken from Baring Gould's Curiosities of olden Times might interest the student of legal history:— Baring Gould's 'Curiosities of olden Times.'

'A bull has caused the death of a man, the brute is seized and imprisoned; a lawyer is appointed to plead for the criminal, another is counsel for the prosecution, witnesses are bound over, the case is heard, sentence is given by the judge declaring the bull guilty of *deliberate and wilful murder* and accordingly it must suffer the penalty of hanging or burning.'

'The first time an ass is found in a cultivated field not belonging to its master, one of its ears is cropped. If it commits the same offence again, it loses the second ear.'

Here are a few concrete instances with dates:—

"A.D. 1266.—A pig was burned near Paris for having devoured a child.

"A.D. 1386.—A judge condemned a sow to be mutilated in its legs and head and then to be hung, for having lacerated and kicked a child. It was executed in the Square, dressed in man's clothes.

"A.D. 1389.—A horse was tried at Dijon on information given by Magistrates of Montbar and condemned to death for having kicked a man."

Even an appeal on behalf of the delinquent beast was not an uncommon thing in those days.

A human being.

In Athens an axe or stone that killed any one by accident was cast beyond the border, and the English law was only repealed in comparatively recent years (1846) 9 & 10 Vict., C. 62, which made a cart-wheel, a tree or a beast, that killed a man forfeit to the State for the benefit of the poor.

In the course of development of legal and juristic ideas these primitive methods have disappeared. Even now vicious animals are destroyed, but the action is preventive and not punitive. When an animal causes an injury we hold the owner of the animal responsible civilly or criminally for such injury. The punishment is not for what the animal has done, but for the omission on the part of the owner to take proper care of his own property and thereby to prevent mischief to others.

A human being 'under a legal obligation to act' and 'capable of being punished' would, by the first restriction, exclude an outlaw who is placed outside the protection and restriction of law. Happily outlawry as an institution has ceased to exist. The second restriction excludes corporations from the operation of the Criminal law. You may punish individuals forming the corporation but that is a different matter. A corporation as such has neither a 'soul to be damned nor a body to be kicked.' A corporation may, however, be punished, for *quasi*-criminal acts, with a fine. These are more of the nature of Civil wrongs but classified as Crimes on grounds of policy. To meet these exceptions I have used the expression '*a fit subject for the infliction of appropriate punishment.*' I shall deal with this subject more fully later on.

The next and by far the most important essential of a Crime is *mens rea* or a criminal design.

In dealing with the difference between a Civil injury and a Crime I have just touched upon this point, but it deserves to be treated at great detail as it really is the corner stone of the whole Criminal Jurisprudence. Austin quoting from Feurbach says, "the application of a Criminal law supposes that the will of the party was determined positively or negatively; that this determination was the cause of a criminal fact. The reference of the fact as effect, to the determination of the will as cause, settles and fixes the legal character of the latter." *Actus non facit reum nisi mens sit rea* (the act itself does not make a man guilty unless his intentions were so) is a well-known legal maxim from which follows the other proposition *actus me invito factus non set meus actus* (an act done by me against my will is not my act). It is this requisite of a Crime that introduces the question of will, intention, motive, malice and various other states of mind. It also brings in questions of compulsion, mistake, insanity, drunkenness, infancy, idiocy and other conditions of mind precluding imputability or what is more commonly called criminal responsibility and which you will find are provided for in Chapter IV of the Indian Penal Code.

When you have got a human being and an evil intent, these two are not sufficient to constitute a Crime. The law does not punish a mere criminal intent. "The thought of man," said Brian, C.J., "is not triable, for the Devil himself knoweth not the thought of man." The criminal intent must manifest itself in some voluntary act or omission. An omission to be punishable must be in breach of a legal duty.

If one allows his wife or young children to die of starvation he commits a crime, because the law casts on individuals the obligation to maintain their wives and young children.

If you examine omissions that are not punishable and those that are, you will, I am sure, be startled at what you would consider a great anomaly. It seems to me that jurists and lawyers have taken an unduly restricted view of our duty to our fellowmen.

Your neighbour, for instance, is dying of starvation. Your granary is full. There is no law that requires you to help him out of your plenty. You are standing on the bank of a tank. A woman is filling her pitcher. All on a sudden she gets an epileptic fit. You may, with a clean legal conscience, allow her to die. You need not raise your little finger to save her.

With the growth of humanitarian ideas the conception of one's duty to others will, I am sure, gradually expand. Saadi, the great Persian poet, gave vent to his conception in the following words:—

"If you see a blind man proceeding towards a well,
If you are silent you commit a crime."

This was in the 13th century, and we must confess that we have moved rather slowly in this direction since. The world has become old and the answer is still the same—"Am I my brothers' keeper?"

Given, a human being, an evil intent and an act in furtherance of such intent you require an injury to another human being or to Society at large of the nature I have already discussed, to complete a criminal offence.

When an offence is committed it leads to the arrest of the offender, his trial and ultimate punishment. What acts constitute an offence and their appropriate punishment are matters dealt with in the substantive penal law, the trial and the determination of punishment in any particular case are matters concerning the law of Procedure. The principles of the law of Crimes mainly arise in connection with the substantive law. The substantive law of Crimes in India is to be found in the Indian Penal Code and the law of Procedure, in the Criminal Procedure Code and in the Evidence Act. There are some special laws which I need not notice here. For the sake of brevity I shall hereafter refer to the Indian Penal Code simply as the Code.

LECTURE II.

I. Capacity to commit Crimes.

I have told you in my introductory lecture that for a crime you first require a human being under a legal obligation to act in a particular way, a fit subject for the infliction of appropriate punishment. I have also told you that the last restriction would exclude corporations. They would also be excluded by the condition that *mens rea* is essential to constitute a crime. The question of the capacity of a corporation to commit a crime and its liability to be punished for a criminal act may be conveniently discussed at this stage. The liability of individual members of a corporate body to be punished for individual part taken in committing an offence is quite distinct from this question. Strictly speaking a corporation cannot be guilty of a crime, because in the first place a corporation as such cannot have a guilty mind. You cannot attribute malice to a body corporate. There is also the further difficulty that imprisonment which is the ordinary punishment for a crime cannot be enforced against a corporation. It would be atrocious to send a man to jail because he was the member of a corporate body which by majority did a criminal act, although possibly that particular member may have disapproved of the action. There are, however, a large class of cases partaking more of the nature of mere civil injury, which for reasons of policy and administrative convenience have been classed as offences and singled out for punishment. These are cases where certain acts are absolutely forbidden whether done

Corporation.

Individual liability.

Imputability.

Punishment.

Quasi-Criminal Cases.

with good or evil intention, and cases where the wrong is not sufficiently serious to call for imprisonment or any other kind of corporal punishment.

The Code does not define a "Corporation," but only lays down that the word 'person' includes any company or association or body of persons whether incorporated or not (Section 11). A corporation is an artificial or juridical person established for preserving in perpetual succession certain rights which if conferred on natural person only would fail in process of time. It is composed of individuals united under a common name the members of which succeed each other, so that the body continues to be the same notwithstanding the change of the individuals who compose it, and is for certain purposes considered a natural person. A corporation viewed in reference to its capacity for crime is a collection of persons or a single individual endowed by law with a separate existence as an artificial being.

Corporation defined.

When I say that a corporation cannot have a *mens rea* I do not mean to suggest that individual members of a corporation cannot entertain a criminal intent, but that only makes its individual members indictable.

From what I have stated above regarding the non-existence of *mens rea*, it follows that a corporation as such could not be guilty of treason or of felony or of perjury or offence against the person or of riot or malicious wrong. In an American case, Weston, C.J., stated the law thus: 'A corporation is created by law for certain beneficial purposes. It can neither commit a crime nor misdemeanour by any positive or

Cannot commit treason or felony.

affirmative act, or incite others to do so, as a corporation. While assembled at a corporate meeting, a majority may by vote, entered upon their records, require an agent to commit a battery; but if he does, it cannot be regarded as a corporate act for which the corporation can be indicted. It would be stepping aside altogether from their corporeal powers. If indictable as a corporation for an offence thus indicated by them, the innocent dissenting minority would become equally amenable to punishment with the guilty majority. Such only as take part in the measure should be prosecuted either as principals, or as aiding and abetting, or procuring an offence to be committed, according to its character or magnitude.' In an annonymous case Lord Holt is

Earlier cases. reported to have laid down generally that a corporation as such is not indictable at all. There are, however, modern cases which go to negative the proposition so broadly laid down and as I have stated before there are *quasi*-criminal offences the essence of which is not the existence of a criminal intent as the existence of an injury to the public or individual. Generally it may be stated that where an offence is punishable by imprisonment or corporal punishment you cannot hold a corporation liable for such an offence. It is obvious that you can neither hang nor imprison nor transport nor whip nor send to reformatory, a corporation. You may only punish a corporation by levying a fine. It may be urged that where an offence can be punished at the option of the Court by fine only, the mere existence of a power to punish otherwise than by infliction of a fine, should not make it impossible to punish a corporation in such cases. It may be answered as to this argument that the existence of power to imprison implies a capacity in the offender to suffer imprisonment. The matter, however, may be based on a broader principle, namely, that where an offence is punishable by imprisonment it is an indication that it is strictly a criminal offence. Generally offences punishable with imprisonment involve a *mens rea*. The offences of which a corporation may be indicted are generally offences against municipal laws or offences of a *quasi*-criminal nature not involving *mens rea*. In such cases very often penalty is inflicted not by way of punishment but by way of compensation for the breach of a duty imposed by a statute. It has been held, for instance, that indictment will lie against a corporation for not repairing a road, a bridge, or a wharf, where by statute or prescription it is bound so to do, or for disobedience to an order of Justices for the construction of works in pursuance of a statute. In England in *R.* vs. *Great North of England Railway* (9 Q.B., p. 315), it was ruled that an indictment lay at common law against an incorporated Railway Company for cutting through and obstructing a high way in a manner not conformable to the powers conferred on it by Acts.

Non-feasance and Misfeasance.

It was at one time thought that a corporation is indictable only for non-feasance but is not indictable for mere misfeasance. The case mentioned above overthrows the distinction, and it seems now to be settled that a charge of trespass or of a nuisance would lie against a corporation.

Later cases.

It was held in a number of English cases that a corporation aggregate may be indicted by their corporate name for breaches of public duty whether in the nature of non-feasance, such as the non-repair of highways or bridges, which it is their duty to repair, or of misfeasance, such as the obstruction of a highway in a manner not authorised by the Act of Parliament. A corporation may also be indicted by its corporate name and fined for a libel published by its orders.

I shall now draw your attention to some of the more important English cases bearing on this point :—

(1) In *Reg.* vs. *Birmingham and Gloucester Railway Company* (1842, 3 Q.B., p. 223), the indictment was for disobedience of an order of Justices whereby the defendants were directed to make certain arches pursuant to certain provisions contained in the statute ; it was argued on the authority of a dictum of Lord Holt in an annonymous case (12 Mod. p. 559), that a corporation is not indictable but the particular members of it are. Patterson J. reviewed the earlier cases and held that a corporation may be indicted for breach of a duty imposed upon it by law, though not for a felony, or for crimes involving personal violence, as for riots or assaults. Reference was made to *Reg*. vs. *Gardner* (1 Cowp. 79), in which an objection that a corporation could not be rated to the poor, because the remedy by imprisonment upon failure of distress was impossible, was considered by the Court to be of no weight, though it was conceded that there might be some difficulty in enforcing the remedy. It was pointed out that the proper mode of proceeding against a corporation to enforce the remedy by indictment, is by distress infinite to compel appearance.

(2) In *Reg.* vs. *The Great North of England Railway Company* (1846, 9 Q.B., p. 315), the defendant company was charged with having cut through a carriage road with the railway, and of having carried the road over the railway by a bridge not satisfying the statutory provisions. Here again it was argued on the dictum of Holt, C.J., that a corporation was not indictable. The points urged were—

(*a*) that a corporation may be indicted for a non-feasance but not for a misfeasance;

(*b*) that the remedy against a corporation was unnecessary as individual members of it could be made liable.

On the first point Lord Denman, C.J., in delivering the judgment of the Court, observed—

"The question is, whether an indictment will lie at common law against a corporation for misfeasance, it being admitted, in conformity with undisputed decisions, that an indictment may be maintained against a corporation for non-feasance. All the preliminary difficulties, as to the service and execution of processes, the mode of appearing and pleading, and enforcing judgment, are by this admission swept away. But the argument is, that for a wrongful act a corporation is not amenable to an indictment, though for a wrongful omission it undoubtedly is; assuming in the first place, that there is a plain and obvious distinction between the two species of offence. No assumption can be more unfounded. Many occurrences may be easily conceived, full of annoyance and danger to the public, and involving blame in some individual or some corporation, of which the most acute person could not clearly define the cause, or ascribe them with more correctness to mere negligence in providing safeguards or to an act rendered improper by nothing but the want of safeguards. If *A* is authorised to make a bridge with parapets, but makes it without them, does the offence consist in the construction of the unsecured bridge, or in the neglect to secure it? But, if the distinction were always easily discoverable, why should a corporation be liable for the one species of offence and not for the other? The startling incongruity of allowing the exemption is one strong argument against it. The law is often entangled in technical embarrassments; but there is none here. It is as easy to charge one person, or a body corporate, with erecting a bar across a public road as with the non-repair of it; and they may as well be compelled to pay a fine for the act as for the omission."

Regarding the case of *R.* vs. *Birmingham and Gloucester Railway Company*, the learned Judge pointed out that though that was a case of non-feasance only, the Court did not intend to lay down that non-feasance was the only disobedience to the law for which a corporation was punishable by indictment.

With reference to the second contention that this remedy is not required, because the individuals who concur in voting the order, or in executing the work, may be made answerable for it by criminal proceedings, the learned Judge pointed out with great force that 'the public would know nothing of the former; and the latter, if they can be identified, are commonly persons of the lowest rank, wholly incompetent to make any reparation for the injury, and that therefore there would be no effectual means of checking an oppressive exercise of power for the purpose of gain, except the remedy by an indictment against those who truly commit it.'

(3) In *Pharmaceutical Society* vs. *London and Provincial Supply Association* (5 App. Cas., 857) the offence charged was that of keeping an open shop for the sale of poisons against the terms of the statute which prohibited the exposure for sale of medical poisons except by properly qualified '*persons*.' The shop belonged to the defendant corporation. The principal share-holder was not a person holding a certificate, and therefore not a person authorised to exercise the business of pharmaceutical chemists. The actual sale was, however, conducted by a duly registered pharmaceutical chemist. This, it was contended, did not affect the case, the offence charged being that of keeping an open shop for the sale of poisons and it was argued that the corporation was a person within the meaning of the statute. The case came ultimately before the House of Lords, and it was there laid down that whether the word 'person' used in a statute included a corporation or not depended upon the context and the subject-matter, and that having regard to the aims and objects of that particular statute, it must be held that the word 'person' was not meant to include an artificial person. Judgment was accordingly entered against the plaintiff. "In such a question of

construction," said Lord Selborne, "it does seem to me to be best to remember the principle, that the liberty of the subject ought not to be held to be abridged any further than the words of the statute, considered with a proper regard to its objects, may require." This was subsequently made clear and in Section 2 of the Interpretation Act of 1889 (52 and 53 Vict., C. 63) it was laid down that in the construction of every enactment relating to an offence punishable on indictment or on summary conviction, the expression 'person' shall, unless the contrary intention appears, include a body corporate. No such saving words are used in Section 11 of the Indian Penal Code, but I apprehend that in construing the various sections of the Indian Penal Code the principle of interpretation laid down by Lord Selborne would be followed.

(4) In the case of *R.* vs. *Tyler* (1891, 2 Q.B., p. 588) Lord Justice Bowen gave strong reasons for overruling the contention that no criminal proceedings can be taken against a company. He thought it was contrary to sound sense and reason that such a technical objection should succeed. 'Where, for instance,' said the learned Judge, 'a statute creates a duty upon individual persons, it would be a strange result if the duty could be evaded by those persons forming themselves into a joint stock company. The point becomes still more incapable of argument where the statute prescribes the duty in the company itself. How can disobedience to the enactment by the company be otherwise dealt with? The directors or officers of the company, who are really responsible

for the neglect of the company to comply with the statutory requirements, might not be struck at by the statute, and there would be no way of enforcing the law against a disobedient company, unless there were in such cases a remedy by way of indictment. It may, therefore, I think, be taken that where a duty is imposed upon a company in such a way that a breach of the duty amounts to a disobedience of the law, then, if there is nothing in the statute either expressly or impliedly to the contrary, a breach of the statute is an offence which can be visited upon the company by means of an indictment.' In support of his views the learned Judge relied on the ruling of Patterson J. in *R.* vs. *Birmingham and Gloucester Railway Company*, but as regards the *dictum* in that case that the liability in the case of a corporation was limited to cases of non-feasance only, the learned Judge preferred to follow the decision in *R.* vs. *Great North of England Railway Company*, to which I have already referred.

The learned Judge also referred to the ruling of Cockburn, C.J., in *Pharmaceutical Society* vs. *London and Provincial Supply Association* (5 App. Cas., 857), where it was pointed out that although a corporation cannot be indicted for treason or felony, it was established by the case of *Reg.* vs. *Birmingham and Gloucester Railway Company*, that an incorporated company might be indicted for non-feasance in omitting to perform a duty imposed by the statute—such as that of making arches to connect lands severed by the defendants' railway. It was also pointed out in the same case that *Reg.* vs. *Great North of England Railway*

Company, was an authority for holding that an incorporated company could be indicted for misfeasance—as in cutting through and obstructing a highway, though they could not be indicted for treason or felony, or offences against the person. Upon a review of all the previous cases the learned Judge thought it was sound common sense and good law that in the ordinary case of a duty imposed by statute, if the breach of the statute is a disobedience to the law punishable in the case of a private person by indictment, the offending corporation cannot escape from the consequences which would follow in the case of an individual by showing that they are a corporation.

(5) The next case of importance is that of *Pearks, Gauston and Tee, Ltd.*, vs. *Southern Counties Dairies Company, Ltd.* (1902, 2 K.B., page 1).

The prosecution was against a joint stock company under The Sale of Food and Drugs Act, 1875. Section 6 of that Act makes it an offence for any person to sell to the prejudice of the purchasers any article of food or any drug which is not of the nature substance and quality of the article demanded by such purchaser, under a penalty not exceeding £20. Channel J. said—" By the general principles of criminal law, if a matter is made a criminal offence, it is essential that there should be something in the nature of *mens rea*, and therefore, in ordinary cases, a corporation cannot be guilty of a criminal offence, nor can a master be liable criminally for an offence committed by his servants. But there are exceptions to this rule in the case of *quasi*-criminal offences, as they may be termed, that is to say, where certain acts are forbidden by law under a penalty, possibly even under a personal penalty, such as imprisonment, at any rate in default of payment of a fine, and the reason for this is, that the legislature has thought it so important to prevent the particular act from being committed that it absolutely forbids it to be done ; and if it is done the offender is liable to a penalty whether he had any *mens rea* or not, and whether or not he intended to commit a breach of the law. Where the act is of this character then the master, who, in fact, has done the forbidden thing through his servant, is responsible and is liable to a penalty. There is no reason why he should not be, because the very object of the legislature was to forbid the thing absolutely. It seems to me that exactly the same principle applies in the case of a corporation. If it does the act which is forbidden it is liable. Therefore, when a question arises, as in the present case, one has to consider whether the matter is one which is absolutely forbidden, or whether it is simply a new offence which has been created to which the ordinary principle as to *mens rea* applies."

Right to maintain action.

The right of a corporation to maintain an action for libel was discussed in *South Hethon Coal Co., Ltd.*, vs. *North-Eastern New Association, Ltd.* (1 Q.B., 1894, p. 133). The case is of importance as a libel gives rise both to Civil and Criminal action. It was there contended *inter alia* that no action would lie by the plaintiffs who were a corporation. With reference to this objection Lopez, L.J., laid down the law as follows :—

Action for libel.

"With regard to the first point I am of opinion that, although a corporation cannot maintain an action for libel in respect of anything reflecting upon them personally, yet they can maintain an action for a libel reflecting on the management of their trade or business, and this without alleging or proving special damage. The words complained of, in order to entitle a corporation or company to sue for libel or slander, must injuriously affect the corporation or company as distinct from the individuals who compose it. A corporation or company could not sue in respect of a charge of murder, or incest, or adultery, because it could not commit these crimes. Nor could it sue in respect of a charge of corruption or of an assault, because a corporation cannot be guilty of corruption or of an assault, although the individuals composing it may be. The words complained of must attack the corporation or company in the method of conducting its affairs, must accuse it of fraud or mismanagement, or must attack its financial position." Pollock, C.B., in *Metropolitan Saloon Omnibus Co.* vs. *Howkins*, said 'that a corporation at common law can sue in respect of a libel, there is no doubt. It would be monstrous if a corporation could maintain no action for slander of title through which they lost a great deal of money. It could not sue in respect of an imputation of murder, or incest, or adultery, because it could not commit those crimes. Nor could it sue in respect of a charge of corruption, although the individuals composing it may. But it would be very odd if a corporation had no means of protecting itself against wrong; and, if its property is injured by slander, it has no means of of redress except by action.' Cases of this nature are expressly provided for in Expl. 2 of Section 499 of the Code which lays down that it may amount to defamation to make an imputation concerning a company or an association or collection of persons as such.

II. Acts—Omissions.

'Act' defined.

Every movement of our body is an act. The striking of a blow is an act. The winking of the eye is an act. A mere expression of the face is an act.

"An action," says Sir Fitz James Stephen, "is a motion or more commonly a group of related motions of different parts of the body. Actions may be either involuntary or voluntary, and an involuntary action may be further subdivided according as it is or is not accompanied by consciousness."

Involuntary actions.

"Instances of involuntary actions are to be found not only in such motions as the beating of the heart and the heaving of the chest but in many conscious acts—coughing for instance, the motions which a man makes to save himself from falling and an infinite number of others. Many acts are involuntary and unconscious, though as far as others are concerned, they have all the effects of conscious acts, as, for instance, the struggles of a person in a fit of epilepsy. The classification of such actions belongs more properly to physiology than to law. For legal purposes it is enough to say that no involuntary action, whatever effect it may produce, amounts to a crime by the law of England. I do not know indeed that it has ever been suggested that a person who in his sleep set fire to a house or caused the death of another would be guilty of arson or murder."

Voluntary action defined.

"Such being the nature of an action," continues the learned author, "a *voluntary action* is a motion or group of motions accompanied or preceded by volition and directed towards some object."

Mercier's criticism.

Mr. Mercier, in his work on criminal responsibility, criticises this definition at some length.

He thinks that the notion of a voluntary act is unduly restricted, if it is held of necessity to include movement. "If a lady is coming out of a door as I am going along a corridor, and I stop to allow her to pass; the arrest of my movement is as much a voluntary act as is the movement by which I start to continue my journey. In customary phrase, the arrest of my movement would be called act of ordinary courtesy, and in this case the custom would, I think, be correct. I take a piece of cabbage on my fork, and as I am conveying it to my mouth, I see a caterpillar on it, and arrest the movement. The arrest of the movement is a voluntary act, as much as the movement itself. My neighbour at the table asks me: 'What are you *doing* that for?' The form of his question is correct. In arresting the movement I do something. In other words, I act."

The criticism so far seems plausible, but is certainly not unanswerable. *Arrest* and *suppression* of movement themselves involve some counter movements, perhaps too quick to be noticed by others, or even for the actor to be conscious of, which bring about a cessation of movement and are in this way included in the definition of Sir Fitz James Stephen. In such cases like the driver of a railway engine we apply the brake to bring about the result. Arrest and suppression of movement are clearly distinguishable from mere abstention or cessation of movement. The learned author's arguments are largely based on naccuracy of language which so often deceives us.

Mr. Mercier would include an intentional abstention from movement in the definition of a voluntary act. " When a person," says he, "in order to commit suicide stands in front of an advancing train he executes a voluntary act by merely standing and abstaining from movement." It is hardly necessary to have recourse to such special pleading. We may either hold the man responsible for going and staying at such a place of danger or on the impossible assumption that he was forcibly taken there, and all he did was not to move out of the place, we may punish him, not for the act but for the omission, for the protection of one's own life is a legal duty.

Indian Penal Code.

The Indian Penal Code recognises this distinction between acts and omissions, but wisely refrains from defining either.

I say " wisely," for an attempt to define with scientific precision elementary ideas often lead to failure, and what is still worse, to confusion.

Act and omission distinguished.

In distinguishing between an act and an omission you must not lay too much stress upon mere forms of expressions commonly used. We often say "you *acted* wisely in not going out." As a matter of fact 'not going out' was not an act but an omission. When we say of a jailor that he starves his prisoners, we apparently charge him with a positive act, but in reality we attribute to him a mere omission to supply food.

I do not think it necessary to dwell at greater length upon the meaning of an act, as I think, every one has a pretty accurate idea of what an act is, and these metaphysical discussions only serve to introduce doubts and difficulties which, but for these discussions, would perhaps not arise at all.

You will observe that in every language acts are often taken along with their consequences and given a separate name. I take up a loaded gun and pull the trigger which causes an explosion—I fire. The explosion *impels* the bullet—I shoot. The bullet comes in contact with another's body and causes loss of life—I kill. These different names are given to the same act but with reference to different consequences. This process enables us to express a number of ideas in a single word and tends to brevity of language.

'Omission' defined.

An omission is the negation of an act. Consequences are referable to an act as result of universal human experience. Apart from the debated question as to whether beyond the invariable sequence, there is any causal connection between an act and what we call its consequences, as a matter of fact, we do, in our minds, believe in the existence of such a connection and act on such a belief, and all laws are based upon that conception. The same thing cannot be said of omissions. When a jailor omits to supply his prisoners with food and the prisoners die of starvation, the jailor does no more cause death than the person who sees a blind man proceeding towards a precipice and does nothing to warn him. Nor is the case different from that of a surgeon who omits to apply a bandage to a bleeding man who dies in consequence. Strictly speaking it cannot be said in either of the last two cases that omission to warn or to apply a bandage was the cause of death. The more correct view of the matter seems to be this: that death could have been prevented and was not. You will, however, find, on an examination of the Indian Penal Code, that *causing* of a consequence has been sometimes loosely attributed to omissions, where what really took place was abstention from prevention of such a consequence.

An omission to be punishable must be an illegal omission or one in breach of a legal duty. This principle is incorporated in Section 32 of the Indian Penal Code which provides that in every part of the Code, except where a contrary intention appears from the context, words, which refer to acts done, extend also to *illegal* omission. Sec. 32, I. P. C.

The word "illegal" is applicable to everything which is an offence or which is prohibited by law, or which furnishes ground for a civil action: and a person is said to be "legally bound to do" whatever it is illegal in him to omit. (Section 43).

Illegal omissions.

I shall now explain what are *illegal* omissions or omissions in breach of a legal duty by a few familiar instances:—

(*a*) A jailor starves to death the prisoners in his charge. He is guilty of murder.

(*b*) A physician in charge of a hospital omits to prescribe for a patient in his ward. The physician is responsible for the consequence of his omission.

(*c*) A station master omits to put up a danger signal with the intention of bringing about a collision in order that it may lead to loss of human life. The other necessary elements of Section 299, Indian Penal Code, being present, he is guilty of murder.

Legal duty.

The important question, to ask in connection with omissoions, is what are *illegal* omissions, or omissions in breach of a legal duty. Now a legal duty may be contractual, it may be statutary or it may be founded on rules of justice, equity and good conscience.

Personal laws of Hindus and Muhammadans in India.

In India we have a large body of what are called personal laws. But the personal law of the Hindus and Muhammadans are not administered by the British Courts, except in matters relating to succession, inheritance, marriage, or caste or any religious usage or institution and even then in the absence of any legislative enactment abolishing or altering it. In other matters the personal law of the parties is administered under similar conditions only in so far as it is consistent with justice, equity and good conscience. A question may arise as to what extent criminal law will recognize the personal law of an accused person to determine his legal obligations. Such recognition would lead to anomalies and undesirable consequences. There would be, to a dangerous extent, an element of uncertainty which cannot be overlooked. The rules of equity, to which, as I have said, such law must conform, are said to "vary with the length of the Lord Chancellor's foot." Should criminal responsibility be judged by such an uncertain standard? To illustrate the above I may refer to the provision of the Muhammadan law which throws upon a rich relation the obligation to maintain a poor and helpless kinsman. I have never heard it suggested that an omission to supply maintenance in such a case is to be considered an illegal omission. In fact the Muhammadan law in this respect is not binding even on the Muhammadans. We cannot, however, altogether avoid reference to personal law in framing a Code of Penal Laws for in certain matters rights are regulated by the personal law of the parties The Chapter dealing with offences relating to marriage will illustrate this. Marriage, though giving rise to numerous rights and obligations of a purely secular character is still looked upon by the largest majority of the human race as a *quasi*-religious institution. In numerous other cases also personal law has an indirect bearing. For instance, in all cases where a question of title to property is involved, directly or indirectly, we have often to refer to personal law in determining such a question.

Apart, however, from personal and statutary laws there are obligations which the penal law has to recognise for the well-being of the human race. The source of this kind of obligation must be traced to the law that exists in the *breast* of the Judges. This law is of very common application in the pursuit of civil wrongs and the law of crimes does not exclude them. This has been enforced frequently in English and American Courts specially in cases of neglect by mothers to provide suitable food and clothing for their children, and it has been laid down that generally in all cases where a grown up person has taken charge of a human creature, helpless either from infancy, simplicity, lunacy or other infirmity, and has been afterwards guilty of wicked negligence, the law will not allow a breach of such obligation to go unpunished. It may be suggested that, in most of these cases, the obligation arises from an implied contract, but this is by no means clear. In English and American Courts the question of illegal omission has been discussed more frequently in connection with the duty of parents to their children and also of others on whom has devolved the duty of maintaining weak and helpless persons. Although these cases would, more properly, be dealt with in connection with offences affecting life, they may be usefully discussed at this stage in illustrating to you the distinction between omissions that are not illegal and those that are.

Bishop in his criminal law states the American law on the subject in these words :—

"If a man neglects to supply his legitimate child with suitable food and clothing, or suitably to provide for his apprentice whom he is under a legal obligation to maintain, and the child or apprentice dies of the neglect, he commits a felonious homicide. But his wife, if she does the same thing, even towards her own offspring, does not incur the guilt: because the law casts the duty of maintenance on him alone, not at all on her, who stands in this respect in no other relation to him than a mere servant. Again, the law imposes on a man no duty to maintain his brother. Therefore if one has abiding in his house a brother who is an idiot, and who through his neglect perishes from want, he is not in law responsible for the homicide; because omission, without a duty, will not create an indictable offence, yet if, however, voluntarily he has taken upon himself the obligation to maintain the brother, he is answerable should death follow from his gross neglect of it, amounting to a wicked mind."

I do not, however, think that a mother can refuse to suckle her new born babe. The Indian Law at any rate takes very serious view of such cases, for the preservation of the human race is still considered to be an important part of the policy of the State in every civilized country.

A number of decided cases both of English and American Courts may be cited in support of these propositions.

In most systems of law a distinction is made as regards the liability to maintain a child between the father and the mother. Under the Muhammadan law the latter has the right to the custody of a child up to a certain age, but the liability to provide maintenance is on the father.

There may, however, be cases in which a mother by her conduct may have assumed the responsibility of maintaining her child, and in such a case she cannot plead the absence of a legal duty. In *R.* vs. *Nichollis* (13 Cox, C. C., 75), an old woman was put upon her trial for the manslaughter of her grandson, an infant of tender years, who was said to have died from the neglect of the prisoner to supply him with proper nourishment. The woman was convicted.

In *R.* vs. *Morley* (8 Q. B. D., 571) the prisoner was one of the " peculiar people " who did not believe in doctors for effecting a cure in cases of illness but only in prayers and anointment. His little boy of eight years old was known to be suffering from confluent small-pox, and yet no medical aid was called in and the child died as the *post mortem* examination showed—of the disease. If the doctor had been sent for at once, the child's life might have been saved, but, on the other hand, it might not have been ; and there being, therefore, no positive evidence that the death was caused or accelerated by the neglect to provide medical aid or attendance, it was held that the father could not be properly convicted of manslaughter. " It is not enough," said Lord Coleridge, " to show neglect of reasonable means for preserving or prolonging the child's life ; but to convict of manslaughter it must be shown that the neglect had the effect of shortening life. In order to sustain conviction affirmative proof is required."

"Under Section 37 of 31 and 32 Vict., C. 122," added Stephen J., "it may be, the prisoner could have been convicted of neglect of duty as a parent, but to convict of manslaughter you must show that he caused death or accelerated it."

In the earlier case of *R.* vs. *Downes* (1 Q. B. D., p. 25) where the facts were somewhat similar it was distinctly shown, and found by the jury that the child's death was caused by the neglect to provide medical aid, and, therefore, the conviction of manslaughter was upheld. "I agree with my Lord Coleridge," said Bramwell, B.,—"as to the difficulty which would have existed had it not been for the statute. But the statute imposes an absolute duty on parents, whatever their conscientious scruples may be. The prisoner wilfully—not maliciously but intentionally—disobeyed the law and death ensued in consequence. It is, therefore, manslaughter." The material words, it may be mentioned, in Section 37 of 31 and 32 Vict., Cl. 22, are as follows:—"When any parent shall wilfully neglect to provide adequate food, clothing, medical aid or lodging for his child, being in his custody, under the age of 14 years, whereby the health of such child shall have been or shall be likely to be seriously injured, he shall be guilty of an offence punishable on summary conviction." There is no such statutary provision in India and I hope we shall never require it.

In the case of *R.* vs. *Rees* a person's death was caused by alleged negligence on the part of a fireman in charge of a fire escape, who was absent from his post when the alarm was given. It was held that there was not sufficient connection between the alleged neglect of the prisoner and the cause of death to warrant a conviction.

Vide also *R.* vs. *Hughes* (D. and B. 248) ; *R.* vs. *Smith* (11 Cox. C. C. 210) ; *R.* vs. *Misselbrook* (Sessions Paper C. C. C., July 1878).

In the case of *R.* vs. *Jeffery* the prisoner and deceased were not married but lived together as man and wife ; the woman died through the alleged neglect of the prisoner. It was held by Hawkins J. that sufficient legal responsibility was made out, but upon the facts it was for the jury to say whether in their opinion death was caused or accelerated by gross and criminal neglect on the part of the prisoner.

In the case of *R.* vs. *Shepherd* (L. and C. 147) a girl of 18 was taken in labour at her step-father's house during his absence. The mother omitted to procure for her the assistance of a midwife in consequence of which the girl died. It was held that the mother was not legally bound to procure the aid of a midwife, and that she could not be convicted of manslaughter for not doing so. The case, however, appears to have turned to some extent on the fact that there was no evidence that the mother had money enough to pay for a midwife.

The case of *R.* v. *Curtis* (15 Cox C. C., 746) should be referred to as regards the responsibility of relieving officers in refusing medical assistance to destitute persons in case of urgent necessity.

There are certain omissions for which the Code specifically provides, *e.g.*—

(1) Omission to produce documents to public servant by a person legally bound to produce. (Section 175).

(2) Omission to give notice of information when legally bound to give it. (Section 176).

(3) Omission to assist a public servant. (Section 187).

(4) Omission to apprehend on the part of public servant. (Sections 221 and 222).

In other cases the question depends upon the applicability of Section 32 as explained by Section 43.

On the subject of omissions I may refer you to the cases of *Thornotte Madathel Poker* (1886, 1, Weir 495) and *Queen-Empress* vs. *Latif Khan* (20 Bom. 394). In the former case it has been held that the word ‘ omission ’ is used in the sense of intentional non-doing. According to Section 32, the word ‘ act ’ includes intentional doing as well as intentional non-doing. The omission or neglect must, it was said, be such as to have an active effect conducing to the result, as a link, in the chain of facts from which an intention to bring about the result may be inferred.

The latter case is not of much importance as it only lays down the law in terms of the section.

LECTURE III.

INCHOATE CRIMES.

ATTEMPTS.

Attempts

I have in my previous lecture discussed the general proposition that a crime is an act or an omission. I have told you that the law does not punish a mere evil intention or design unaccompanied by any overt act in furtherance of such a design. This indeed follows from what has been said before. You must not, however, think that criminal law only deals with the last proximate act that actually produces the evil consequence which determines its penal character. It often happens that the last proximate act has not been done or has failed to produce the contemplated evil consequence. No injury to the individual may have been caused and yet the act may be sufficiently harmful to society by reason of its close proximity to the contemplated offence to be classed as a crime. Thus, unlike civil law, criminal law takes notice of attempts to commit punishable wrongs and punishes them with more or less severity according to the nature of the act attempted. A distinction is drawn between an *attempt* and a *preparation*. The relative proximity between the act done and the evil consequence contemplated, largely determines the distinction. Whereas an attempt is punishable, a preparation is not. This distinction is based on sound reason. In the first place a preparation, apart from its motive, would generally be a harmless act. It would be impossible in most cases to show that the preparation was directed to a wrongful end or was done with

Distinguished from preparation.

an evil motive or intent, and it is not the policy of law to create offences that in most cases it would be impossible to bring home to the culprit or which may lead to harassment of innocent persons. Besides a mere preparation would not ordinarily affect the sense of security of the individual intended to be wronged, nor would society be disturbed and its sense of vengeance roused by what to all outward appearances would be an innocent act. Take a case of murder. In many cases there will be first the stage of contemplation, and I have told you the law would not punish mere evil thoughts. Then would come the stage of preparation. For instance, the procuring of a gun or other deadly weapon. In most cases you will not suspect that your neighbour has procured the gun for any evil purpose, and no one would feel at all alarmed or even concerned about it. If such an act were made punishable, it would be impossible in ninety-nine out of hundred cases to prove that the object of it was murder. On the other hand, it will be possible to harass a man who has procured a gun for a perfectly legitimate purpose. The acts done up to this stage are not penal. The case will, however, be different where the man having procured the gun pursues his enemy with it, but fails to overtake him or is arrested before he is able to complete the offence or fires without effect. These would clearly be attempts and obviously none of the considerations which justify the exclusion of preparations from category of crimes will apply.

I have said that a preparation is *generally* not punished. There are, however, exceptional cases where the contemplated offence may be so grave that it would be of the utmost importance to stop it at its earliest stage. Instances of such exceptional cases are to be found in Sections 122 and 126, Indian Penal Code, whereby preparing to wage war against the Sovereign or to commit depredation on the territories of any friendly power are made punishable. There are also other cases of mere preparations which are made punishable, although the mere gravity of the contemplated offence would perhaps not have been considered sufficient to justify a departure from so well established a doctrine, but for the fact that the preparations are of so peculiar a nature as to preclude the likelihood of their being meant for innocent purposes. The provisions against making or selling or being in possession of instruments for counterfeiting coins (Sections 233, 234, 235, Indian Penal Code) are instances of this kind.

You will also notice that there are a number of acts which we have come to regard as substantive offences which are in reality mere preparations to commit other offences. Possession of counterfeit coins, false weights and forged documents, etc., are nothing but preparations to cheat or commit other offences. The classification of these acts as crimes are based on one or other of the considerations I have enumerated above.

Having considered the matter generally, I shall now draw your attention to the difficulties that have arisen both in this country and in England in the application of the doctrine to facts of particular cases. It has not been always easy in practice to draw the line between preparations and attempts. The Indian Penal Code has not defined an attempt. This is probably due to the fact that the word is not used in any technical sense. Even in the matter of differentiation between a preparation and an attempt a great deal has been left to be determined with reference to the general import of the word.

When a man merely purchases implements of burglary we never say he attempted to commit burglary, or when a man procures a *lathi* to beat another we never say that he attempted to cause hurt. Many difficulties would, I think, be solved if we asked the simple question "Is this an act that we will describe as an attempt in common parlance?"

The Code deals with attempts in three different ways. In some cases the commission of an offence and the attempt to commit it, are dealt with in the same section, the extent of punishment being the same for both. (*See* Sections 196, 198, 213, 239, 240, 241, 250, 251, 254, 385, 387, 389, 391, Indian Penal Code.)

The other way of dealing with attempts are exemplified by Sections 307, 308, 393. In these sections attempts for committing specific offences are dealt with side by side with the offences themselves but separately, and separate punishments are provided for the attempts from those of the offences attempted.

As for the cases not provided for in either of the two modes above mentioned you have the general Section 511, which has been placed somewhat illogically at the end of the Code. That section provides as follows :—

> "Whoever attempts to commit an offence punishable by this Code with transportation or imprisonment, or to cause such

> an offence to be committed, *and in such attempt does any act towards the commission of the offence*, shall, where no express provision is made by this Code for the punishment of such attempt, be punished with transportation or imprisonment of any description provided for the offence, for a term of transportation or imprisonment which may extend to one-half of the longest term provided for that offence, or with such fine as is provided for the offence, or with both."

The language of the section seems to me somewhat redundant. The very essence of the idea of an attempt is something done towards the commission of the act attempted to be done, and in this view the words " and in such attempt does any act towards the commission of the offence " seem unnecessary. Could there be any attempt at all unless something had been done towards the commission of the offence attempted ? And yet you will find when I come to discuss the Indian case law on the subject that in some reported cases, considerable stress has been laid on these words in determining whether certain acts are punishable under Section 511 or not. That the words are redundant seems also clear from the fact that in dealing with attempts in the two other modes mentioned above no such qualifying words are used. Can it be reasonably contended that the legislature intended to deal with a different and more limited class of attempts in Section 511 ? You will find similar restrictive words used in Section 309.

I shall quote two sections of the Code to enable you to realise more fully the difference of language used in the treatment of attempts in connection with different offences.

I have already quoted Section 511.

Section 393.—Whoever attempts to commit robbery shall be punished with rigorous imprisonment for a term which may extend to seven years and shall also be liable to fine.

Section 309.—Whoever attempts to commit suicide and *does any act towards the commission of such offence,* shall be punished with simple imprisonment for a term which may extend to one year, or with fine or with both.

Although, on the one hand, having regard to the extremely careful drafting of the Indian Penal Code, it is difficult to believe that the difference of language was the result of inadvertence, on the other hand, it is equally difficult to discover the reason for the difference. It seems clear that the omission of the words in italics would have made no difference in the law relating to attempts. They have probably been introduced out of abundance of caution to emphasise the difference between a preparation and an attempt in cases where such caution was thought more necessary than in others. This is not a very satisfactory explanation, but I can think of no other.

The difference between a preparation and an attempt is thus explained by Lord Blackburn in *Reg.* vs. *Cheesman* (1 L. & C. 140, 1862): "There is no doubt a difference between a preparation antecedent to an attempt and the actual attempt, but if the actual transaction has commenced which would have ended in the crime if not interrupted, there is clearly an attempt to commit the crime."

"The word attempt," said Chief Justice Cockburn, "clearly conveys with it the idea that *if the attempt had succeeded the offence charged would have been committed.* An attempt must be to do that which if successful would amount to the felony charged." (M'cpherson's case, D. and B. 202). Following this definition it was held in a Calcutta case, that where the accused had printed some forms similar to those used by a Coal Company, but had done nothing to forge the signature or seal of the Company he was held not guilty of an attempt to commit forgery; all that he did, consisted in mere preparation for the com mission of the crime.

Neither of the two cases cover the whole ground of difference between preparation and attempt. They deal with two different aspects of the question. Lord Blackburn deals with cases where the offender had not gone through all the steps necessary to constitute the complete offence. For instance, it covers the case of an accused who pursued his enemy with a gun and was arrested before he got near enough to shoot. It ignores a case in which the offender has taken all the necessary steps to commit the complete offence, but has failed to produce the consequence without which the offence is not complete. It does not, for instance, apply to the case of the man who fires at his enemy, but misses either for his want of skill or because of a defect in the gun or because he had mistaken something else for his enemy. In all these cases there is no question of any interruption at all. On the other hand, Chief Justice Cockburn's definition fixes the mind more upon consequences than upon the acts. The principle laid down in *R.* vs. *McPherson* (D. & B., p. 197) was that a prisoner could not be properly convicted of breaking and entering a building and attempting to steel goods which were not there. Upon such a view of the meaning of an attempt it was held in *Queen* vs. *Collins* (9 Cox, C. C. 407) that if a person put his hand into the pocket of another with intent to steal what he can find there, and the pocket is empty, he cannot be convicted of an attempt to steal. The principle laid down in *Reg.* vs. *McPherson* and *R.* vs. *Collins* was applied in a subsequent case *R.* vs. *Dodd* (18 Law Times N. S. 89, 1868), wherein it was held that a person could not be convicted of an attempt to commit an offence which he could not actually commit. These cases were reviewed in *R.* vs. *Brown* (24 Q. B. D. 357) and Lord Coleridge declared that these cases were decided on a mistaken view of the law. Finally in *R.* vs. *Ring* (17 Cox, p. 491) a conviction for an attempt to steal from a woman by endeavouring to find her pocket was held good, although as in the case of *R.* vs. *Collins* there was nothing in the pocket, and it was clearly stated that *R.* vs. *Collins* was overruled. But though overruled, the case is still important, as I shall presently show, and I need make no apology in quoting a portion of Chief Justice Cockburn's judgment :—

" We are all of opinion that this conviction cannot be sustained ; and, in so holding, it is necessary to observe that the judgment proceeds on the assumption that the question, whether there was anything in the pocket of the prosecutrix which might have been the subject of larceny, does not appear to have been left to the jury. The case was reserved for the opinion of the Court on the question, whether, supposing a person to put his hand into the pocket of another for the purpose of larceny, there being at the time nothing in the pocket, that is, an attempt to commit larceny? We are far from saying that, if the question whether there was anything in the pocket of the prosecutrix had been left to the jury, there was no evidence on which they might have found that there was, and in which case the conviction would have been affirmed. But, assuming that there was nothing in the pocket of the prosecutrix, the charge of attempting to commit larceny cannot be sustained. The case is governed by that of *Reg.* vs. *McPherson*, and we think that an attempt to commit a felony can only be made out *when, if no interruption had taken place, the attempt could have been carried out successfully, and the felony completed, of the attempt to commit which the party is charged.* In this case, if there is nothing in the pocket of the prosecutrix, in our opinion the attempt to commit larceny cannot be established. It may be illustrated by the case of a person going into a room, the door of which he finds open, for the purpose of stealing whatever property he may find there, and finding nothing in the room, in that case no larceny could be committed, and therefore no attempt to commit larceny could be committed. In the absence, therefore, of any finding by the jury in the case, either directly or inferentially by their verdict, that there was any property in the pocket of the prosecutrix, we think that this conviction must be quashed."

Illustrations (*a*) and (*b*) to Section 511, Indian Penal Code, clearly show that the law in India is the same as that laid down in *Reg.* vs. *Ring.* The absurdity of the law as laid down in *R.* vs. *Collins* was thus commented upon by Butler, J., a learned American Judge. "It would be a novel and startling proposition that a known pick-pocket might pass around in a crowd in full view of a policeman, and even in the room of a police station, and thrust his hands into the pockets of those present, with intent to steal, and yet not be liable to arrest or punishment until the policeman has first ascertained that there was in fact money or valuables in some one of the pockets." Although *R.* vs. *Collins* was rightly overruled it cannot be said that the entire principle upon which that case was based has been abandoned. For instance, in *R.* vs. *McPherson* which laid down a principle similar to *R.* vs. *Collins*, the facts being also similar, Lord Bramwell strengthened his position by instancing the case of a person who mistaking a log of wood for an enemy fires at it intending to cause death, and he laid down that this will not amount to an attempt. Can it be said that *R.* vs. *Collins* and by parity of reasoning *R.* vs. *McPherson* being overruled the case of firing at a log of wood will constitute an attempt at murder. No case so far as I am aware has gone so far. On the other hand, I have never seen it suggested in any recent case that the principle of *R.* vs. *Collins* should be applied to the case of a person who administers a drug to cause miscarriage, and it afterwards transpired that the woman was not pregnant at all. In *R.* vs. *Goodall* (2 Cox C. C. 41) it was decided that this amounted to an attempt. "The acutest understanding," says Bishop, "could not reconcile these two cases, the one for putting the hand into the pocket, but not finding there anything to be removed and the other for penetrating the womb and yet not discovering an embryo or fœtus to be taken away."

To reconcile these inconsistencies other theories have been propounded, and it has been suggested as a doctrine of general application that an impossible attempt is not punishable, and that, there fore, it is not an offence to shoot at a shadow, to administer sugar mistaking it for arsenic or to try to kill a man by witchcraft. The impossibility must, however, be absolute not relative, so that the doctrine would not cover the case of an adequate dose of arsenic. It is also said that the means must be adapted to the end. The question still remains on what principle are these reservations based. It cannot be said that there is any want of evil intent in such cases. It is not the absence of *mens rea.* It is not also the absence of an overt act. Perhaps the doctrine may be defended on the same ground on which a mere criminal intent is not punishable, *viz.*, that such an act causes no alarm, no sense of insecurity to society—no consequence following the act which would in vast majority of cases remain undetected and unknown.

A differentiation has also been made between cases where the object is merely mistaken and cases where the object is merely absent. The case of the empty pocket is said to belong to the former and of shooting at a shadow to the latter. The distinction seems to be without a difference. In both cases there is both mistake and the absence of the object. In the case of the shadow the man is absent and by mistake he is supposed to be present, and in the case of the empty pocket the money is absent, but the criminal thinks by mistake that money is there, though it is absent. It appears that till the time of Feurback it was considered that cases of impossible attempts were outside the scope of criminal attempts and that such attempts whether impossible owing to the absence of the object or owing to inadaptability of the means to the end were on the footing of mere preparations or of mere intention which has not led to any overt act. But Feurback in his anxiety to base his conclusions on clear logical grounds thought that the peasant who prayed to God to strike his neighbour dead in the belief that it was the surest means of effecting his object must be punishable. Too much insistance on the subjective elements of a crime would furnish adequate reasons for such a conclusion.

Although the decision in *R.* vs. *Ring* has the effect of removing this anomaly, we must discover some new principle upon which to exclude from the category of attempts the shooting at an enemy's big coat or striking a log of wood, and including in it the case of an attempt to steal property where none existed, or the case of attempted abortion in the case of a woman who was found not to be pregnant at all. In the one case there was no man to kill and in the other no property to steal or no fœtus to remove, and the same principle should therefore apply to both. I shall try to differentiate the principles to be applied to these two cases. The Indian Penal Code will not materially help you in finding out the point of distinction. Before coming to the point I shall analyse the ideas involved in an attempt.

An act or series of acts constitutes an attempt—

(*a*) If the offender has completed all or at any rate all the more important steps necessary to constitute the offence, but the consequence which is the essential ingredient of the offence has not taken place.

(*b*) If the offender has not completed all the steps necessary to constitute the offence, but has proceeded far enough to necessitate punishment for the protection of society.

Regarding (*a*) the non-production of the consequence may be due solely to want of skill on the part of the accused or it may be due to other causes operating on the offender personally or it may be due to causes in no way connected with the offender.

In all these cases attempt in the legal sense is complete.

Illustration.—*A* shoots at *B* intending to kill him, but misses his mark for want of skill or for any defect in the gun. It is clearly an attempt.

Illustration (*a*), *Section 511.*—*A* makes an attempt to steal some jewels by breaking open a box and finds after so opening the box that there is no jewel in it. He has done an act towards the commission of theft, and therefore is guilty under this section.

Illustration (*b*), *Section 511.*—*A* makes an attempt to pick the pocket of *Z* by thrusting his hand into *Z's* pocket. *A* fails in the attempt in consequence of *Z's* having nothing in his pocket. *A* is guilty under this section.

These cases present no difficulty, and have been discussed before in connection with *Collin's* case.

Take, however, another case also falling in the same class to which I have already averted more than once.

A intending to kill *B* fires at *B's* big coat hanging in his room mistaking it for *B*. Will *A* be guilty of an offence ? So far as the language of Section 511 is concerned, it seems to me that if it covers the case of the pick-pocket in illustration (*a*) as it certainly does, it ought to cover this case also. And it may very justly be said that in the forum of conscience such a case is as bad as any other ordinary case of an attempted murder, and that any instinctive abhorrence at such a conviction may be overcome by passing a light sentence upon the offender. It seems to me, however, that in spite of the language of Section 511, which wholly ignores the objective element of an offence, there are grounds for distinguishing the present case from that of the pick-pocket. True all the subjective elements of the contemplated offence are present there, but it will be well to remember that there are offences the gravity of which lies not so much in their subjective as in their objective elements, and in this class we may include the various offences grouped in the Indian Penal Code under the head of offences against the human body. The gradation between assault, hurt, grievous hurt and murder are all indications of the stress laid upon the objective element, *viz.*, the amount of injury inflicted upon the individual. In offences against property, such as theft, criminal misappropriation, criminal breach of trust, little or nothing turns upon the extent of the injury caused, *i.e.*, upon the amount of property taken. That shows that different principles have been adopted in determining the penal character of offences against human body and offences against property, and from this point of view a distinction based on principle may be drawn between the case of the pick-pocket and the person who shoots at his enemy's big coat based on the impossibility of the evil consequence happening in either case. But as I have said before the language of Section 511 does not recognise any such distinction and the words of the section applied literally may warrant the conviction for attempt at murder in the case above mentioned.

It may, however, be argued that the words "and in such attempt does any act towards the commission of the offences" are intended to exclude these cases, but this is far from being clear. I have not found this point of view clearly stated anywhere and put it forward with certain amount of diffidence. The distinction, however, seems fairly deducible from reported cases and reconciles the apparent conflict between many of them.

There are, I must admit, cases to which the doctrine of attempt would be inapplicable on the basis of the distinction I have suggested, which, however, from the risk they involve and other considerations of the like nature, have been considered sufficiently serious to be punished. One of these cases is mentioned by Wharton, *viz.*, shooting at an empty carriage the offender supposing it to be occupied to which may be added the case of shooting at a coat hanging in a man's bed room. Cases of this kind may be treated as exceptions on the ground of the alarm that such acts will cause to the individual and to society at large, and the disturbance they are likely to cause to public peace. On similar reasoning and also on grounds of public policy the case of an attempted abortion where the woman was not pregnant at all, may be treated as an exception.

I have so far discussed cases of attempt where the offender has done all that he could to commit the offence attempted, but it has not been completed, because the consequence which is essential to constitute it has not accrued for reasons other than the act or will of the offender. I have told you such cases present no difficulty and on them no question of mere preparation arises. The cases where the difficulty arise are those belonging to the second of the two classes I have enumerated before, I mean cases where the offender has not gone through the whole series of acts necessary to complete the offence apart from the resulting consequence. These cases have to be dealt with from various standpoints. The offender may have stopped of his own free-will abandoning the idea either as the result of penitence, or in view of the consequences that might befall him. In these cases whether the stage arrived at is that of preparation or attempt the law allows the offender a *locus pœnitentiæ*. If, however, the offender has desisted from proceeding further owing to the attempt being discovered, or the presence of police, the law will not excuse, for the evil will is still there.

You will observe that the question whether what the offender has done has reached merely the stage of preparation or has amounted to an attempt to commit the offence, arises only in the class of cases I am now discussing, namely, where the whole series of acts necessary to complete the offence has not been completed or gone through. It seems to me that in these cases the principle upon which the distinction is or should be based is either the possibility of the act, so far as it is completed, being meant for an innocent purpose or of the probability of the offender desisting of his own accord from committing the offence without external compulsion, mental or physical. I have said that the law allows the offender a *locus pœnitentiæ* in certain cases, and it may be stated as a general principle that so long as the steps taken leave room for a reasonable expectation that the offender may of his own free-will still desist from the contemplated attempt, he will be considered to be still on the stage of preparation. Such an expectation may be based upon the remoteness of the act done from the last proximate act that would complete the offence.

To illustrate the above, suppose, *A* purchases a gun and it is proved that he had held out a threat that he will kill *B* with a gun and intended to do so. Still it is the stage of preparation only, for the purchase of a gun may be for quite an innocent purpose. Besides the purchase of a gun may be far removed both as regards time and space from the last act necessary to kill or by the intervention of several other acts without which the accused could not effect his purpose. The intended victim may be miles off, and even if near it might take a long time to procure the powder and shot and other things necessary which alone could enable the accused to effect his purpose. You cannot say with any confidence that either he will walk the several miles or complete the rest of the process to accomplish his object. The probability of the man giving up his design is not negatived in such cases. This probability should, in every case, be a question of fact and cannot be determined by any rigid rules of general application. Suppose, however, having purchased the gun the man loads it, goes out with it, meets his victim and chases him, but is unable to overtake him, he must, I think, be held guilty of an attempt. His act will cause as much alarm as if he had fired and missed his aim. In all human probability he would have fired, if he could overtake his victim. This probability, along with the alarm that the act causes, takes it beyond the limits of a mere preparation.

Take again the case of a man who orders a machine from France at considerable cost, takes delivery of it and sets it up in a secluded place. (We had a recent instance here in Calcutta.) Following the principle laid down in several cases he will perhaps be said to be in the stage of preparation still. I would hesitate to accept such a decision for the nature of the preparation is such as to preclude the possibility (*a*) of a change in the intentions of the accused and (*b*) of the preparation being meant for an innocent purpose.

But if a man merely purchases a stamp paper with the intention of forging a document, even if the intention is proved, he should not be punished for his act only amounts to a preparation both because the presumption of innocence is not negatived and because of the remoteness and consequent probability of a change of intention. But as soon as he begins to write on the paper, the stage of preparation is exceeded, and it should be considered to be an attempt when the forgery is not completed. For in such a case, it is not reasonable to suppose that having commenced the writing he will not complete the document. But suppose a man is found to have commenced writing on a stamped paper a year ago and to have left the work unfinished, it would not be right to punish him, for his conduct is clear indication of a change of intention.

As regards the distinction between a preparation and an attempt it has been said that where there has been merely the procuring of means for the commission of an offence and there is a gap between this and the commencement of an act that would, in all likelihood, lead to the offence, the mere procuring of means is not punishable as an attempt. This also is based mainly on the ground that in most cases of this kind the acts so far as they are accomplished may, to the outside world, look perfectly innocent, and partly on the ground that in the interval that must elapse between the preparation and the commencement of the acts leading up to the offence there may be a change in the mind of the wrong-doer. Where, therefore, both of these elements are excluded and where from the very nature of the preparation made it may be inferred that in all human probability the offender is not likely to desist from putting his intention into final execution, such an act, call it by any name, ought to be punished as an attempt. It is upon these considerations that whilst the man who procures poison to kill another is only considered to be at the stage of preparation the man, who purchases a die for counterfeiting the King's coin, has been held to be guilty of an attempt to counterfeit such coin. One of the reasons for thinking that such a person will not desist from final execution of his object is the secrecy with which the operation of coining can be carried on, and the comparative immunity from detection that the coiner enjoys, so that the motive of gain may be assumed to impel the man to further action in the same direction, in the absence specially of any serious impediment in his way. But if the intending coiner has only purchased the silver for preparing the coin that would only amount to the stage of preparation, for the purchase of silver is quite an innocent act and the silver could be used in various other profitable ways. It is the violent presumption of an evil intent arising from the nature of the preparation that makes the possession of a die an attempt to counterfeit coin but not the possession of silver. It is not, therefore, the mere proximity to the completion of the intended offence in point of time or space, which may negative any reasonable expectation of a change of intention, that determines the line between the preparation and the attempt, but also the consideration arising from the act up to a particular stage being *per se* innocent. I venture to think, you will find in this somewhat lengthy discussion some help in understanding the principles which have guided courts in deciding the very difficult questions that have arisen in determining whether certain acts have amounted to an attempt or not.

I shall now give a few concrete instances taken mostly from reported decisions to illustrate the principles that I have attempted to elucidate.

Illustrative Cases.

(1) *A* makes an attempt to steal some jewels by breaking open a box and finds after so opening the box that there is no jewel in it. He is guilty of an attempt to commit theft. Section 511, illustration (*a*)., See also *Reg.* vs. *Ring* (17 Cox 491).

(2) *A* makes an attempt to pick the pocket of *Z* by thrusting his hand into *Z's* pocket. *A* fails in the attempt in consequence of *Z's* having nothing in his pocket. *A* is guilty of an attempt. Section 511, illustration (*b*). Also *Reg.* vs. *Ring*

(3) *A* writes and sends to *B* a letter inciting *B* to commit a felony. *B* does not read the letter. *A* has attempted to incite *B* to commit a felony. *R.* vs. *Ransford*, 31 I. J. (N. S.) 488.

(4) *A* procures dies for the purpose of coining bad money. *A* has attempted to coin bad money. (Robert's case, Dearsley, C. C. 539).

(5) *A* goes to Birmingham to buy dies to make bad money. *A* has not attempted to make bad money. (Per Jervis, C. J., in Robert's case, Dearsley 551).

(6) *A* procures indecent prints with intent to publish them. *A* has attempted to publish indecent prints (Semble). (*Dugdale* vs. *R.*, I. E. & B., 435 ; *R.* vs. *Dugdale,* Dear C. C. 64).

(7) *A* having in his possession indecent prints, forms an intent to publish them. *A* has not attempted to publish indecent prints. (*Per* Bramwell, B., in *R.* vs. *McPherson*, D. & B. 201).

(8) *A* mistaking a log of wood for *B* and intending to murder *B,* strikes the log of wood with an axe. A has not attempted to murder *B.* (Per Bramwell, B., in *R.* vs. *McPherson*, D. & B. 201).

(9) *A* attempts to suborn a witness *B*, though *B* was of such a high character as to make success impossible, or though the witness was incompetent, *A* has attempted. (Wharton, p. 210.)

(10) *A* administers to *B* a drug with the intent of producing abortion. The drug is found to be harmless. *A* has not attempted. (Wharton, p. 210.)

(11) *A* takes null oath before *B*, an incompetent officer. He has attempted. (Wharton, p. 210.)

(12) *A* intending to kill *B* shoots at an empty carriage supposing it to be occupied. *A* has attempted. (Wharton, p. 213.)

(13) *A* attempts to commit a miscarriage. It turns out the woman was not actually pregnant. *A* has attempted. *Reg.* vs. *Goodall* (2 Cox, C. C. 41).

(14) *A* shoots at a shadow *sufficiently near another person* as to put that person in peril. The attempt is made out. (Wharton, p. 213.)

(15) *A* in order to forge a document purporting to be executed by one *C* takes a deed writer to a place *G*, where it was represented that *C* will execute the document. Having gone to the place *G* he sends his servant to a stamp vendor who is induced by false representation to put on the stamp paper an endorsement to the effect that *C* was the purchaser of the stamp. At this stage the servant was arrested and this stopped further progress. Nothing as a fact was written on the blank form. Held not to be an attempt to commit forgery, but *semble* an attempt to fabricate false evidence (*R.* vs. *Ramsarem*, 4 N. W. P. 46).

16. *A* procures the printing of forms similar to those used by a company in forwarding accounts of goods supplied by it. *A* has done nothing towards forging the signature or seal of the company. Held this was no attempt to commit forgery (*R.* vs. *Raisat Ali*, 7 Cal. 352).

(17) *A* buys a stamp in the name of one *K* which the vendor endorses upon it and commences to write a bond out in *K's* name. This is an attempt to commit forgery (*R.* vs. *Kalyan Singh*, 16 All. 409).

I shall shortly comment on some of these illustrations.

Illustrations (3), (9) and (11) show that where a person has done all that he can to bring about the commission of an offence the fact that by reason independent of his will the offence has not been committed, does not exculpate him.

Illustration (4) shows that although the acts so far as they are accomplished may merely amount to preparation, but if the nature of the act precludes the possibility of the preparation being directed towards an honest purpose, it may be punished as an attempt. In connection with this case you may, however, consult *Reg.* vs. *Sutton* (2 Strange 1074) in which a man was convicted for having in his custody and possession two iron stamps with intent to impress the sceptres on six pence and to colour and pass them off for half-guineas. The defendant was sentenced to pay a fine of 6*s.* 8*d.* and to stand in the Pillory at Charring Cross.

This case was followed in *Reg.* vs. *Scofield* (1784 Cald 397), but was not followed in *Reg.* vs. Charles Stewart (1814 R. and R. 288).

The cases are, however, not quite similar for whilst procuring is an act, mere possession is not and the criminal law does not ordinarily punish merely an existing state of things. It may be argued that the very fact that the possession of any instrument of counterfeiting coin is made punishable by the Code (Section 235), and so also the procuring thereof (Section 234) is an indication that these cases do not fall within the definition of an attempt and are, therefore, to be separately provided for. On the other hand, it may be urged with equal force that the general doctrine relating to preparations is defective and fails to afford adequate protection to society or the public.

Illustration (5) shows that where an act so far as it is accomplished is *per se* an innocent act, the mere evil intention with which it was done in a particular case will not make it punishable as an attempt to commit an offence specially where by reason of remoteness between the acts done and the final execution the possibility of repentance is not excluded.

The correctness of illustration (6) is not free from doubt. I am rather inclined to think that it represents a mere stage of preparation and is not distinguishable from the case of a person who purchases a gun or poison to cause the offence of murder nor is it covered by one of those exceptional cases to which I have referred.

Illustration (7) is an instance of a mere evil intent which has not manifested itself in an overt act.

Illustration (8) I have already discussed.

Illustration (9) also shows that the mere impossibility of producing the desired consequence is not enough in cases where the impossibility is not absolute.

Illustration (10) is an instance of absolute inadaptability of means adopted to bring about an evil consequence. I would put it on the ground that such an action will cause no alarm to society.

Illustration (11) is also an instance showing that an attempt may be made out even where if it had succeeded, the offence charged would not have been committed.

Illustrations (12) and (14) show that the mere absence of the object is not enough to negative an attempt where the act was likely to create alarm and a sense of insecurity.

Illustration (13) I have already discussed.

The other illustrations are based on Indian decisions which I shall discuss in dealing with those cases.

The important Indian cases dealing with the interpretation of Section 511 are—

(1) *Queen* vs. *Dayal Bauri.*

(2) *Queen* vs. *Ramsaran.*

(3) *Queen* vs. *Peterson.*

(4) *Empress* vs. *Baldeo Sahay.*

(5) *Queen* vs. *Dhundi.*

(6) *Empress* vs. *Riasat Ali.*

(7) *In the matter of the petition of R. MacCrea.*

(8) *Queen* vs. *Kalyan Sing.*

1. *Queen* vs. *Dayal Bauri* (4 B. L. R., A. Cr., p. 55, 1869) was an important case which unfortunately led to a difference of opinion between the two learned Judges who formed the Court of Appeal. The facts found against the accused were that there had been about the time of the occurrence attempts at incendiarism in the locality, the active agent of which was a ball of rag enclosing a piece of burning charcoal. The villagers were suspecting the Bauries. The prisoner himself was a Bauri and defended himself and others of his caste and abused the villagers. The villagers

threatened to take him to the Thana, and whilst they were hustling him about, a ball of rag of the same kind fell from his *Dhoti* which on being opened was found to contain a piece of burning charcoal. Mr. Justice Glover thought that if it were a piece of unlighted charcoal only there would not have been a sufficient commencement of any act tending towards the commission of mischief by fire, and that the prisoner would, in that case, have been in the same position as a person who, intending to murder some other person whether by shooting or poisoning him, buys a gun or poison and keeps the same by him, such act being ambiguous, and not so immediately connected with the offence as to make the parties punishable under Section 511 of the Penal Code. But, since the instrument for causing mischief by fire was completely ready and was not used, only because the party carrying it had no opportunity, it must, thought the learned Judge, be assumed that a person going about at night provided with an apparatus specially fitted for committing mischief by fire intends to commit that mischief and that he has already begun to move towards the execution of his purpose, and that was sufficient to constitute an "attempt." On this view of the case he was for upholding the conviction. Mitter J. dissented from his colleague. He was of opinion that the mere fact of being in possession of a ball, like the one which was found with the prisoner, was by no means sufficient to warrant a conviction for attempting to cause mischief by fire. "In order," said the learned Judge, "to support a conviction for attempting to commit an offence of the nature described in Section 511, it is not only necessary that the prisoner should have done an overt act 'towards the commission of the offence,' but that the act itself should have been done 'in the attempt' to commit it." "Suppose," proceeded the learned Judge, "a man goes out of his house into the street with a loaded gun in his possession, and suppose even that there is evidence to show that he did so with the intention of shooting *Z*, if *Z* is not found in the street, or when found no attempt is made to shoot him either from fear or repentance, or from any other cause, can it be said that the man is guilty of attempting to murder *Z?* The going out of one's house with a loaded gun and with the intention of shooting a particular individual might be in one sense considered as an act done towards the shooting of that individual; but so long as nothing further is done, so long as there is no attempt to shoot him, and no overt act done 'in such attempt,' it is impossible to hold that there has been an attempt to murder." The learned Judge relied, in support of his view on a passage in Russell on Crimes, in which it was stated that acts in furtherance of a criminal purpose may be sufficiently proximate to an offence, and may sufficiently show a criminal intent to support an indictment for a misdemeanour, although they may not be sufficiently proximate to the offence to support an indictment for an attempt to commit it; as where a prisoner procures dies for the purpose of making counterfeit foreign coin, or where a person gives poison to another and endeavours to procure that person to administer it.

The decision of Mr. Justice Mitter has been accepted as correct by many writers on Indian Criminal law, notably by Mr. Mayne, and I admit it is conformable to the principles upon which preparations and attempts have been distinguished in many cases. The question, however, is one of great difficulty and one's inclination would, perhaps, be to hold that an offence had been committed and the accused deserved to be punished. Judging by the tests which I have suggested the preparation was in the first place of such a peculiar character that it could not be reasonably supposed to have been meant for an innocent purpose, and the fact that there had been about that time attempts at incendiarism in the village with balls of this description, would preclude the possibility of the ball having been meant for any purpose other than incendiarism. The presumption was violent that the accused intended to commit incendiarism, and that if not caught he would not have desisted from his purpose. What was said by Butler J. of the policeman and the pickpocket would apply with equal force to this case. The decision of Mr. Justice Glover may also be supported on the principle enunciated in Bishop's Book on Crimes that "the act was sufficient both in magnitude and in proximity to the fact intended to be taken cognisance of by law and was near enough to the offence intended, to create apparent danger of its commission."

As a matter of fact nothing remained to be done except the last proximate act, namely, the application of the fire-ball to some property which undoubtedly the accused wanted to destroy.

Mr. Justice Glover's view is also to a certain extent in conformity with the law laid down in the case of *Reg.* vs. *Taylor* (1 F. F., p. 511, 1859) tried before Chief Baron Pollock where the accused having lighted a lucifer match to set fire to a stack desisted on discovering that he was watched. It was held that the act amounted to an attempt. An argument in favour of Mr. Justice Mitter's view may be based on those cases where preparations have been made specifically punishable. It may be argued that if Mr. Justice Glover's decision were correct there would hardly have been any necessity to provide specifically for a case of possession of instrument for counterfeiting coin as has been done by Section 235 of the Code, as cases of this kind would have fallen under the general provision of attempts under Section 511 of the Code, and that the fact that those cases had to be specially provided for leads to the inference that they would otherwise not have been covered by the general provisions of the law relating to attempts. It may be urged that the accused could not have been charged for mere possession of an instrument for incendiarism as an attempt must always be an act. But it was not a case of mere procuring of means to commit the offence or of possession thereof, but there was a good deal more than that in the case inasmuch as the prisoner had come out of his house at a particular hour of the night, and was moving towards the object or objects which he intended to set fire to when he was interrupted by the villagers. One cannot but regret at the result, but our laws are defined with scientific precision and hedged round by too many general principles not always elastic. 'Happy is the nation,' says Baccaria, 'whose laws are not a Science.'

The result of the decision was as unfortunate as that in *Reg.* vs. *Collins*, and indicates that there is something wrong in the generally accepted principles.

2. *Queen* vs. *Ramsaran* (4, N. W. P. H. C. R., p. 46, 1872) was a case, the material facts of which are given in illustration 15 (page 68). Sir Charles Turner laid down that the word "attempt" indicated the actual taking of those steps which lead immediately to the commission of the offence, although nothing be done or omitted which of itself is a necessary constituent of the offence committed. It is perhaps unsafe to generalise in a matter of this kind. The question, as Sir Fitz James Stephen points out, can only be determined with reference to the facts of each case. In this case the nature of the preparation was such and it had reached a stage when if left to himself, and if not interrupted the accused would have, in all probability, completed the forgery. 'If a word of the document had been written,' said Turner J., 'the offence would have been complete.' The non-completion was the result of interruption and not of remorse. I doubt if there was not in that case a sufficient beginning of the offence charged to make the accused liable. Technically the decision may be right, but it cannot be defended on any intelligible principle.

3. *Queen* vs. *Peterson* (1 All., p. 316, 1876) was a case of a conviction for attempt to commit bigamy and the attempt consisted of the

publication of the banns of marriage. The learned Judge (Pearson J.) quoted with approval the following passage from Mayne's Indian Penal Code :—

> "Preparation consists in devising or arranging the means or measures necessary for the commission of the offence; the attempt is the direct movement towards the commission after the preparations have been made."

Accordingly the learned Judge held that the publication of the banns did not constitute an attempt, but only a preparation for such an attempt. 'The publication of the bann,' said the learned Judge, 'may or may not be in cases in which a special license is not obtained, a condition essential to the validity of the marriage, but common sense forbids us to regard either the publication of the banns or the procuring of the license as a part of the marriage ceremony.' The learned Judge also referred to what he described as the rule laid down in America, that an attempt can only be manifested by acts, which would end in the consummation of the offence but for the intervention of circumstances independent of the will of the party, and that in the case under consideration the accused might have willed not to carry out his criminal intention. The last is perhaps the strongest argument in favour of the view taken by the learned Judge if the Code leaves any room for such an argument, a point not wholly free from doubt.

4. In *Empress* vs. *Baldeo Sahay* (2 All., p. 253, 1879) it was held that to ask for a bribe is an

attempt to obtain one. The learned Judge having regard to the facts elicited in the case observed, "the intention had been conceived, the plans had been matured, and all preparations made, and though no specific sum had been asked for, the transaction had so far advanced that Abbas Ali had thoroughly understood what was being done, and put a stop to what might have been successful, if he had not refused to enter into any arrangement and intimated to him that he would not give anything."

5. In *Queen* vs. *Dhundi* (8 All., p. 304, 1886), the accused had made a false statement in order to obtain a certificate which would have enabled him to obtain a refund of *octroi* duty. The certificate, however, was not granted and in consequence the attempt failed. It was held by the learned Sessions Judge who referred the case to the High Court that the prisoner had not completed an attempt to cheat, but had only made preparations for it. "Even supposing," said the learned Sessions Judge, "that Dhundi by false representation had succeeded in getting a refund certificate, yet he still had a *locus pœnitentiæ*. He had to get it endorsed at the outpost and had to present it on the following Saturday for encashment before he finally lost all control over it, and could no longer prevent the commission of the offence. Before that time he might have altered his mind even from prudence, if not from penitence and torn up the certificate and no cheating could then have happened." Brodhurst J. agreed with this view and acquitted the prisoner.

6. The next case *Empress* vs. *Riasat Ali* (7 Cal., p. 352, 1881) was a comparatively important

case—important not only because it laid down a definite principle, but also important because of the reputation of the Judges who decided the case. That was a case in which the prisoner was found to have given orders to a particular press to print 100 forms similar to those formerly used by the Bengal Coal Company, to have corrected one of the proofs and to have suggested further corrections in a second proof in order to assimilate the form to that then being used by the Company. At this stage his activities were interrupted by his arrest by the Police. Sir Richard Garth held in the first place that the printed form without the addition of the seal or signature would not be a false document as that was technically what is meant by the words 'making a document.' It was urged that the printing and correcting of the form which was intended by additions to be a false document was in itself the making of the part of a false document within the meaning of Section 464 and therefore amounted to forgery. The learned Judge was, however, of opinion that this was not so, and if it were the mere printing or writing of a single word upon a piece of paper, however innocent the word might be, would be the making of a part of a false document, when coupled with an intention to add such other words as it would make it eventually a false document. "In my opinion," observed the learned Judge, "this is very far from the meaning of section 464, and I think that such a construction of the section involves a misconception not only of the word 'make,' but also of the sense in which the phrase 'part of a document' is used in the section." In coming to the conclusion that the act did not amount to an attempt, the learned Judge relied on *Reg.* vs. *Cheeseman* and also on Macpherson's case which I have already discussed. On the authority of those cases the learned Judges held that the attempt could not be said to be complete until the seal or the signature of the Bengal Coal Company was affixed to the document, and consequently what was done was not an act towards making one of the forms of false document, but if the prisoner had been caught in the act of writing the name of the Company upon the printed forms and had only completed a single letter of the name, then in the words of Lord Blackburn the actual transaction would have commenced which would have ended in the crime of forgery, if not interrupted. Prinsep J. concurred in the dictum of Lord Blackburn quoted by his colleague.

I feel considerable doubt regarding the correctness of this decision. A great deal depends upon the question as to what constitutes the making of a false document or part of a document. Assuming, however, that it is only constituted by the act of signing or sealing a document the point is lost sight of, that the mere signing or sealing cannot constitute a forged document without the writing which the seal or signature is intended to authenticate. The whole of the writing as the result of the signature becomes a part and parcel of the false document. The order in which the forgery is completed is immaterial. Supposing in accordance with the Indian practice of signing at the top a person begins with the signature, would it not be open to him to urge with equal force that the signature was meaningless without some other writing which the signature would authenticate, and then perhaps we will be told that unless a beginning is made with the writing of the body of the document there is no offence. It may, therefore, be said that as soon as the writing has commenced whether of the body of the deed or of the signature a beginning has been made with the actual transaction which, if not interrupted, would have ended in the crime. To hold that the actual transaction commences only when the signature is begun is taking a very narrow view of the meaning of a forged document and of an attempt to commit forgery. The definition of forgery itself shows that it contemplates the existence of a document to which the forged seal or the signature is attached. Therefore the forged seal or signature alone does not constitute the false document, and as the writing has commenced the actual transaction which would have ended in the offence may be said to have commenced. It has no doubt been held that the mere purchase of a particular kind of paper necessary for forging a document does not amount to an attempt, but the paper is not a material part of the document and the purchase of the paper is clearly a preparation and not an attempt. The definition of an attempt given by Lord Blackburn in *Reg.* vs. *Cheeseman* or by Cockburn C. J. in *Reg.* vs. *Macpherson* led to an erroneous decision in *Reg.* vs. *Collins* which was overruled in *Reg.* vs. *Ring*, and as I have already pointed out, the provision of the Indian Penal Code has followed the case last mentioned. The actual transaction, it may be remembered, is not the last act proximate to the offence. This case is also in conflict with the decision I have already referred to that a person who procures dies for the purpose of coining bad money, attempts to coin bad money. The surer tests are the extent of the presumption of evil intent arising from the act and the possibility of a change of intention. Whereas the purchase of a paper or for the matter of that of a stamped paper is fully consistent with an honest intention and cannot give rise to a presumption that an offence was contemplated, the printing of forms and the correcting of proofs in the manner disclosed in this case gave rise to a violent presumption that the accused could not have intended by these acts to serve any honest purpose, and in point of time the beginning with the writing was in such close proximity to the offence attempted that it was very unlikely that after having gone so far the accused would desist from carrying out his purpose. I do not place much stress on the case relating to the purchase of dies for that case is inconsistent with several other cases in England. This case was followed in *Chandi Pershad* vs. *Abdur Rahaman* (22 Cal., p. 131, 1894), but the correctness of the decision has been challenged in the case of *MacCrea* to which I shall refer later.

7. *In the matter of the petition of R. MacCrea* (15 All., p. 173, 1893) was a case in which the prisoner was charged among others of having attempted to cheat, it being his intention fraudulently to induce delivery of a valuable security. As is usual with Indian reports it is stated that the facts sufficiently appear from the judgment of the Court, but unfortunately they do not. The few facts so far as can

be gathered by piecing together the various parts of the judgment dealing with them appear to be the following:

There was a Government Promissory Note which was the property of one Mahomed Hosain Ali Khan. MacCrea with the intention of getting possession of that note from the Controller General entered into correspondence with his office, and then obtained in favour of one Asad Ali, a letter-of-administration to the estate of his deceased brother in which this particular note was falsely entered as belonging to the deceased. He forwarded this letter-of-administration and a draft notice for publication in the *Calcutta Gazette* with the object of inducing the Controller General to make over the note to Asad Ali Khan, to whom it did not belong. It was argued on behalf of the prisoner that the acts done by him amounted to preparation only and did not reach the stage of an attempt under Section 511 of the Indian Penal Code. Mr. Justice Nox in holding that the conviction was right distinguished *Queen* vs. *Ramsaran Chaubey* and expressed a dissent from *Empress* vs. *Riasat Ali*. I have already commented on this case and need not repeat what I have said. The learned Judge held—

(*a*) that 'attempt' within the meaning of Section 511 of the Indian Penal Code covers a much wider ground than the definition given either by Lord Blackburn in *Reg.* vs. *Cheeseman* or Chief Justice Cockburn in Macpherson's case;

(*b*) that Section 511 was not meant to cover only the penultimate act towards the completion of an offence and not acts precedent, if these acts are done in the course of the attempt to commit the offence, and are done with intent to commit it, or done towards its commission ;

(c) that the question is not one of mere proximity in time or place, that the time that may elapse between the moment when the preparations made for committing the fraud are brought to bear upon the mind of the person to be deceived and the moment when he yields to the deception practised upon him may be very considerable interval of time ;

(d) that an attempt once begun and a criminal act done in pursunce of it towards the commission of the act attempted does not cease to be a criminal attempt, because a person committing the offence does or may repent and abstain from completing the attempt. Blair J. generally agreed with these views.

The last observation is important. In England and America at any rate a change of intention even at the last moment would exculpate the offender, provided it was not the result of external compulsion moral or physical. Sir Fitz James Stephen states the English law thus :

'The offence of attempting to commit a crime may be committed in cases in which the offender *voluntarily* desists from the actual commission of the crime itself.' The learned author illustrates his proposition thus: '*A* kneels down in front of a stack of corn and lights a lucifer match intending to set the stack on fire, but observing that he is watched blows it out. *A* has attempted to set fire to the stack.' The illustration is based on the case of *Reg.* vs. *Taylor*, (1859, 1 F. and F. 511). Although the principle of *locus pœnitentiæ* is not expressly recognised in the Indian Penal Code, yet you will observe that it was recognised in the case of *Queen* vs. *Dhundi*. Whether a general principle like this can be admitted in derogation of the words of the section is extremely doubtful. You will have to strain the words of Section 511 a good deal to squeeze in such a principle into it. It is one thing to say that so long as there is room for the expectation of a change in the intention to commit an offence, the stage of a punishable attempt has not been reached at all, but once that stage is reached punishment cannot be avoided by proof that the accused is penitent.

8. *Queen* vs. *Kalyan Sing* (16 All., 409, 1894) is the case referred to in illustration 17. Briefly stated the facts are as follows:—

"One Chaturi calling himself Kheri, the son of Bhopal Kachhi, went to a stamp-vendor accompanied by a man, named Kalyan Sing, and purchased from him in the name of Kheri a stamp paper of the value of four annas. The two men then went to a petition-writer and Chaturi again gave his name as Kheri, they asked the petition-writer to write for them a bond for Rs. 50 payable by Kheri to Kalyan Sing. The petition-writer commenced to write the bond, but his suspicion being aroused, did not finish it, but took Chaturi and Kalyan Sing to the nearest thana."

It was contended on behalf of the defence that the acts committed by the accused amounted to no more than a preparation for an attempt to commit the offence and did not in themselves constitute an attempt, but Burkitt J. held that the acts alleged and proved amounted to much more than a preparation, and they were acts done towards the commission of an offence within the meaning of Section 511 of the Indian Penal Code. In taking this view reliance was placed on the dictum of Turner J. in *Queen* vs. *Ramsaran Chaubey* which I have already discussed.

Before leaving the subject I wish to repeat what I have already said, that the almost hopeless conflict of decisions both here and in England is conclusive evidence that the test usually adopted in determining the line of demarcation between preparations and attempts have not been infallible, and it is worth while to examine those tests somewhat closely to find out wherein they fail. It is not possible in the variety of human actions to draw the precise line between preparations and attempts. It often happens that in a series of acts culminating in an offence each step is a preparation for the next. In such cases it would be unduly restricting the meaning of the word to say that an attempt must preclude all stages of preparation, and be the last proximate act to that which would complete the offence, or to say that it must be the one immediately preceding that with which the acts constituting the offence begin.

In the absence of a clear dividing line the question must, to a great extent, be decided with reference to the facts of each particular case, and the general nature of the offence attempted. It is seldom that an offence consists of one single act. In every offence the whole series of preliminary acts that lead up to those that complete the offence are not essential parts thereof, a great many are innocent acts, innocent in that they are not harmful either to individual or to society. They are acts from which no evil intent can be inferred, they cause no disturbance to society, and are, therefore, not sufficient in magnitude to attract law's notice. What may appear to be a mere preparation need not necessarily be outside the scope of an attempt or even of a complete offence. But only such preparations as preclude the possibility of innocent intention should, on principle, be singled out for punishment.

LECTURE IV.

INCHOATE CRIMES.

II—Abetment.

When several persons are concerned in a criminal act and take different parts in it, it has been considered necessary to make a distinction between them according to the degree of culpability of each. Having regard to the fact that the Judge in most cases has been given great latitude in awarding punishment, the distinction does not appear by any means to be essential and its abolition is not likely to cause any hardship or injustice. The distinction, however, exists both in English and the Indian law, much more in the former than in the latter. Under the English law distinction is made between principals and accessories, between principals of first and second degrees, and between accessories before and after the fact.

Principals & accessories.

Whoever actually commits or takes part in the actual commission of a crime is a principal in the first degree.

Whoever aids or abets the actual commission of a crime is a principal in the second degree.

An accessory before the fact is one who directly or indirectly incites, counsels, procures, encourages or commands any person to commit a felony which is committed in consequence thereof. Such a person when present at the actual commission of the crime is a principal in the second degree.

An accessory after the fact to a felony is one who knowing a felony to have been committed by another receives, comforts, or assists him, in order to enable him to escape from punishment.

I have taken these definitions substantially from Stephen's Digest.

The distinction between principals and accessories has reference only to felonies. In treasons and misdemeanours all persons who aid or abet in the commission of a crime are regarded as principals, whether they are present or absent when it is committed. Similarly, an accessory after the fact in treasons is deemed as principal, but in misdemeanours such a person is not guilty of any offence. Here it may be useful to tell you that under the English law crimes are classified under three heads, treasons, felonies and misdemeanours.

Treasons, felonies and misdemeanours.

The name treason is given to certain crimes which are more particularly directed against the safety of the Sovereign and the State.

All indictable crimes below the degree of treason are either felonies or misdemeanours.

Felonies are those crimes which are such by common law or have been made such by statute.

All crimes which are not treasons or felonies are misdemeanours either by common law or by statute.

I need not go into further details regarding this classification. The distinctions based on them are more or less arbitrary and have not been followed in this country, and I do not think we have lost anything by doing so. Even in England the distinction is gradually disappearing, and there is now a feeling in favour of abolishing it. One step in this direction was taken in the year 1861 when the Accessories and Abetters' Act (24 and 25 Vict., C. 94) was passed, which enacted that " accessories before the fact, principals in the second degree and principals in the first degree are each considered as having committed the crime," and may be tried as if they had committed it.

As regards different degrees of criminality between persons taking different parts in the commission of a crime, the Indian Penal Code makes a broad distinction between principals and abettors.

Accessory after the fact not recognised in Indian Penal Code.

The Code does not recognise accessories after the fact, except that it makes a substantive offence of it in a few cases. For instance, a person who knowing or having reason to believe that an offence has been committed causes any evidence of the commission of that offence to disappear with the intention of screening the offender (Section 201), a person who conceals an offender with similar intent (Section 212), or a person who harbours a State prisoner or prisoner of war (Section 130), or harbours deserters (Section 136), or harbours offenders who have escaped from custody or whose apprehension has been ordered (Section 216), or harbours robbers or dacoits (Section 216A), is guilty of a substantive offence. It is also a substantive offence to resist the lawful apprehension of a person for an offence or to rescue an offender under arrest or to suffer an offender under custody to escape. I may state in passing that harbouring is explained for purposes of Sections 212, 216, and 216A to include supplying shelter, food, drink, money, clothes, arms, ammunition or means of conveyance or assisting a person in any way to evade apprehension. Even the simple distinction in Indian law between principal and abetter is without a difference in cases in which the punishment for abetment is the same as the punishment for the actual perpetration of the crime.

Three forms of abetment in the Indian Penal Code.

Under the Indian Penal Code abetment is constituted by instigation, by conspiracy or by aid intentionally rendered. I shall first deal with the more complicated subject of criminal conspiracies.

Instigation ordinarily means inciting or urging a person to do a thing.

Conspiracy is generally understood to mean an agreement between two or more persons to do or cause to be done anything illegal or to do a legal act by illegal means. A criminal conspiracy under Section 107 has a more restricted meaning. 'A person is said to abet the doing of a thing by conspiracy if he engages with one or more other person or persons in any conspiracy for the doing of that thing, if an *act or illegal omission takes place in pursuance of that conspiracy*, and in order to *the doing of that thing*.' The difference between the English and the Indian law was thus explained by Bhashyam Ayyanger J. in *Emperor* vs. *Tirumal Reddi* (24 Mad. 523).

" Under the English law, the agreement or combination to do an unlawful thing by unlawful means amounts in itself to a criminal offence. The Indian Penal Code follows the English law of conspiracy only in a few exceptional cases which are made punishable under Sections 311 (Thug), 400 (belonging to a gang of dacoits), 401 (belonging to a gang of thieves), 402 (being a member of an assembly of dacoits) and 121A (conspiring to wage war). In these cases, whether any act is done or not or offence committed in furtherance of the conspiracy, the conspirator is punishable; and he will also be punishable separately for every offence committed in furtherance of the conspiracy. In all other cases, conspiracy is only one species of abetment of an offence, as that expression is defined and explained in Section 108 and stands on the same footing as 'abetment by intentional aiding.' In regard to both these species of abetment, an act or illegal omission, in pursuance of the conspiracy or for the purpose of intentional aiding, is essential. If two or more persons conspire, the gist of the offence of abetment by conspiracy is not only the conspiracy, but the taking place of an act or illegal omission in pursuance of the conspiracy and in order to the doing of the thing abetted."

I shall discuss later on the change effected in this respect by the Criminal Conspiracies Act of 1913.

The third form of abetment consists in intentionally aiding by any act or illegal omission the doing of a thing. I shall deal with these three forms of abetment separately. I shall first deal with the two simpler forms, *viz.*, the first and the third.

INSTIGATION.

Instigation. Instigation, as the word itself implies, is the act of inciting another to do a wrongful act. It stands for the words counselling, procuring or commanding as generally used in English law.

Mere acquiescence or silent assent or words amounting to bare permission would fall short of instigation. *A* tells *B* that he is going to murder C. *B* says "You may do as you like and take the consequence." *A* kills *C*. *B* cannot be said to have instigated *A* to murder *C*. In order to constitute instigation it is necessary to show that there was some active proceeding which had the effect of encouragement towards the perpetration of the crime. So where two men having quarrelled agreed to fight with their fists, and each one deposited £1 with the prisoner who held the amount as a stake-holder to be paid to the winner, and it was found that beyond holding the stakes the prisoner had nothing to do with the fight and he was neither present at it, nor had any reason to suppose that the life of either man would be endangered, it was held that the prisoner was not guilty of any offence. Each such case must be decided on its merits. Lord Coleridge observed that to support an indictment there must be an active proceeding on the part of the prisoner. A stakeholder is perfectly passive, all he does is to accept the stakes (*R.* vs. *Taylor*, 44, L. J. M. C. 67).

Similarly, it has been held that such encouragement and countenance as may be lent by persons of influence who, aware of the object of an unlawful assembly, deliberately absented themselves from the locality to express sympathy with the object of the assembly cannot be said to be abetters —*Etim Ali Majumdar* vs. *Emp.* (4, C. W. N. 500). A mere request to do a thing may amount to abetment by instigation, *e.g.*, the offer of a bribe to a public servant even when it is refused. A person who had offered a bribe to a servant to sell his master's goods at less than their value was held guilty of incitement to commit an offence—*Reg.* vs. *De Kromme* (17 Cox, 492).

It has also been held that the mere receipt of an unstamped instrument does not constitute the offence of abetment of the execution of such an instrument—*Emp.* vs. *Janki* (7 Bom. 82).

In order to convict a person of abetting the commission of a crime by instigation, there must be proof of direct incitement; it is not enough that a person has taken part in those steps of the transaction which are innocent, but it is absolutely necessary to connect him in some way or other with those steps of the transaction which are criminal—*Queen* vs. *Nimchand* (20, W. R. Cr. 41).

But silent approval shown in a way that had the effect of inciting and encouraging the offence is abetment. Accordingly it was held that when a woman prepared herself to be a *Sutti* those that followed her to the pyre and stood by her crying '*Ram, Ram,*' and thereby actively connived and countenanced the act, were guilty of abetment—*Queen* vs. *Mohit* (3, N. W. P. 316). An instigation or incitement or aid rendered to an act which is a mere preparation to commit an offence not amounting to a commencement thereof does not constitute either a substantive offence or an attempt or abetment of the same—*Emp.* vs. *Baku* (24, Bom. 288). A person who by wilful misrepresentation or by wilful concealment of a material fact which he is bound to disclose voluntarily causes or procures or attempts to cause or procure a thing to be done is said to instigate the doing of that thing. (Section 107, Explanation 1). The following example is given to illustrate the case :

A, a public officer, is authorised by a warrant from a Court of Justice to apprehend *Z*. *B* knowing that fact and also that *C* is not *Z*, wilfully represents to *A* that *C* is *Z*, and thereby intentionally causes *A* to apprehend *C*. Here *B* abets by instigation the apprehension of *C*. This hardly calls for any comment.

AIDING.

It is explained that any one who, either prior to or at the time of the commission of an act, does anything in order to facilitate the commission of that act, and thereby facilitates the commission thereof, is said to aid the doing of that act. The explanation shows that the mere intention to facilitate, even coupled with an act calculated to facilitate, is not sufficient to constitute abetment, unless the act which it is intended to facilitate *actually* takes place and is facilitated thereby. It seems pretty clear from Explanation 2, Section 107, that one cannot be held to have aided the doing of a thing when that thing has not been done at all. For instance, if a servant keeps open the gate of his master's house, so that thieves may enter, and thieves do not come, he cannot be held to have abetted the commission of theft. But if such a person, after having opened the door or before it, informs possible thieves that he is going to keep the door open, he encourages them by his conduct to commit theft and is guilty of abetment; or if prior to the opening of the gate he had entered into an agreement with the thieves to keep the door open he would be guilty of abetment by conspiracy.

Whoever encourages, urges, provokes, tempts, incites or induces another to do a thing is said to instigate it. Whoever prior to or at the time of the commission of an act does anything in order to facilitate the doing of it is said to aid it.—Explanation (2), Section 107. For instance, if a person incites another to commit an assault by saying *maro maro* he only instigates the assault, but the man, who puts a *lathi* into the hands of another with the object of that other committing an assault with it, aids in the commission of the assault. Both abet the offence, one by instigation and the other by aid rendered.

Aid may be rendered by act as well as by illegal omission. Where a head-constable, who knew that certain persons were likely to be tortured for the purpose of extorting confession, purposely kept out of the way, it was held that he was guilty of abetment within the meaning of Explanation 2—*Queen* vs. *Kali Churn* (21 W. R. Cr. 11). But in such cases it is necessary to show that the accused intentionally aided the commission of the offence by his non-interference—*Khaja Noorul Hossein* vs. *Fabre-Tonnere* (24 W. R. Cr. 26). An omission to give information that a crime has been committed does not amount to aiding, unless such omission involves a breach of a legal obligation—*Queen* vs. *Khadim* (4 B. L. R. A. Cr. 7). When the law imposes on a person a duty to discharge, his illegal omission to act renders him liable to punishment—*Emp.* vs. *Latif Khan* (20 Bom. 394). This case follows *Queen* vs. *Kali Churn*

(21 W. R. Cr. 11). But the mere fact, however, of a village chowkidar being present when an extortion was being committed without eliciting any disapproval on his part, will not render him liable as an abetter of the offence—*Gopal* vs. *Foolmani* (8 Cal. 728). Such conduct neither amounted to incitement nor to aid, as it was not his legal duty to interfere or report such a case. A zemindar who lent a house to a police officer who was investigating a case, knowing that the house would be used for torturing a suspected thief, is guilty of abetment—*Emp.* vs. *Faiyaz Hossain* (16 A. W. N. 194).

In a recent *Sutti* case (*Emp.* vs. *Ram Lal*, 36 All. 26) persons were held guilty of abetment, who had done their best to dissuade the woman from becoming a *Sutti* and had even given information to the nearest police station, but finding it impossible to dissuade her complied with her wishes and helped her in effecting her object. In a somewhat similar case in England, where a pregnant woman anxious to procure abortion took a dose of corrosive sublimate and died, and it was found that this was procured at her desire by the prisoner who knew the purpose for which it was to be used, but did not administer the poison or cause it to be taken, but had only procured it at her instigation and under a threat by her of self-destruction, and the facts were consistent with the supposition that he hoped and expected that she would change her mind and not resort to it, the prisoner was held not guilty of being an accessory before the fact (*R.* vs. *Fretwell*, L. & C. 161).

The facility given must, however, be such as is essential for the commission of the crime. The mere act of allowing an illegal marriage to take place at one's house does not amount to abetment —*Queen* vs. *Kudum* (W. R. 1864, 13); so also mere consent to be present at an illegal marriage or actual presence in it, or the grant of accommodation in a house for the marriage, does not necessarily constitute abetment of such marriage; but the priest who officiates and solemnizes such illegal marriage is guilty of abetting an offence under Section 494—*Emp.* vs. *Umi* (6 Bom. 126).

CRIMINAL CONSPIRACY.

Conspiracy. Questions relating to conspiracy have, in recent years, assumed very great importance in this country, specially in Bengal, by reason of the prevalence of what are known as anarchical crimes, and there have been numerous cases dealing with the subject, and I propose to dwell on it at some length.

A conspiracy under the English law, and also under the Indian law as it now stands, is the agreement of two or more persons to do an illegal act or to do a legal act by illegal means. Before the passing of the Criminal Law Amendment Act of 1913 a conspiracy to do an illegal act was punishable only when such act amounted to an offence. It was also essential in the words of Section 107 of the Indian Penal Code, 'that an act or illegal omission should have taken place in pursuance of the conspiracy and in order to the doing of the act which was the object of the conspiracy.' The

Criminal Law Amendment Act, 1913. Criminal Law Amendment Act has, however, introduced two rather drastic changes in this respect. By Section 120B punishment is provided for criminal conspiracies of all kinds, whether, according to the requirement of Section 107, an overt act has or has not taken place in pursuance of such conspiracy, or whether, as required by Sections 109, 115 or 116, the object of the conspiracy is or is not the commission of ano ffence. Section 120A defines a criminal conspiracy thus :—

When two or more persons agree to do or cause to be done an illegal act or an act which is not illegal by illegal means, such an agreement is designated a criminal conspiracy.

It also provides that no agreement, except an agreement to commit an offence, shall amount to a criminal conspiracy, unless some act besides the agreement is done by one or more parties to such agreement in pursuance thereof.

The first part of the definition brings the English and the Indian law on a line, in so far as they differed regarding the nature of the act with reference to which the conspiracy was formed, the Indian law confining conspiracies to agreements to commit punishable wrongs, the English law only insisting on such wrongs being merely illegal. The second is a compromise between the Indian law and the English law. The Indian law insisted on some overt act, the English law did not. But now an overt act is necessary only where the object of the conspiracy is the commission of an illegal act not amounting to an offence. I may, however, observe that even under the English law an overt act is necessary in an action of tort for conspiracy (*Moghul Steam Ship Co.* vs. *Mcgregor*, L. R. 21, Q. B. D. 549).

The position now is this. Conspiracies now fall into two classes not wholly exclusive of one another—

A. Conspiracies falling within the definition of abetment in Section 107 of the Indian Penal Code.

B. Conspiracies outside the definition of abetment, but falling within the words of Section 120A.

All conspiracies falling under class A and also such conspiracies under class B as are for the commission of offences punishable with death, transportation or rigorous imprisonment for a term of two years or more are governed by the law relating to abetment as contained in Chapter V, Section 120B, sub-section (1). With reference to cases of the latter class the distinction is maintained but without any difference. In Chapter V a distinction is made between abetments which are followed by the act abetted and as the result of such abetment and abetments which are not so followed. These, for the sake of brevity, I shall distinguish as successful and unsuccessful abetments. A successful abetment in the absence of any special provision to the contrary is punishable in the same way as the offence which it abets or is intended to abet (Section 109).

Unsuccessful abetments may be divided into three classes according to the nature of the offence abetted :—

(*a*) Where the offence abetted is punishable by death or transportation for life ;

(*b*) Where it is punishable by imprisonment;
(*c*) Where it is not punishable by death or transportation for life or by imprisonment.

In the case of (*a*) the punishment may extend to seven years or fine (Section 115).

In the case of (*b*) the punishment may extend to one-fourth of the longest term provided for the offence abetted, or with the fine provided for that offence or with both (Section 116).

In the case of (*c*) the law provides no punishment at all.

There remain conspiracies which may or may not fall within the meaning of abetment defined in Section 107 but which fall within the scope of Section 120A, but are not punishable with death, transportation or rigorous imprisonment for two years or more. These are punishable with imprisonment of either description for a term not exceeding six months or with fine or with both. Section 120B, sub-section (2). In these cases no distinction is made between successful and unsuccessful conspiracies, and none of the provisions of Chapter V will apply.

Although, you will observe, the amendment does not expressly affect conspiracies falling within Section 107, its effect is to do away with the limitations provided in that section, in all cases falling under Section 120B, sub-section (1). One result of maintaining the distinction without maintaining the difference is this: That with reference to offences punishable with death or transportation or rigorous imprisonment for two years the wider definition of a conspiracy in Section

120A practically replaces the more limited definition in Section 107. But as regards offences not so punishable the following effect seems to follow :-

(*a*) Where an offence is punishable with imprisonment of less than two years or with simple imprisonment only a punishment of six months replaces the punishment provided under Section 116.

(*b*) In case of offences punishable with fine only they are for the first time made punishable when the conspiracy is an unsuccessful one and irrespective of the question whether the conspiracy is one under class A or class B.

(*c*) A conspiracy to commit a mere illegal act not amounting to an offence which was outside the scope of Chapter V has been for the first time made punishable, the punishment provided being six months or fine or both.

The anomalies that the new method of treatment involves are that in cases falling within Section 120A and not falling under Section 107 and not punishable under Section 120B, sub-section (1), the provisions of Chapter V are inapplicable, and some of the matters specially provided for in Chapter V will have to be dealt with on general principles without reference to those specific provisions, and the argument based on their not being made expressly applicable will have considerable force, and it is difficult to say how Courts will decide them. The inconvenience arising from the necessity of introducing doctrines of English common law in the interpretation of laws carefully and exhaustively codified is obvious, and this inconvenience was recognised when a decision of Sir Barnes Peacock on the interpretation of Section 34 was followed somewhat rapidly by amending the section so as to incorporate that principle.

In the statement of objects and reasons for the Criminal Law Amendment Act, VIII of 1913, the necessity for the amendment has been thus explained :

" Under Section 107 abetment includes the engaging with one or more person or persons in any conspiracy for the doing of a thing, if an act or illegal omission takes place in pursuance of that conspiracy, and in order to the doing of that thing. In other words, except in respect of the offences particularized in Section 121A, conspiracy *per se* is not an offence under the Indian Penal Code.

" On the other hand by the common law of England if two or more persons agree together to do anything contrary to law, or to use unlawful means in the carrying out of an object not otherwise unlawful, the persons who so agree commit the offence of conspiracy. In other words conspiracy in England may be defined as an agreement of two or more persons to do an unlawful act or to do a lawful act by unlawful means, and the parties to such a conspiracy are liable to indictment.

" Experience has shown that dangerous conspiracies are entered into in India which have for their object aims other than the commission of the offences specified in Section 121A of the Indian Penal Code, and that the existing law is inadequate to deal with modern conditions. The present Bill is designed to assimilate the provisions of the Indian Penal Code to those of the English law with the additional safeguard that in the case of a conspiracy other than a conspiracy to commit an offence some overt act is necessary to bring the conspiracy within the purview of the criminal law. The Bill makes criminal conspiracy a substantive offence, and when such a conspiracy is to commit an offence punishable with death, transportation or rigorous imprisonment for a term of two years or upwards, and no express provision is made in the Code, provides a punishment of the same nature as that which might be awarded for the abetment of such an offence. In all other cases of criminal conspiracy the punishment contemplated is imprisonment of either description for a term not exceeding six months or with fine or with both."

The Indian Penal Code contained no definition of a conspiracy up to the year 1913. The definition given for the first time by the amending Act, as pointed out in the statement of objects and reasons, assimilated the provisions of the Indian Penal Code to those of the English law with one small difference.

It would be useful to refer to the exposition of the law of criminal conspiracy by eminent Judges in England. In *Reg.* vs. *Gill*, 2B. & Ald. 204, Lord Holrayed said that conspiracy was itself the offence, and it was quite sufficient to state only the act of conspiracy and the object of the conspiracy in the indictment. He pointed out that a conspiracy to cheat, for instance, was indictable even when the parties had not settled the means to be employed.

In *Mulchay* vs. *Reg.* (3 L. R. H. L. R. 306) Willes J. guarded against the common belief, of which I have found expression in some Indian cases also, that conspiracy is an exception to the general principle that criminal law takes no notice of an evil intent so long as it has not manifested itself in an overt act. 'A conspiracy,' observed the learned Judge, 'consists not merely in the *intention* of two or more but in the *agreement* of two or more to do an unlawful act by unlawful means. So long as such a design rests in intention only it is not indictable. When two agree to carry it into effect, the very plot is an act in itself and the act of each of the parties promise against promise, *actus contra actum* capable of being enforced if lawful, punishable if for a criminal object or for the use of criminal means. The number and the compact give weight and cause danger.' In the same case Lord Chelmsford explained that agreement was an act in advancement of the intention which each person has conceived in his mind. The definition given by Willes J. was accepted by the House of Lords in subsequent cases and was quoted as an authority in *Barindra Kumar Ghose* vs. *Emperor*, more commonly known as the Alipore Conspiracy Case, 14 C. W. N., 1114. 'To establish the charge of conspiracy,' said Jenkins, C.J., 'there must be agreement, there need not be proof of direct meeting or combination nor need the parties be brought into each other's presence; the agreement may be inferred from circumstances raising a presumption of a common plan to carry out the unlawful design. As was pointed out in *Pulin Behary Das* vs. *Emperor*,

Agreement is the gist of the offence.

16, C. W. N. 1105, on the authority of *Reg.* vs. *Gill*, 2 B. and Ald. 204, combination is the gist of the offence, there is nothing in the word conspiracy, it is the agreement which is the gist of the offence.

Passive cognizance of conspiracy no offence.

It is well established that mere passive cognizance of a conspiracy is not sufficient, there must be active co-operation; in other words, joint evil intent is necessary to constitute the offence. This is implied in the meaning of the term conspiracy itself (Wharton, Vol. II, Art. 1341*a*). In Pulin Behary's case it appeared that certain members of a society found to be revolutionary were not acquainted with the real object of the society, not having been admitted to its secrets, and it was held that it would not be proper to convict such members of the charge of conspiracy. In such cases there is no agreement of two minds and not even mental participation in each other's designs.

The difficult question, however, as pointed out by Russell, is to find out when a particular combination becomes unlawful. We get very little assistance on this point from the reported decisions. An agreement implies the meeting of two minds with reference to a particular matter, and so long as matters are discussed and views are interchanged, but the plan of action has not been settled by the concurrence of any two or more of the conspirators, the stage of criminal conspiracy would not be considered to have been reached. I have already told you more than once that a mere criminal intention formed in a man's mind and never getting beyond that stage is never criminally cognisable. The forum of conscience alone can take notice of such cases, but municipal law can only deal with matters and not merely with mind save as manifested by action. So long as the design to do a wrongful act rests in intention only it is not criminal, but as soon as two or more agree to carry it into effect the agreement goes beyond mere mental conception of a design and is an offence. You have, however, seen that in the case of an attempt not only is intention insufficient, but intention even, where coupled with an act which merely discloses the *mens rea*, but goes no further to carry it out or in other words merely amounts to a preparation and is not a link in the chain of circumstances that would immediately lead to the crime, would not constitute an attempt. Consistency, therefore, required that a mere conspiracy should be considered a substantive offence, only when the object of the conspiracy is so serious as the waging of war against the sovereign and other acts of equally grave nature, and thato ther cases of conspiracy should be deemed an offence, only when they fall within the definition of abetment, *i.e.*, when the agreement has led to some overt act which does more than merely disclose the *mens rea*, or to use the words of Section 107 'if an act or illegal omission takes place in pursuance of the conspiracy and in order to the doing of that thing, *i.e.*, the thing which is the object of the conspiracy.' Not only has consistency secured by the original framers of the Code now been sacrificed, but the pecularities of the English law have been reproduced at a time when feeling in other countries is veering just the other way.

Special features of the law of conspiracy.

Although a conspiracy is not confined to the mind only, there are still circumstances which make the law of conspiracy something apart from the general principles of criminal law. You have seen that the law does not punish a mere preparation to commit an offence. You will also observe that for an assembly to be unlawful you require at least five persons sharing in one common object. In conspiracies, however, you require only two to complete the offence and yet you punish before even the stage of preparation is reached. Take, for instance, the case of five persons agreeing to commit a theft. If they assemble with that common object and are caught they would only be held guilty of an unlawful assembly and would be punishable with not more than six months' imprisonment. Even if they had proceeded to the stage of preparation to commit theft they could not be punished for an attempt to commit that offence, but if they were caught when they had just entered into the agreement they are punishable as conspirators and would be exposed to more severe punishment than that for being member of an unlawfully assembly. One of the grounds upon which a preparation is not punished is that it causes no alarm to society, and also because ordinarily it does not disclose the existence of a criminal intent. Similarly a conspiracy, though it may itself technically be an overt act, has not the publicity of an overt act and does not produce the same disturbing effect on society as an ordinary overt act towards the commission of a crime. Conspirators often work in secret, and it is seldom that a conspiracy is revealed until something is done in pursuance of it. That this is so ordinarily will appear from the facts of the various cases relating to conspiracy that have recently come before the courts here. There probably would have been no danger and no inconvenience if the law in India were left exactly where it was before the Conspiracy Act was passed. But although the law is changed in practice it can make very little difference, for even though you declare a conspiracy to be complete without an overt act, you cannot prove a conspiracy without it. Again I may refer to what I have already told you that it is not the policy of law to create offences that cannot ordinarily be proved. It is also an inconsistency that whereas any individual attempting to commit an offence is given a *locus pœnitentiæ*, the conspirator has none. The conspiracy is complete as soon as the agreement or combination is formed. No repentance, no desire to withdraw protects him. As observed by Brett J. the crime of conspiracy is completely committed, if it is committed at all, the moment two or more have agreed that they will do, at once or at some future time, certain things. It is not necessary in order to complete the offence that any one thing should be done beyond the agreement; the conspirators may repent and stop, or may have no opportunity, or may be prevented, or may fail; nevertheless, the crime is complete; it was completed when they agreed. You have seen that in cases of attempts the adoption of means absolutely unadapted to the end excuses the criminal, for instance, a person who attempts to kill his enemy by witchcraft is not punishable, but it seems that once an agreement is entered into to commit murder, even if the means agreed upon is absolutely insufficient, that is no excuse.

The peculiar doctrine about conspiracies has been defended on the ground, that the combination of two or more persons to commit an illegal act gives a momentum to the act which justifies its punishment at the earliest possible stage. Bowen J. in *Moghul Steam Ship Company* vs. *Mcgregor Gow & Co.*, 23 Q. B. D. 598, observed as follows :—"Of the general proposition that certain kinds of conduct not criminal in any one individual may become criminal if done by combination among several there can be no doubt. The distinction is based on sound reason, for a combination may make oppressive or dangerous that which if it proceeded only from a single person would be otherwise and the very fact of the combination may show that the object is simply to do harm to the exercise of one's just right." This may be sound with reference, for instance, to the offence of rioting and other offences relating to the disturbance of public peace, but has very little weight in relation to an offence like forgery, and still less so in relation to acts which are merely illegal. The true justification for punishment of all kinds of inchoate crimes will be found in the following passage from Bentham : "The more these preparatory acts are distinguished, for the purpose of prohibiting them, the greater the chance of preventing the execution of the principal crime itself. If the criminal be not stopped at the first step of his career, he may at the second, or the third. It is thus that a prudent legislator, like a skilful general, reconnoitres all the external posts of the enemy with the intention of stopping his enterprises. He places in all the defiles, in all the windings of his route, a chain of works, diversified according to circumstances, but connected among themselves, in such manner that the enemy finds in each, new dangers and new obstacles."

If this policy had been consistently followed the deplorable result that might have followed the decision of Mitter J. in Doyal Bauri's case would be avoided.

It has also been suggested that the secrecy with which conspirators generally act is another ground for departing from ordinary principles in dealing with the few that are caught. But whatever may be the value of the explanation or attempt at explanation, one finds it difficult to be convinced that there is any justification for treating as an offence, the agreement to commit an act, that is merely illegal and not an offence when done by a single individual. "The application of this theory," says Russell, "has caused much controversy, especially as to combinations with reference to trade or of employers against workmen or workmen against employers." The point is fully discussed by Wharton, and it is stated by him that conspiracy as a distinct offence has been stricken from the revised codes of Prussia, Oldenburg, Wurtemburg, Bavaria, Austria and North Germany. I do not think this will give rise to any inconvenience, for the law relating to attempts, if freed from some of those meaningless technical limitations, which have no better basis than unbroken tradition, will fully serve the purpose of punishing offences at their inception. Those who were responsible for the Indian Penal Code must have realised how difficult it was to defend the law of conspiracy as it then existed, and had the courage to alter the law, in order that it may conform to reason and common sense and be consistent with its other provisions, and with all respect for those who are responsible for the legislation of 1913 I must say that it is difficult to see the justification for the change.

The late Chief Justice Cockburn made the following suggestions for the amendment and consolidation of the law of conspiracy, in which he justified the punishment of persons conspiring to do an act which if committed by a single individual would have amounted merely to a mere civil injury:—

Three classes of conspiracies according to Cockburn, C. J.

"Conspiracy may be divided into three classes—First, where the end to be accomplished would be a crime in each of the conspiring parties, a class which offers no difficulty. Secondly, where the purpose of the conspiracy is lawful, but the means to be resorted to are criminal, as when the conspiracy is to support a cause believed to be just, by perjured evidence. Here the proximate or immediate intention of the parties being to commit a crime the conspiracy is to do something criminal; and here again the case is consequently free from difficulty. The third and last case is where with a malicious design to do an injury the purpose is to effect a wrong, though not such a wrong as, when perpetrated by a single individual, would amount to an offence under a criminal law. Thus an attempt to destroy a man's credit, and effect his ruin by spreading reports of his insolvency, would be a wrongful act, which would entitle the party whose credit was thus attacked to bring an action for a civil wrong, but it would not be an indictable offence.......The law has wisely and justly established that a combination of persons to commit a wrongful act with a view to injure another shall be an offence, though the act, if done by one, would amount to no more than a civil wrong." (Wharton, Vol. 2, p. 177.)

This peculiarity in the treatment of criminal conspiracies and the departure from some of the ordinary principles of criminal law have led to various other peculiarities which I shall briefly discuss. Of these the most important are the special rules of evidence which have been exhaustively discussed in some of the recent cases in Bengal.

Special rules of evidence in trials for onspiracy.

One of the peculiar features of the rules of evidence relating to conspiracies is that anything said or done by any one of the conspirators, having reference to their common intention, is under certain circumstances evidence against the others. The reason of the law is that, within the scope of the conspiracy, the position of the conspirators is analogous to that of partners, one being considered the agent of the other. Russell states the law on the subject thus: " when several persons are proved to have combined together for the same illegal purpose, any act done by one of the party in pursuance of the original concerted plan, and with reference to their common object, is in the contemplation of law the act of the whole party and therefore the proof of such act would be evidence against any of the others who were engaged in the same conspiracy; and declarations made by one

Act or declaration of one conspirator when and how far evidence against others.

of the party at the time of doing such illegal act seem not only to be evidence against himself as tending to determine the quality of the act, but against the rest of the party who are as much responsible as if they had themselves done the act."

Existence of conspiracy must be proved first.

But before you can give in evidence the acts of one conspirator against another, you must prove the existence of the conspiracy, *viz.*, that the parties were members of the same conspiracy and that the act in question was done in furtherance of the common design. The prosecutor may, however, either prove the conspiracy which renders the acts of the conspirators admissible in evidence or he may prove the acts of the different parties and so prove the conspiracy (Archbold, p. 307, 1288). You will notice that in a case of conspiracy it is open to the prosecutor to go into general evidence of the nature of the conspiracy before he gives evidence to connect the defendant with it. This is a course which is not ordinarily permissible in a criminal trial, but the peculiar nature of the indictment of conspiracy necessitates this departure.

In Hardy's trial, 24 How St. Tr. 451, for high treason, letters written by one conspirator to another were held to be evidence against the prisoner after his complicity in the conspiracy had been established.

You must bear in mind, however, that although on a charge of conspiracy statements made by any conspirator for the purpose of carrying the conspiracy into effect are admissible in evidence against the others, statements by one not made in pursuance of the conspiracy are not so admissible.

nor are statements made after the conspiracy has been abandoned or its object attained. In *R.* vs. *Blake*, 6 Q. B. 137, the prisoner was tried for conspiracy with one Tye to defraud the Customs. Tye was an agent to pass goods through the Customs and pay the proper duties. Blake was an official of the Customs called a "landing waiter." Passing goods through the Customs was effected as follows:—Tye made a list of the goods he wished passed. This was copied into the official Customs House record and the original given to Blake to check the goods by as they came ashore. Blake tallied the goods with the list, and if the list was accurate his duty was to write "correct" across it and add his initials. The duty payable was then calculated according to the list thus checked and paid. Tye made a false list which Blake certified as correct. Blake was caught; Tye absconded. To prove the conspiracy Tye's day book was tendered in evidence showing that the list Blake certified as correct could not have tallied with the goods actually put ashore and received, also Tye's cheque book, the counterfoil of which showed the amount of which the Crown had been defrauded by the conspiracy. Both documents were admitted, but on an application for a new trial, on the ground of improper reception of evidence, it was held that the day book was properly admitted, but that the counterfoil of the cheque book was inadmissible and should have been rejected, as no declaration of Tye could be received in evidence against Blake which was made in Blake's absence and did not relate to the furtherance of the common object.

Blake's case.

Hardy's case.

In Hardy's case, referred to above, evidence was tendered by the prosecution of a letter written by one of the conspirators Thelwall, not then on trial, to his wife who was not a party to the conspiracy, in which he simply detailed the part he had taken in the crime. Eyre, C.J., refused to admit the evidence and summed up the whole matter thus :—

"I doubt whether we ought to consider this private letter as anything more than Mr. Thelwall's declaration, and Mr. Thelwall's declaration ought not to be evidence of anything, which though remotely connected with this plot, yet still does not amount to any transaction done in the course of the plot for the furtherance of the plot, but is a mere recital of his, a sort of confession of his, of some part he had taken. It appears to me that that is not like the evidence of a fact which is a part of the transaction itself."

Husband and wife if can be conspirators.

It may be mentioned in passing that in English law a man and his wife cannot be indicted for conspiring together alone, because legally they are deemed to be one person, but such an indictment will not be barred in this country.

Section 10, Indian Evidence Act.

The Indian law regarding evidence to prove conspiracy is practically the same and Section 10 of the Indian Evidence Act provides as follows :—

> 'Where there is reasonable ground to believe that two or more persons have conspired together to commit an offence, or an actionable wrong, anything said, done or written by any one of such persons in reference to their common intention, after the time when such intention was first entertained

> by any one of them, is a relevant fact as against each of the persons believed to be so conspiring, as well as for the purpose of proving the existence of the conspiracy as for the purpose of showing that any such person was a party to it.

The following is the illustration given to show the meaning and scope of the section :—

> 'Reasonable ground exists for believing that *A* has joined in a conspiracy to wage war against the Queen. The facts that *B* procured arms in Europe for the purpose of the conspiracy, *C* collected money in Calcutta for a like object, *D* persuaded persons to join the conspiracy in Bombay, *E* published writings advocating the object in view at Agra, and *F* transmitted from Delhi to *G* at Cabul the money which *C* had collected at Calcutta, and the contents of a letter written by *H* giving an account of the conspiracy, are each relevant, both to prove the existence of the conspiracy, and to prove *A's* complicity in it, although he may have been ignorant of all of them, and although the persons by whom they were done were strangers to him, and although they may have taken place before he joined the conspiracy, or after he left it.'

This section is intended to make evidence, communications between different conspirators, while the conspiracy is going on with reference to the carrying out of the conspiracy. The section is perhaps wider than the English law as to evidence Scope of the section.

in cases of conspiracy ; but it is not intended to et in the confession of a co-accused and put it on the same footing as a communication passing between conspirators or between the conspirators and other persons with reference to the conspiracy—(*Emp.* v. *Abani Bnushan,* 15 C. W. N. 25). You will notice that what is to be established under the section to make documents found in the possession of one of several persons accused of conspiracy admissible against the others is that there is reasonable ground to believe in the existence of a conspiracy amongst such persons. It is not necessary for this purpose to establish by independent evidence that they were conspirators—(*Puiln Behary Dass* vs. *Emp.*, 16 C. W. N., 1107). In an earlier case (*Kalil Munda* vs. *King Emp.*, 28 Cal. 797), Ghosh and Brett JJ. laid down that where it is shown that there is reasonable ground to believe that two or more persons have conspired together to commit an offence anything said done or written by any one of such persons in reference to the common intention may be proved both for the purpose of proving the existence of the conspiracy as also for showing that any such person was a party to it. *In re Chedambaran Pillai*, 32, Mad. 3, it was held that if *C* engaged with *S* in a conspiracy to excite disaffection towards the Government and if in pursuance of such conspiracy and in order to the exciting of disaffection an overt act took place, then *C* would be guilty of having abetted the excitement of disaffection and the speeches of *C* would be admissible in evidence to prove the object of the conspiracy. In *Pulin Behary Dass* vs. *Emperor* it was held that if the facts proved are such that the Jury as reasonable men can say that there was a common design and the prisoners were acting in concert to do what is wrong, that is evidence from which the Jury may suppose that a conspiracy was actually formed. In the same case the learned Judges pointed out that once reasonable grounds are made out for belief in the existence of the conspiracy amongst the accused, the acts of each conspirator in furtherance of the common object are evidence against each of the others, and this whether such acts were done before or after his entry into the combination, in his presence or in his absence. Acts done prior to the entry of a particular person into the combination are evidence to show the nature of the concert to which he becomes a party, whilst subsequent acts of the other members would indicate further the character of the common design in which all are presumed to be equally concerned. In this case the discovery of certain arms made after the arrest of the accused was held to be admissible, in view of the case made by the prosecution that the arms belonged to the association of the conspirators and were deposited in the place where they were found many months earlier when the activities of the association were in full operation. The same case is an authority for the proposition that it is not necessary that all the conspirators should have joined the scheme from the first; those who come in at a later stage are equally guilty provided the agreement is proved. In *Barirdro Kumar Ghosh* vs. *Emperor* (14 C. W. N. 1114) evidence of the association of an individual accused with the place of conspiracy and correspondence with or relating to the members of the conspiracy, as also connection with newspapers and pamphlets published in furtherance of the object of the conspiracy, was held to be admissible.

Evidence in conspiracy case generally circumstantial.

The evidence in support of an indictment for conspiracy is generally circumstantial; and it is not necessary to prove any direct concert or even any meeting of the conspirators (Russell, Vol. I, p. 191). The existence of a conspiracy is in most cases a matter of inference, deduced from criminal or unlawful acts done in pursuance of a common criminal purpose. The agreement which is the gist of the offence may be inferred from circumstances raising a presumption of a common concerted plan to carry out the unlawful design; direct evidence, which is almost impossible in such cases, is not necessary. In *R.* vs. *Duffield* (5 Cox 404) Earle J. told the Jury that 'it does not happen once in a thousand times when the offence of conspiracy is tried that any body comes before the Jury to say that he was present at the time when the parties conspired together, and when they agreed to carry out their unlawful purposes; but the unlawful conspiracy is to be inferred from the conduct of the parties, and if several men are seen taking several steps, all tending towards one obvious purpose, and they are seen through a continued portion of time taking steps that lead to one end, it is for the Jury to say whether those persons had not combined together to bring about that end which their conduct appears so obviously adapted to effectuate.' In another case (*R.* vs. *Cope*, 1 Str. 144) a husband and wife and their servants were indicted for conspiring to ruin the trade of the King's card maker. The evidence against them was, that they had at several times given money to his apprentices to put grease into the paste which had spoiled the cards; but there was no account given that more than one at a time was ever present, though it was proved that they had all given money in their turns; it was objected that this could not be a conspiracy on the ground that several persons might do the same thing without having any previous communication with each other. But it was ruled that the defendants being all of a family and concerned in making of cards, it would amount to evidence of a conspiracy.

Whatever these peculiarities may be regarding evidence of conspiracy, there is, and there can be no relaxation of, the fundamental principle of criminal jurisprudence that the onus of proving an indictment is entirely on the prosecution, and a man must be presumed to be innocent until he is proved to be legally guilty beyond doubt, and if there is any doubt at all he must be given the benefit of it and acquitted, although the greatest suspicion may exist against him. The responsibility and difficulty of Courts of Law in admitting and weighing the evidence adduced in support of a conspiracy are thus greater than in any other case owing to the wide scope and nature of the evidence permissible to be brought before the Court. I may here aptly quote the words of Jenkins, C.J., in *Barindro Kumar Ghosh* vs. *Emperor*—"There is always the danger in a case like the present that conjecture or suspicion may take the place of legal proof, and therefore it is right to recall the warning addressed by Baron Alderson to the Jury in *Reg.* vs. *Hodges*, 2 Lewis C. C. 227 (1838), when he said ' the mind was apt to take a pleasure in adapting circumstances to one another, and even in straining them a little, if need be, to force them to do some parts of one connected whole ; and the more ingenious the mind of the individual, the more likely was it, in considering such matters, to over-reach and mislead itself, to supply some little link that is wanting, to take for granted some fact consistent with its previous theories and necessary to render them complete.' "

One alone cannot conspire.

It follows from the very nature of the offence of conspiracy that there must be at least two to complete the offence. So where two persons are indicted for conspiring together (no other parties being alleged) if one is convicted and the Jury is for the acquitting of the other, the conviction of the one cannot stand. In *Reg.* vs. *Manning* (42 Q. B. 241) defendant Manning and a person named Hannam were indicted at the Winchester Summer Sessions for conspiring together to cheat and defraud. Lord Coleridge, C.J., tried the case and directed the Jury that they might find one prisoner guilty and acquit the other. This was afterwards held to have been a misdirection and the principle was clearly laid down. " The rule appears to be this," said Mathew J., " in a charge for conspiracy in a case like this when there are two defendants the issue raised is whether or not both the men are guilty, and if the Jury are not satisfied as to the guilt of either then both must be acquitted." This rule has been carried so far that when three were charged jointly with conspiring together and one pleaded guilty, but the other two were tried and acquitted, even then it was held that the conviction of the confessing accused could not stand—*R.* vs. *Plummer* (1902, 2 K. B. 397).

In one case some cannot be found guilty of one and some of another conspiracy.

It has been held that where several persons are indicted for a conspiracy it is a legal impossibility that any verdict should be found which implies that some were guilty of one conspiracy and some of another (per Stephen J. in *R.* vs. *Manning*). See also *Emperor* vs. *Noni Gopal Gupto*, 15 C. W. N. 593.

Effect of the acquittal of some on other co-conspirators.

As a matter of procedure it would seem that if *A* be indicted and tried alone for conspiring with others he could be lawfully convicted, though the others referred to or indicted in the indictment had not appeared or pleaded or were dead before or after the indictment was preferred or before pleading not guilty or were subsequently and separately tried. But it is not settled whether in cases of separate trials of the conspirators the acquittal of those tried later would avoid the conviction of an earlier trial and for the same conspiracy (Russell, Vol. I, 147, 148). In consequence of the nature of the crime, it has been held, when an indictment for conspiracy was tried in the Court of King's Bench a new trial granted as to one of several, convicted of conspiracy, operated as a grant of a new trial as to the others convicted, although the grounds for the grant of the new trial applied only to the one. But where of those indicted for conspiracy some were convicted and some acquitted, the grant of a new trial in favour of those convicted did not affect the verdict of acquittal. A new trial can no longer be granted in England on conviction of any criminal offence (7 Edw. VII, c. 23, S. 20).

but the principles noticed above may have to be considered in the event of an appeal by one conspirator where several have been convicted.

It has been held that a judgment of not guilty against an accused person fully establishes his innocence and the incident in respect of which the charge was brought cannot be used against the acquitted person in a subsequent trial for conspiracy (*Emp.* vs. *Nonigopal*, 15 C. W. N. 593). But the fact that proceedings for participation in a dacoity against certain individuals were dropped owing to insufficiency of evidence does not preclude a charge of conspiracy in respect of such dacoity being brought against the same persons and others, for the criminality of a conspiracy is distinct from and independent of the act which the conspiracy was intended to promote (*Pulin Behary* vs. *Emp.*, 15 C. W. N. 1107).

Instances where conspiracy punishable under the Penal Code.

Although a conspiracy has been generally made punishable under Section 121A there are other cases where specific acts, which can only be regarded as a conspiracy to commit an offence, have been made punishable, as pointed out by Bhashyam Ayyangar J. in *Emp.* vs. *Tirumal Reddi*, 24 Mad. 523. For instance, Section 310 read with Section 311 makes it punishable for any person to be habitually associated with any other or others for the purpose of committing robbery or child-stealing by means of or accompanied with murder. Similarly Section 400 says " whoever at any time after the passing of this Act shall belong to a gang of persons, associated for the purpose of habitually committing dacoity, shall be punished, etc." Section 402 is also of the same nature. These cases, however, strictly speaking are not punished as conspiracies, but as cases of association for habitual commitment of offences, *i.e.*, the association being of such a character as to lead to irresistible presumption of antecedent guilt. You will note that in all those sections the object of the association is the habitual committing of some offence. Habitual association for the purpose of committing an offence implies a great deal more than a mere agreement. These sections will operate only after several such offences have already been committed. An unlawful assembly may be looked upon as one particular phase of a criminal conspiracy. But there is the distinction that an assembly is a good deal more than a mere criminal agreement. It does not amount to an attempt, it is at any rate one of those preparations which the law has expressly made punishable.

Trade combinations and combinations of workmen.

I would, before leaving the subject of conspiracies, refer shortly to its application to trade combinations for the purpose either of creating monopolies and thereby to raise prices or to combinations of workmen in order to raise wages. The law of conspiracy has been invoked in aid of what are termed free trade principles which, as Sir Fitz James Stephen has pointed out, have meant different things at different times. At a certain stage of commercial development in England, free trade ideas have led to the enactment of laws which had the effect of keeping down wages by penalising combinations among workmen and artisans. A statute enacted in 1349 laid down "that every man and woman of what condition he be, free or bond, able in body, and within the age of three-score years and not having means of his own, if he in convenient service (his state considered) be required to serve, he shall be bounden to serve him which so shall him require." By a similar statute passed next year the wages of the most important classes of mechanics were fixed. Things have now greatly changed. The struggle between labour and capital has brought out the strength of both sides and the workman is no longer under the heels of the capitalist. Public conscience in America has been aroused against the mischievous effect of the gigantic combinations of capitalists which have enabled them to dominate the market by killing all competition and thereby to place the public entirely at their mercy. The struggle will inevitably lead to a readjustment of the claims of labour and capital in a way that would be fair to both. How far combinations, either of labour or of capital, are legal have been discussed both in England and in America. These cases are important even here, for our workmen have not been slow to imitate the methods of workmen in other parts of the world. We have had very recently strikes among butchers, strikes among ghariwalas and the solution even here cannot be long deferred. It was said by Earle J. in *R.* vs. *Rowlands* (17 Q. B. 671 and 871) of workmen and of masters: "The intention of the law is, at present, to allow either of them to follow the dictates of their own will with respect to their own actions and their own property, and either, I believe, has a right to study to promote his own advantage or to combine with others to promote their mutual advantage." The general question of the legality of trade combinations was also discussed in the case of *Moghul Steam Ship Company* vs. *McGregor Gow & Co.* to which I have already referred. That was a case in which an associated body of traders had combined to create in their favour a practical monopoly of a certain trade, by offering very favourable terms to their customers, with the object of killing competition. The competition was held to be not indictable. Lord Justice Bowen cautioned against pressing the doctrine of illegal conspiracy 'beyond that which is necessary for the protection of individuals or of the public.' "The truth is," said the learned Judge, "that the combination of capital for purposes of trade and competition is a very different thing from such a combination of several persons against one with a view to harm him as falls under the head of an indictable conspiracy. There is no just cause or excuse in the latter class of cases. There is such a just cause or excuse in the former. There are cases in which the very fact of a combination is evidence of a design to do that which is hurtful without just cause, is evidence (to use the technical expression) of malice. But it is perfectly legitimate, as it seems to me, to combine capital for all the mere purposes of trade for which capital may, apart from combination, be legitimately used in trade ...... Would it be an indictable conspiracy to agree to drink up all the water from a common spring in a time of draught ; to buy up by preconcerted action all the provisions in a market or district in times of scarcity (see *R.* vs. *Waddington*, 1 East 143) ; to combine to purchase all the stores of a company against a coming settling day, or to agree to give away articles of trade gratis in order to withdraw custom from a trade ? May two itinerant match-vendors combine to sell matches below their value in order by competition to drive a third match-vendor from the street ? The question must be decided by the application of the test I have indicated Assume that what is done is intentional and that it is calculated to do harm to others. Then comes the question. Was it done without just cause or excuse ? If it was *bona fide* done in the use of a man's own property, in the exercise of a man's own trade, such legal justification would, I think, exist not less because what was done might seem to others to be selfish or unreasonable (see *R.* vs. *Rowlands*, 17 Q. B. 671). But such legal justification would not exist when the act was merely done with the intention of causing temporal harm, without reference to one's own lawful gain or the lawful enjoyment of one's own rights. The good sense of the tribunal which had to decide would have to analyse the circumstances, and to discover on which side of the line each case fell." This decision was approved of by the House of Lords on appeal (1892, A. C. 25) and was followed in *Allen* vs. *Flood* (1898, A. C. 1) and *Quinn* vs. *Leathem* (1901, A. C. 495). In *South Wales Miners Federation* vs. *Glamorgan Coal Co.* (1905, A. C. 239) Lord Lindley said :—" It is useless to try and conceal the fact that an organised body of men working together can produce results very different from those which can be produced by an individual without assistance. Moreover laws adapted to individuals, not acting in concert with others, require modification and extension, if they are to be applied with effect to large bodies of persons acting in concert. The English law of conspiracy is based on this undeniable truth." Admitting that this is so, the constitution of a conspiracy by a combination of two persons can hardly be said to fall within the reason of the law. That large conspiracies by the very fact of the combination produce consequences of a grave nature may be true. From this point of view the penalisation of large combinations on strikes, be they of the gharriwalas or railway employees or any other class of workmen or even of capitalists may perhaps be defended. But it would be ridiculous to punish two gharriwalas because they agree to go upon a strike. It might interest you to know that a combination between Military Officers of the East India Company to resign their Commissions in order to coerce the Company into granting them certain allowances was held punishable. In an American case Judge Agnew held that a combination between miners in a particular market controlling the coal in that market to hold up the price of coal is indictable at common law. "When competition is left free," said he, "individual error or folly will generally find a correction in the conduct of others. But here is a combination of all the companies operating in the Blossburg and Barclay mining regions and controlling their entire productions. They have combined together to govern the supply and the price of coal in all the markets from the Hudson to the Mississippi rivers and from Pennsylvania to the lakes. This combination has a power in its confederated form which no individual action can confer.......The influence of a lack of supply or the rise in the price of an article of such prime necessity, cannot be measured. This permeates the whole mass of the community and leaves few of its members untouched by its withering blight. Such a combination is more than a contract; it is an offence." *Morris Run Coal Co.* vs. *Barclay Coal Co.*, 68 Pa. 173. It has, however, been urged that if there is no fraud or no intimidation, in the means adopted, rulings making penal agreements between particular owners to keep up prices are open to the objections (*a*) that they would be futile, as combinations may be made without formal agreement by a tacit understanding; (*b*) that if effective, such rulings would cover every combination to obtain remunerative prices; (*c*) that they put a prerogative which can be best exercised by individuals, as the exigencies of the time prompt, into the hands of the State; (*d*) that they establish a standard which is fixed and therefore often harsh and oppressive, in place of one which is elastic, yielding to the necessities of the market. I have discussed this question at some length, not because it is of any importance, so far as the Indian Criminal Law is concerned, but of its possible importance in the future.

Indictment of conspiracy how to be framed.

As regards the form of indictment in a trial for conspiracy, you must remember that in a criminal trial an indictment is the basis of the prosecution; it should enable the prisoner to know what is the charge against him. The Code of Criminal Procedure provides that the charge shall contain such particulars as to the time and place of the alleged offence and the person, if any, against whom or the thing, if any, in respect of which it was committed as are reasonably sufficient to give the accused notice of the matter with which he is charged (Section 222), and if the nature of the case is such that those particulars do not give the accused sufficient notice of the matter with which he is charged, the charge shall also contain such particulars of the manner in which the alleged offence was committed as will be sufficient for that purpose (Section 223).

It has been held that an indictment for conspiracy may be framed in a general form (*R.* vs. *Gill*, 2 B. and Ald. 204), but there are numerous instances in which the Court has made an order for particulars being furnished to the accused.

Although in stating the object of a conspiracy the same degree of certainty is not required as in an indictment for the offence conspired to be committed, the charge of conspiracy must not be indefinite. The counts must state the illegal purpose and design of the agreement entered into between the defendants with such proper and sufficient certainty as to lead to the necessary conclusion that it was an agreement to do an act in violation of the law (*Amritalal Hazra* vs. *Emperor*, 19 C. W. N. 676). In *Jogjiban Ghosh* vs. *Emperor*, 13 C. W. N. 861, the charge was to the effect that the accused on or between certain dates mentioned in the charge, unlawfully and maliciously conspired to cause by an explosive substance, *viz.*, a bomb, an explosion in British India, etc., and Jenkins, C.J., and Mookerji J. held that the charge should have specified with what other persons the accused had conspired. In *Emperor* vs. *Lalit Mohan*

Chakravarti, 15 C. W. N. 98, the accused were charged with conspiracy with persons known and unknown and it was held that the charge could not be maintained without the persons who were known being definitely named.

Abetment when complete.

I, now return to the general question of abetments. It is inferable from Section 107, clause *thirdly*, as well as from Explanation 2 of that section, that abetment constituted by intentional aiding presupposes that the act aided has been consummated or at any rate commenced. In the other two forms of abetment, *viz.*, abetment by instigation and abetment by conspiracy, the abetment is complete as soon as the instigation or conspiracy has taken place and is quite independent of such consummation or commencement. In this connection it will be useful to consider the provisions of Section 34 and to determine the relative culpability of those who merely abet and those whose case falls within that section. Section 34 provides that 'when a criminal act is done by several persons in furtherance of the common intention of all, each of such persons is liable for that act in the same manner as if it were done by him alone.' Section 114, on the other hand, provides that one who, if absent, would be liable to be punished as an abettor, is present when the act or offence for which he would be punishable in consequence of the abetment is committed, he shall be deemed to have committed such act or offence. It is obvious that both Sections 34 and 114 contemplate cases where an offence has been consummated. The effect of Section 114 seems to be to confine the punishment for abetment, as provided in Sections

Difference between abetment and cases under Section 34.

Sections 34 and 114 distinguished

109, 115 and 116, to persons who abet an offence and are absent when the offence abetted takes place, those who are present being deemed as principals. Cases under Section 114 must fall under Section 107 and have the additional element of presence at the commission of the crime. Cases falling under Section 34 are, however, distinct from cases of abetment, for otherwise the section would apparently serve no useful purpose.

No illustration is given to Section 34, but apparently it incorporates the principle laid down in 1838 in the case of *Reg.* vs. *Cruse* (8 C. and P. 541), which, in Stephen's Digest, Article 39, has been reproduced almost in the words of Section 34 and illustrated thus :—

" A constable and his assistants go to arrest *A* at a house in which are many persons. *B*, *C*, *D*, and others come from the house, drive the constable and his assistants off, and one of the assistants is killed, either by *B*, *C*, *D*, or one of their party. Each of their party is equally responsible for the blow whether he actually struck it or not." From the general accuracy of the Indian Penal Code and the care taken in defining offences to keep in view all their distinct phases, we may presume that Sections 34 and 114 were not intended to overlap.

Act of abetment distinct from act abetted.

The definition of abetment shows that two distinct acts are contemplated, the act abetted and the act constituting the abetment ; the one is detached from the other with a clear line of demarcation between them. The idea of joint action which is an essential element in a case under Section 34 is excluded by the very definition of abetment. In a case under Section 34 there is no question of abetment. It clearly excludes the case in which one commits an offence and another merely instigates or aids. In the illustration I have given all come out together to effect a common purpose. It is uncertain who actually caused the death of the constable, and even where this could be ascertained it is immaterial, for it was a mere matter of accident what part each played in the transaction. All were prepared to commit the offence and take such part in it as circumstances required. Take again the case of several persons going out to commit a theft, some of whom actually move the articles, some stand by ready to help, whilst others wait some way off to give alarm if any one comes, every one has committed theft and there are no grounds for any differentiation between them. So also in a case of murder there is no reason to differentiate between persons of whom one holds the victim by the legs, another by the head, whilst the third applies the knife to the victim's throat. In such a case the knife with which the throat was cut might have been as well in the hand of *A* as in that of *B*, and Section 34 applies to all of them. Although under the English law, in the case of theft, the actual mover of the articles would be the principal in the first degree and the others would be principals in the second degree, the distinction even under that law is without a difference. Under Section 34 all of them will be considered *pacticipes criminis* to the same extent and in the same degree, and no distinction between abettors and principals would arise in such cases.

Where, however, some are prepared only to facilitate the commission of the crime and to stop there and to take no further part in the actual commission of the crime they are only abettors. If present they will be dealt with under Section 114 and if absent under Sections 109, 115 or 116, as the case may be.

Necessity of Section 34 discussed.

Mr. Justice Stephen of the Calcutta High Court, in discussing the question of the necessity and utility of Section 34 in a letter published in the *Calcutta Weekly Notes*, Vol. 18, page 222N, takes a case somewhat of a different nature. He thinks that where *A*, *B* and *C* all fire at *D* and kill him, and it is found that *B* and *C* missed, and it was the shot fired by *A* that caused death, the case does not fall under Section 34. If it does not fall under Section 34 it can hardly be said to fall under Section 107 or under Section 114. In such a case as in the illustrative cases I have discussed, all go out to effect a common purpose, and it is purely a matter of accident that death is actually caused by one rather than the other. In most cases it would be impossible to find out whose shot proved fatal. The Court in such a case may very well decline to consider who is actually responsible for the consequence. It may, however, be urged that if in the illustration given the criminal act mentioned in Section 34 is the causing of death, it was caused by *A* alone, and it cannot be said that the criminal act was done by all the three. From this point of view the case may not be covered by Section 34, but if so, the case of those who missed would not come under any of the three forms of abetment in Section 107 and would go unpunished. It may in some cases afford evidence of a conspiracy and thereby the case may be brought under abetment, but that is a different matter altogether. If there is any force in the argument against the application of Section 34 those that missed may be held guilty of an attempt to commit murder, and the case would then fall under Section 307 of the Code. But even as against this it may be urged that there is no reason why those who missed should receive the lesser punishment. But this argument may be urged with equal force against the whole policy of Section 307. The inclination of my mind is to treat the whole firing as one act and to hold every one jointly liable for the consequence in which case Section 34 would apply. It would, as I have already said, be idle in such a case to require evidence to show who aimed correctly and who did not. The participants in the crimes would in most cases not know it themselves.

In *Nibaran Chandra Ray and others* vs. *King-Emperor* (11 C. W. N. 1085), their Lordships Mitra and Fletcher JJ. observed :—

"If, however, two persons are found under circumstances as assumed in the hypothetical case with gun in their hands, and they have been acting in concert, or that each was an assenting party to the action of the other, the criminal act done by one must be presumed to have been done in furtherance of the common intention, and Section 34 of the Indian Penal Code may be invoked to impose penal liability on any one of the persons in the same manner as if the act was by him alone."

In the opinion I have expressed that Section 34 relates to joint acts directed towards a common purpose and forming as it were, a single transaction and thereby excluding cases of abetment. I am also fortified by the observations of Holmwood and Sharfuddin JJ. in the case of *Manindra Chandra Ghose* vs. *King-Emperor* (18 C. W. N. 580). Their Lordships observed: "Section 34 does not involve abetment and therefore does not imply any conspiracy and does not require proof that any particular accused was responsible for the commission of the actual offence." The same view was held in *Keshwar Lal Shaha* vs. *Girish Chandra Dutt* (29 Cal. 496). A servant had received money for *ganja* sold by his master in contravention of the terms of his license, both being present at the sale. Prinsep and Stephen JJ. held that Section 114 did not apply and that the servant was guilty of the offence of selling *ganja* without a license by the operation of Section 34.

As I understand Section 114, it only means that if a man abets an act and is present at the commission of the act abetted, he is punishable as principal, but if he is absent he is only punishable as an abettor. The words in Section 114, "*who, if absent, would be liable to be punished as an abettor,*" have been differently interpreted, and it has been said that there must be an antecedent abetment, and a subsequent presence at the commission of the act which had been previously abetted. This was apparently the view taken in the case of *Ram Ranjan Ray* vs. *King-Emperor* (19 C. W. N. 28). Before coming to this case I should like to draw your attention to several earlier cases on the applicability of Section 114.

Queen vs. *Mussammat Nironi and Moniruddin* (7 W. R. 49) is an important case on the interpretation of this section. Moniruddin was convicted of having abetted the murder of one Bulai, he being present when the murder was committed. After rejecting a confession of Moniruddin the learned Judges (Jackson and Glover JJ.) were of opinion that all that was left to prove Moniruddin's complicity were—

(*a*) The fact of his intrigue with the wife of the deceased;

(*b*) The statement of a witness who says he saw Moniruddin running away from the spot.

Upon these facts they held that a case under Section 114 had not been made out. The learned Judges observed:

"The Court of Sessions has not convicted the prisoner of the murder, but of abetment and being present at the commission of the murder so as to make him liable (under Section 114, Indian Penal Code) to be deemed to have committed the murder. It is clear that to bring the prisoner within this section it is necessary first to make out the circumstances which constitute abetment, so that 'if absent' he would have been 'liable to be punished as an abettor,' and then to show that he was present when the offence was committed.

"Now we find no evidence of any fact or facts which would amount to abetment of either kind. The only fact really in evidence against the prisoner would support a case of suspicion, not of the strongest kind, against the prisoner Moniruddin, that he had himself committed the murder, if we had not the admission of Niruni herself that the deed was her own.

"The whole case for the prosecution appears to point to Moniruddin as a principal offender and not a mere abettor, but he has not been convicted or even charged as such, and whatever may be the inclination of our minds as a matter of private opinion, we cannot now direct the prisoner to be tried on that charge."

In this case there was no evidence as to any act constituting abetment and mere presence of Moniruddin at the occurrence, without some evidence as to his attitude towards the crime and the effect of his presence on the actual perpetrator of the crime, was rightly held to be insufficient to constitute abetment.

If, however, there were evidence that Moniruddin and the woman Niruni had gone together to commit the murder and that Moniruddin's presence had the effect of encouraging the woman or to facilitate the commission of the murder, he would have been clearly an abettor. On the other hand if it could be shown that Moniruddin and the woman went together to commit the murder and Moniruddin took any part in its actual commission, he would have been liable under Section 34.

This case was followed in *Abhi Missir* vs. *Lachmi Narayan* (27, Cal. 566). That was a case in which grievous hurt was caused to a police officer by Abhi Misser and a number of other persons. The finding of the Sessions Judge was that if the accused all joined together to beat the Inspector, so as to cause him grievous hurt, all would by the provision of Section 114 of the Indian Penal Code be guilty of an offence under Section 325. The learned Judges (Prinsep and Stanley JJ.) observed :

"We think that the law has been properly expressed in the case of *Queen* vs. *Mussammat Niruni and another*, in which it was held that to bring a prisoner within Section 114 of the Penal Code, it is necessary first to make out the circumstances which constitute abetment, so that 'if abesnt' he would have been liable to be punished as an abettor; and then to show that he was also present when the offence was committed. Under such circumstances we think that the conviction and sentence passed by the Magistrate and confirmed by the Sessions Judge should be set aside."

The facts of this case are the same as those in the illustration to Article 39 in Stephen's Digest taken from *Reg.* vs. *Cruse*, to which I have already referred.

The decision is right so far as it holds that the accused having all joined in the assault on the Sub-Inspector there was no question of abetment or of the applicability of Section 114. In explaining, however, a previous case (*Queen-Empress* vs. *Chhatardhari*, 2, C. W. N. 49), the learned Judges say that it was not intended in that case to lay down, that mere *presence as an abettor of any person would under the terms of Section 114 render him liable for the offence committed*, and that it was found in that case that the *abetment had been committed before the actual presence of the accused at the commission of the offence abetted.* From a reference to the facts of that case it will appear that the mere presence of one of the accused had the effect of facilitating the commission of the crime and constituted such encouragement as rendered the act at least one of abetment, even if it fell short of the requirements of Section 34, and the decision was quite correct and consistent with the case law both here and in England. That case required no explanation in this case, but the learned Judges in trying unnecessarily to differentiate it, made the observations I have quoted which are not warranted by the words of Section 114. Although these observations do not seem to have been expressly relied on in Ram Ranjan's case, it is not unlikely that the ball set rolling by Prinsep and Stanley JJ. was taken up by Jenkins, C.J., and his colleague.

In *Hansa Pathak* vs. *Banshi Lal Dass* (8, C. W. N. 519) the accused was found to have been a member of an unlawful assembly which went armed with *lathies* and axes and looted the house of the complainant. The accused himself did not remove any property nor did he make any preparation for committing any theft or aiding any one in the commission of the theft. He was convicted under Sections 114 and 379 of the Indian Penal Code. The learned Judges Bannerji and Harrington JJ. held that on these facts the accused if he had been absent would not have been punishable as an abettor. His connection with the offence of theft arose from his being a member of the unlawful assembly, the common object of which was to commit theft and some members of which assembly actually committed theft. That being his only connection with the case, Section 114 did not apply.

If this reasoning is correct, then if there were not more than five in the assembly, and the accused who is said to have been the leader of the party had, with three others, gone out armed to loot the complainant's house and the house were looted, the accused standing aside and taking no part, he could not be convicted of any offence at all. There being no unlawful assembly, Section 149 would not apply, and in the absence of a joint action in furtherance of the common intention of the others, Section 34 also would not be applicable. I do not think the view of law taken in this case is correct. There may be circumstances under which mere presence may amount to abetment. The accused, it was found, shared the common intention of his party and was their leader. He was with them. His presence alone, whilst he approved what was going on, was sufficient to constitute him an abettor.

I have the authority of Wharton, Article 211, in support of this view. The learned author says :

"Although a man be present while a felony is committed, yet if he take no part in it, and do not act in concert with those who commit it, he will not be a principal in the second degree, merely because he does not endeavour to prevent the felony or apprehend the felon. Something must be shown in the conduct of the bystander which indicates a design to encourage, incite, or in some manner afford, aid or consent to the particular act ; though when the bystander is a friend of the perpetrator, and knows that his presence will be regarded by the perpetrator as an encouragement and protection, presence alone may be regarded as an encouragement. When presence may be entirely accidental, it is not even evidence of aiding and abetting. Where presence is *prima facie* not accidental, it is evidence, but no more than evidence, for the jury. It is not necessary, therefore, to prove that the party actually aided in the commission of the offence; if he watched for his companions in order to prevent surprize, or remained at a convenient distance in order to favour their escape, if necessary, or was in such a situation as to be able readily to come to their assistance, the knowledge of which was calculated to give additional confidence to his companions, in contemplation of law he was aiding and abetting."

I now come to the case of *Ram Ranjan Ray* vs. *King-Emperor* (19, C. W. N., 28) to which I have referred more than once. The zemindar Ram Ranjan had sent for one of his tenants and had assaulted him by one of his servants for not agreeing to pay an enhanced rent; while this was going on, the uncle of the tenant came and protested whereupon the zemindar gave order to the servant saying '*maro sala ko*,' and the latter wounded the tenant by kicking him first and then striking him with a *lathi* on the head with the result that he died. The zemindar was convicted under Section 302 read with Section 114, Indian Penal Code, but it was held by Jenkins, C.J., and N. R. Chatterjee J. that the conviction could not stand for this single reason that 'the only abetment charged necessarily required the presence of the accused, while to come under Section 114 the abetment must be complete apart from the presence of the abettor.'

I confess I fail to appreciate the force of the learned Judges' reasonings in this case. Here was a man who had ordered his servant to beat the deceased (*maro sala ko*). The servant on the command of his master assaulted the deceased and caused his death. If it were found that he did not mean that the deceased should be killed outright or that the death of the deceased was not a probable consequence of the order, the master might have been held guilty of a lesser offence, but there seems to be no ground for holding that the case did not fall under Section 114, because the only abetment charged "necessarily required the presence of Ram Ranjan while to come within Section 114 the abetment must be complete apart from the presence of the abettor." The conclusion seems to be wholly unwarranted. Why the words "*maro sala ko*" which constitutes the most common form of incitement in this country, should have required the presence of the abettor is not intelligible, and it is equally unintelligible why it should be necessary in order to bring a case under Section 114 to prove a previous abetment away from the scene of occurrence and a subsequent presence at the occurrence itself. I do not see anything in the words of Section 114 to justify such a view.

In *Emperor* vs. *Amrita Govinda* (10, Bom. H. C. R., 497) it was held that if the abettor of an offence is on account of his presence at its commission to be charged under Section 114 as a principal, his abetment must continue down to the time of the commission of the offence. If he distinctly withdraws at any moment before the final act is done, the offence cannot be held to have been committed under his continuing abetment.

In *Queen* vs. *Shib Chandra Mundal* (8, W. R. Cr. 59) it was held that when a number of armed men came and carried off a crop they must, even if they took no part in the actual taking, be considered guilty of the substantive offence under Section 378. Leaving aside the question of interpretation, it may be useful to enquire whether, if the view taken by Jenkins, C.J., is correct, there is any reason for separately dealing with the case of a person who having abetted an offence is subsequently present at its commission. Such a person either takes an active part in the commission of the offence or does not. If he does, he comes within the scope of Section 34 and is dealt with as a principal. If he does not and his presence amounts to encouragement or aid, he is an abettor and his case would fall under Section 109, and here also he receives exactly the same punishment. But if he is present and his case does not fall under Section 34 or 114, his presence may be disregarded, and he will still be liable under Section 109 by reason of the antecedent abetment. It is clear that in a case falling under Section 114 the provisions of sections 115 and 116 can have no application, for there can be no presence at the commission of a crime in a case where the crime is not committed at all. For these reasons the necessity of Section 114 even on the interpretation placed on it by Jenkins, C.J., is not clear. This, however, is a difficulty which is not removed even if the other interpretation which I have suggested is accepted, and it seems to me that upon any view of the interpretation of Section 114 its utility cannot be clearly demonstrated. Why make separate provision for an abettor present at the commission of a crime when even if he were absent his punishment would have been the same under Section 109. It may perhaps be suggested that Section 114 is not subject to any special provision in the Code relating to the punishment of an abettor, whereas Section 109 is. The explanation seems plausible at the first sight, but an examination of these special provisions show that in no case there is any separate provision for the punishment of abetment where the offence abetted is itself punishable by the Code. The only special cases, it would be observed, are those in which the original offence is dealt with under other laws, or is not by its very nature punishable at all. The special provisions are, so far as I can gather, the following, *viz.*, those relating to the abetment of offences against the State and His Majesty's Army and Navy (in Chapters VI and VII of the Code) and abetment of suicide (Sections 305, 306).

Taking the case of suicide first, neither Section 114 nor Section 109 can have any application for suicide cannot and is not punishable as a substantive offence except where it is a mere attempt to commit it (Section 309). To that Section 109 will apply and so will Section 114. In the other cases Section 109 will not be applicable by reason of the special provisions, and Section 114 will be equally inapplicable for there is no punishment prescribed in the Code for the substantive offence, those being offences under military laws and the provisions of Section 5 show that the Code does not affect any of the provisions of any act for punishing mutiny and desertion of officers and soldiers in the service of His Majesty, these being exactly the offences for the abetment of which there are special provisions in the Code. Although I have expressed a doubt as to the correctness of the view expressed non-judicially by Stephen J. regarding the scope of Section 34, I think, the conclusion arrived at by him, that Section 114 is a surplusage is correct and the explanation which he has suggested seems extremely probable. The only difference between Sections 109 and 114, as pointed out by the learned Judge, is that in one case the accused is punished as if he had done a thing and in the other as being deemed to have done it.

Section 34 distinguished from Section 149.

Section 34 has also to be differentiated from Section 149. One patent difference is, no doubt, the necessity for five persons or more to constitute an unlawful assembly, in order to bring into play the provisions of Section 149. There are, however, other more important and less obvious differences. In the case of Section 149 there need be neither joint action nor abetment, but all that is required is a common object to render liable one member of an unlawful assembly for an act done by another in prosecution of such common object. Here also joint action tending to one particular consequence is excluded. In *Riazuddin* vs. *King-Emperor* (16, C. W. N., 1077) five accused were in ambush and attacked the complainant simultaneously. Reaz caught hold of the complainant's neck and threw him down on the ground. Reaz, Khoaz and Tamiz beat him and Khoaz broke his 8th rib.

The other two were standing close by with *lathies* in their hands. The accused were originally charged under Sections 147 and 325 read with 149, Indian Penal Code. The Sessions Judge on appeal convicted the accused under Section 325 only. The conviction was set aside and Holmwood and Imam JJ. observed as follows :—

" When a Court draws up a charge under Section 325 read with Section 149, it clearly intimates to the accused persons that they did not cause grievous hurt to anybody themselves, but that they are guilty, by implication, of such offence, inasmuch as somebody else in prosecution of the common object of the riot in which they were engaged did cause such greivous hurt.

" *Section 34 can only come into operation where there is a substantive charge of causing grievous hurt.* The considerations which govern Section 34 are entirely different and in many respects the opposite of those which govern Section 149, and it is now settled law that when a person is charged by implication under Section 149, he cannot be convicted of the substantive offence."

You may note that in Section 34 as it was originally framed the words 'in furtherance of the common intention of all' did not occur. Sir Barnes Peacock in *Queen* vs. *Gora Chand Gopi* (5, W. R. Cr. 45) held that mere presence of persons at the scene of an offence is not *ipso facto* sufficient to render them liable to any rule such as Section 34 enunciates, and that 'the furtherance of a common design' was an essential condition before such a rule applied to the case of an individual person. The law was accordingly amended by Act XXVII of 1870 and the words referred to were added.

It is noticeable that whilst Section 34 speaks of acts in furtherance of the common intention of all, Section 149 speaks of acts in prosecution of the common object of the unlawful assembly or such as the members of that assembly knew to be likely to be committed in prosecution of that object. Mahmood J. in the case of Dharam Rai (7, A. W. N., 237) differentiated the two sections thus :—

" While Section 34 limits itself to the furtherance of the common intention Section 149 goes further, inasmuch as it renders every member of an unlawful assembly guilty of the offence when it is likely that such an offence might have been committed in prosecution of the common object. I have referred to this section to show that it is more strongly worded than Section 34, and even upon this section a Full Bench of the Calcutta High Court in *Queen* vs. *Sabed Ali* (11, B. L. R., 347, F. B.) held that any sudden and unpremiditated act done by a member of an unlawful assembly would not render all the other members liable therefor, unless it was shown that the assembly did understand and realize either that such offence would be committed or was likely to be necessary for the common object."

In the case of *Nibaran Chandra Ray* (11 C. W. N. 1085) Mitra and Fletcher JJ. expressed the opinion that 'Section 149 of the Indian Penal Code lays down the same principle as Section 34, with this difference that Section 149 refers to an assembly of five or more persons, while Section 34 has no limitation as to the number of persons who may have been acting in pursuance of a common intention.' With all respect for the learned Judges, it seems to me, that this is only a part and the least important part of the difference between the two sections. As I have pointed out, Section 34 deals with joint action in the furtherance of a common intention, and Section 149 only insists on a common object and an act done by one in prosecution of the common object of all. It does not insist on any act at all by those members of the assembly who are to be dealt with under it. In fact where there is joint action or any participation by any one in the actual commission of the offence, Section 149 as pointed out by Holmwood and Imam JJ. would cease to apply.

What constitutes presence.

What constitutes presence is a matter of some difficulty. Presence is not a question of mere proximity in point of time or space. Suppose *A* incites *B* to assault *C* by crying '*maro maro*' when *C* is passing by. *B* pursues *C* and overtakes him at a distance of 500 yards from the place of instigation and causes hurt to *C*. Is *A* present or absent within the meaning of Section 114? The true test seems to be whether *A* was so situated with reference to *B* or *C* at the time of the assault that he could effectively help *B* or take part in the assault on *C*. If the answer is in the affirmative, *A* is present. If in the negative, he is absent. The law is thus stated by Russell (p. 108, vol. I)—

"The presence need not be a strict actual immediate presence, such a presence as would make him (the abettor) an eye-witness or ear-witness of what passes, but may be a constructive presence.

So that if several persons set out together or in small parties upon one common design, felonious or unlawful in itself, and each takes the part assigned to him ; some to commit the fact, others to watch at proper distances and at stations to prevent surprise, or to favour, if need be, the escape of those more immediately engaged ; they are all, provided the fact be committed, in the eye of the law, present at it ; for it was made a common cause with them ; each man operated in his station at one end and the same instant, towards the same common end, and the part each man took tended to give countenance, encouragement and protection to the whole gang, and to ensure the success of their common enterprise."

The point was considered in several English cases. *R.* vs. *William Stewart and Ann Dicken* (Russell and Ryan, 363) was a case in which prisoners *S* and *D* had agreed to sell forged Bank notes to one *P* and had met him several times and negotiated with him. Ultimately by arrangement *D* went to a place with the forged notes and *S* took the purchaser near her and pointing her out from a distance of about 100 yards said 'you see *D* there, she will deliver you the goods and I wish you good luck' and left. The purchaser and *D* then walked together a short distance and *D* brought out the forged notes from her reticule and made them over to the purchaser. The interval between the time when *D* was pointed out by *S* and the time of delivery was about three minutes. It was not shown whether the prisoners were or were not in sight of each other when *D* delivered the notes to the purchaser, nor which way he had gone. It was held that *S* was only an accessory before the fact and not being present could not be treated as principal. The case is perhaps open to doubt.

The case, *Regina* vs. *Howell* (9 C. and P., 437), is authority for the proposition that those who are present when a felony is committed and abet the doing of it are principals in the felony. Where persons combine to stand by one another in a breach of the peace with a general resolution to resist all opposers and in the execution of their design a murder is committed, all of the company are equally principals in the murder, though at the time of the fact some of them were at such a distance as to be out of view. The facts were these:

A mob of 2,000 or 3,000 persons met at Hollowayhead. The prisoner Wilkes addressed the mob in violent language. He said: "Too much time has been lost in speaking. The time was now come to act, they must act now decisively; there were 200,000 men completely armed ready to march and join them at Birmingham at a moment's notice." Wilkes led the mob, who were armed with sticks, iron rods, etc., in a direction towards a police office, some of the mob from time to time leaving and others joining. The mob then went and attacked the house of Messrs. Bourne, wholesale and retail grocers, where they broke the shop shutters, destroyed the windows, got into the warehouse, brought out the goods and burnt them, and then set fire to the house.

There was no evidence to show that the prisoner Wilkes was present at the attack on Messrs. Bourne's house though it was proved that when with the mob at an earlier period he had pointed to the house. On an indictment for feloniously demolishing the house of Messrs. Bourne, it was held that on the state of facts Wilkes ought not to be convicted of the demolition, as it did not sufficiently appear what the original design of the mob at *H* was, nor whether any of the mob who were at *H* were the persons who demolished *B's* house. In coming to this decision Littledale J. relied on the passage from Russell already quoted and on the following passage from Hawkin's Pleas of the Crown:

"I take it to be settled at this day, that all those who assemble themselves together with a felonious intent, the execution whereof causes either the felony intended or any other to be committed, or with an intent to commit a trespass, the execution whereof causes a felony to be committed, and continuing together, abetting one another, till they have actually put their design in execution; and also all those who are present when a felony is committed, and abet the doing of it, as by holding the party while another strikes him; or by delivering a weapon to him that strikes, or by moving him to strike, are principals in the highest degree, in respect of such abetment, as much as the person who does the act, which in judgment of law is as much the act of them all, as if they had all actually done it."

Persons acting through a material agent.

When a person acts through a material agent, such as poison, which does not require the presence of a guilty director, he is constructively present; nor is it necessary to constitute presence that the party should be actually present, an ear or eye witness, in order to make him principal in the second degree.—(Wharton).

If a person aiding and abetting with the intention of giving assistance, is near enough to afford it, should the occasion arise, he is constructively deemed to be present. Such constructive presence is sufficient to make an accessary liable as principal in the second degree.

Actual presence is not necessary if there is direct connection between the actor and the crime, thus a confederate, who aids the commission of a robbery by a signal on a distant hill notifying approach of the parties to be attacked, is a principal in the robbery.

The question as to what constitutes presence is interesting, but having regard to the fact that the punishment of an abettor is ordinarily the same as that of the actual perpetrator of the crime, this question as well as questions relating respectively to the applicability of Section 109 or 114 is more or less of an academic interest.

Innocent agent.

I shall now deal with some other phases of the law of abetment. It is not necessary that the person abetted should be capable of committing an offence. It is expressly stated in Section 108, Explanation 3, that it is not necessary that the person abetted should be capable by law of committing an offence, or that he should have the same guilty intention or knowledge, as that of the abettor, or any guilty intention or knowledge at all. One may employ a child or a lunatic to commit an offence and he cannot escape liability by pleading that the person he has abetted is not punishable, not being capable of committing a crime—*Reg.* vs. *Manley*

(1 Cox 104). In such a case the innocent agent is only the instrument with which the abettor effects his illegal act. If we look to the reason of the thing, the so-called abettor is in reality a principal. The position is exactly the same as if a person were to let loose a wild animal on another. If this is not abetment, why should the other be? Nor is it different from the case of a man who pushes and throws another over a third person and causes hurt to the latter. In such a case there is a double offence, one against the man pushed and the other against the man on whom he is pushed. The man pushed is only the instrument used for the purpose of causing hurt.

Apart from incapacity to commit a crime an agent may be innocent by reason of the want of *mens rea.* The case of a nurse who is asked by a physician to administer poison to a patient telling her that it was medicine is an instance in point.

The person abetted may do the act with an intention or knowledge different from the intention or knowledge of the abettor, and in such a case each will be dealt with from the point of view of his intention or knowledge and the intention or knowledge of one will not be imputed to the other. *A* orders *B* to beat *C* with a *lathi*; *B* uses the *lathi* and causes hurt. The *lathi* had an iron knob of which *A* was not aware. *A* cannot be held guilty of the offence of causing hurt with a dangerous weapon under Section 324, although *B* would be guilty of an offence under that section.

Liability for probable consequence of abetment.

The act done under the influence of the abetment may be different from the act contemplated by the abettor; in that case, the abettor is only liable for the act which he intended to abet and not for the act actually done, unless the latter is a probable consequence of the act abetted (Sections 111 and 113). Where *A* instigates *B* to murder *C*, but *B* by mistake murders *C's* twin-brother, *A* is liable, for the mistake was natural and might have been anticipated, but there would have been no liability if *B* had killed *C* intentionally and without any mistake regarding his identity.

But the fact that a crime has been committed in a manner different from the mode which the abettor had advised or instigated, will not preclude liability. Where there is compliance in substance with the instigation of the accessory, but the variation is only in circumstances of time or place or in the manner of execution, the accessory will be involved in his guilt. If *A* commands *B* to murder *C* by poison and *B* does it by shooting him, *A* is accessory to the murder. For the murder of *C* was the object principally in contemplation and that is effected. It is not necessary that the specific material or machinery contributed or counselled by the abettor should be used by the principal. Although there is no liability where an entirely different offence is committed, there is liability if the act committed was a probable consequence of the abetment. Section 111 of the Code provides :—

Act abetted different from act committed.

" When an act is abetted and a different act is done, the abettor is liable for the act done, in the same manner and to the same extent as if he had directly abetted it :

Provided the act done was a probable consequence of the abetment, and was committed under the influence of the instigation, or with the aid or in pursuance of the conspiracy which constituted the abetment."

The following instances may be quoted as illustrations :—

If *A* advises *B* to rob *C* and in robbing him *B* kills him either upon resistance made or to conceal the fact or upon any other motive operating at the time of the robbery, in such a case *A* is accessory to the murder as well as to the robbery.

If *A* solicits *B* to burn the house of *C* and *B* does it accordingly, and the flames taking hold of the house of *D*, that likewise is burnt, *A* is accessory to *B* in the burning of the houses both of *C* and of *D*. This is based upon sound reason for a man must be held responsible not only for his acts, but also for the consequences which he knows to be likely to ensue from them. A person is said to cause an effect voluntarily when he causes it by means whereby he intended to cause or by means which at the time of employing those means he knew or had reason to believe to be likely to cause it (Section 39, Indian Penal Code).

More difficult questions, says Russell, arise when the principal by mistake commits a different crime from that to which he was solicited by the accessory. If *A* orders *B* to kill *C* and he by mistake kills *D*, will *A* be accessory to the murder ? Applying the test in Saunders' case (Plowd 475) it may be doubtful whether he will be. Saunders with the intention of killing his wife by the instigation of one Archer had given her a poisoned apple to eat. The wife having eaten a small part of it gave the remainder to their child. Saunders (making a faint attempt to save the child whom he loved and would not have killed) stood by and saw it eat the poison of which it soon afterwards died. It was held that though Saunders was clearly guilty of the murder of the child, yet Archer was not accessory to that murder.

" *B* is a stranger to the person of *C* ; *A* there fore takes upon him to describe him by his stature, dress, age, complexion, etc., and acquaints *B* when and where he may probably be met with. *B* is punctual at the time and place, and *D*, a person possibly in the opinion of *B* answering the description, unhappily comes by and is murdered, upon a strong belief on the part of *B* that this is the man marked out for destruction. Here is a lamentable mistake—but who is answerable for it ? *B* undoubtedly is ; the malice on his part *egriditur personam*. And may not the same be said on the part of *A* ? The pit which he with a murderous intention dug for *C*, *D* through his guilt fell into and perished. For *B* not knowing the person of *C* had no other guide to lead him to his prey than the description *A* gave of him. *B* in following this guide fell into a mistake, which it is great odds any man in his circumstances might have fallen. into." *A* was therefore held answerable for the consequence of the flagitious orders he gave, since that consequence in the ordinary course of things was highly probable. (Fost, pp. 370, 371).

The case of *Queen* vs. *Mathura Das* (6 All. 491) is important on the question of the liability of the abettor when one act is abetted and a different act is committed and generally on the interpretation of Section 111.

One Hira Sing accompanied by his servant was carrying a lot of money with him. On their way they were murdered by three men. It appears that the accused Mathura Dass and Chattarjit knew of the design of these men to *rob* Hira Sing, that one of them gave information of the departure of the deceased with the money, and that after the murder was committed by the three men, they took a share of the money robbed from the deceased. Mathura Das and Chattarjit were convicted by the Sessions Judge of abetment of murder. The judgment of Straight J. is worth quoting *in extenso* :—

" With respect to Mathura Das and Chattarjit it is not easy to arrive at a conclusion. The question that I have to ask myself with respect to these two accused is ' Can I properly adopt the Judge's view that both these persons must be held guilty of abetment of murder since the murder was a probable consequence of the intention known and abetted ?' I do not think I can and I will explain why. It seems to me that the Judge has scarcely appreciated how close and strict are the tests that should be applied to the interpretation of a penal statute, and specially of a section such as section 111 of the Penal Code, for construed loosely, it is difficult to see to what limits it might be stretched. Now, it is clear law, that if one man instigates another to perpetrate a particular crime, and that other, in pursuance of such instigation, not only perpetrates that crime, but in the course of doing so commits another crime in furtherance of it, the former is criminally responsible as an abettor in respect of such last mentioned crime, if it is one which, as a reasonable man, he must, at the time of the instigation, have known, would, in the ordinary course of things, probably have to be committed in order to carry out the original crime. For example, if *A* says to *B* 'You waylay *C* on such and such a road and rob him, and if he resists, use this sword, but not more than is absolutely necessary,' and *B* kills *C*. *A* is responsible as an abettor of the killing, for it was a probable consequence of the abetment. To put in plain terms the law virtually says to a man 'If you choose to run the risk of putting another in motion to do an unlawful act, he, for the time being, represents you as much as he does himself; and if in order to effect the accomplishment of that act, he does another which you may fairly, from the circumstances, be presumed to have foreseen would be a probable consequence of your instigation, you are as much responsible for abetting the latter act as the former.' In short, the test in these cases must always be whether, having regard to the immediate object of the instigation or conspiracy, the act done by the principal is one which, according to ordinary experience and common sense, the abettor must have foreseen as probable. The determination of this question as to the state of a man's mind at a particular moment must necessarily always be a matter of serious difficulty, and conclusions should not be formed without the most anxious and careful scrutiny of all the facts." His Lordship altered the convictions of the two accused to abetment of robbery.

If *A* commands *B* to burn *C's* house and he in so doing commits a robbery, *A*, though accessory to the burning, is not accessory to the robbery, for the robbery was a distinct act and not a probable consequence of the burning. And if *A* counsels *B* to steal goods of *C* on the road and *B* breaks into *C's* house and steels them, then *A* is not accessory to the house-breaking but is accessory to the stealing.

Offence is complete with the instigation.

To constitute the offence of abetment, it is not necessary that the act abetted should be committed, or that the effect requisite to constitute the offence should be caused (Section 108, Explanation 2.) But under the Code such abetment is punishable only in the graver offences referred to in Sections 115 and 116. The offence is complete with the instigation, notwithstanding that the person abetted refuses to do the thing or doing it, the excepted result does not follow. It is also immaterial that the means which are intended to be employed are such that it is physically impossible that the effect requisite to constitute the offence should take place.

Countermanded advice.

Advice, before it operates in any way, if countermanded, excludes responsibility, but if after starting the ball the abettor changes his mind and tries when too late to stop the act his responsibility does not cease. To exculpate himself he must have acted in time and done everything practicable to prevent the consummation, and then even if it takes place and is imputable to some independent cause he is not liable.

Abettor changing his mind.

If an abettor changes his mind after having gone as far as an attempt, he is indictable for the attempt.

Unlike attempts the entire inadaptability of the means is no defence. For instance, if *A* incites *B* to cause the death of *C* by invoking on him the curse of God, he is guilty as an abettor. The proposition perhaps requires qualification and it may largely depend on the question whether the instigation had reference directly to the means to be adopted or to the consequence to be aimed at. What I mean is this. If *A* goes to a witch an old woman and tells her to kill *B* by incantation knowing full well that the witch can take no other means, I doubt if *A* can be held guilty of abetment of murder. But suppose *A* goes to *B*, a *lathial*, and tells him 'I want you to kill *B* and you may do so by invoking the curse of God on him.' The instigation is really an instigation to commit murder and the means proposed is only a suggestion, and *B* may effect the purpose by adopting a different means. In such case *A* ought to be held criminally liable. On the analogy of attempts a distinction between partial and absolute inadequacy of means would make the law more consistent.

Causa connection between abetment and act committed.

When the act abetted has taken place the causal connection between the abetment and the act abetted must be shown. Section 109 insists that the act abetted should take place in consequence of the abetment. It is explained that an act or offence is said to be committed in consequence of abetment when it is committed in consequence of the instigation or in pursuance of the conspiracy or with the aid which constitutes the abetment. Where the causal connection is established, it is immaterial how long a time or how great a space intervenes between the instigation and the consummation, provided there is an immediate causal connection between the instigation and the act.

In order to constitute abetment it is not necessary that there should be any direct communication between the abettor and the principal. It is an incontrovertible principle of law, says Russell, that he who procures the commission of a felony is a felon, and when he procures its commission by the intervention of a third person, he is an accessory before the fact; for there is nothing in the act of commanding, hiring, counselling, aiding or abetting which may not be effected by the intervention of a third person without any direct immediate connection between the first mover and the actor. Thus in the case of the Earl of Sommerset (2 St. Tr. 951) who was indicted as an accessory before the fact to the murder of Sir Thomas Overbury, the evidence showed that he had contributed to the murder by the intervention of his Lady and of two other persons who were themselves no more than accessories without any sort of proof that he had ever conversed with the person who was the only principal in the murder or had corresponded with him directly by letter or message. The accused was found guilty. Direct communication not necessary.

The publication of obscene literature is a crime and a newspaper publishing an advertisement for the sale of obscene books is guilty of abetment as the advertisement is likely to encourage their sale. An article or letter to a newspaper may be incitement of murder within the meaning of the Offences against the Person Act (24 and 25 Vict., C. 100, S. 4), though no particular person be named, if the incitation be directed against the members of a particular class, R. V. Most (7, Q. B. D. 244).

Counselling must be special.

The view has prevailed in America that counselling must be special. Free love publications will not constitute abetment of sexual offences which the publications may have stimulated.

Communication containing incitement must be proved to have reached the person intended to be incited but it is not necessary to prove that his mind was affected by it. (R. V. Fox, 19 W.-R. (Eng.) 109 ; R. V. Krause 1902, 66 J. P. 121, per Lord Alverstone, C. J.).

If communication cannot be proved it may constitute an attempt to commit the crime (R. V. Krause).

A letter of incitement which did not reach the person (R. V. Banks, 12 Cox 393) or which he did not read (R. V. Ransford, 13 Cox 9) were held to be attempts to an indictable misdemeanour.

Abetment of abetment.

Abetment of an abetment of an offence is itself an offence, and to illustrate, the following example is given :—

A instigates *B* to instigate *C* to murder *Z*. *B* accordingly instigates *C* to murder *Z* and *C* commits the offence in consequence of *B's* instigation, *B* is liable to be punished for his offence with the punishment for murder, and as *A* instigated *B* to commit the offence, *A* is also liable to the same punishment (Section 108, Expl. 4).

In *Emp.* vs. *Trylokhonath Chowdhury*, 4 Cal. 366, it was held that abetment may be complete without the offence abetted being committed, so it is not necessary to an indictment for the abetment of an abetment of an offence to show that such offence was actually committed.

Section 113 makes an abettor liable for the effect caused by the act abetted, although it is different from that which was intended by the abettor. It provides—

"When an act is abetted with the intention on the part of the abettor of causing a particular effect, and an act for which the abettor is liable in consequence of the abetment causes a different effect from that intended by the abettor, the abettor is liable for the effect caused in the same manner and to the same extent as if he had abetted the act with the intention of causing that effect, provided he knew that the act abetted was likely to cause that effect."

In these sections dealing with abetments the sort of conduct which constitutes abetment is explained, but no rule is or could be laid down to indicate the degree of incitement or the force of the persuasion used which would suffice to make a person an abettor.

The provisions of this chapter of the Penal Code must be read with the chapters of general explanations and general exceptions. Construed with reference to the latter chapter it is clear that those who cannot commit offences cannot be abettors of offences; therefore infants, insane persons and others excepted from criminal liability cannot be abettors.

THE TRIAL.—Principals and accessories may be tried together both in England and in this country. In England the procedure is regulated by the Accessories and Abettors Act, 1861, and in this country by the Code of Criminal Procedure, Section 239 of which expressly provides for the joint or separate trial of principals and abettors as the Court thinks proper.

Abetment itself being a substantive offence under the Penal Code, the conviction of the abettor is in no way dependent on the conviction of the principal and the acquittal of the principal does not necessarily involve the acquittal of his abettors —(*Q.* vs. *Dada Maruti*, 1 Bomb., 15).

Where the principal and accessory are tried separately, the conviction of the principal is *prima facie* evidence of his guilt on the trial of the accessory, but may be collaterally disputed when the issue is the guilt of the accessory.

PUNISHMENT.—Abetment of petty offences not punishable with imprisonment is by itself not punishable, unless the act abetted actually takes place (see Sections 109, 115, 116). In other cases in the absence of any special provision the punishment of the abettor is the same as that of the principal if the act abetted has taken place (Section 109). But if it has not, the punishment for abetment is lighter than the punishment for the offence itself (Sections 115, 116). The explanation 2 of Section 108 must, therefore, be read as applying only to the graver offences mentioned in Sections 115 and 116. The explanation may be misleading, and so also explanation 4 which lays down that abetment being a substantive offence, the abetment of an abetment is also an offence. Abetment of offences punishable with death or transportation for life or with imprisonment is punishable in different degrees of severity (Sections 115, 116 of the Code), even if the act abetted be not committed in consequence of the abetment. So that if one abets such an offence and the person abetted refuses to act the abettor is punishable, but if he acts and it can be shown that the person abetted did not act in consequence of the abetment, he is not. The position seems to be rather anomalous. To explain more clearly, suppose *A* instigates *B* to murder *C*. If *B* refuses to act, *A* is punishable (Section 115). But if *B* acts and murders *C*, and it can be shown that *B* was not influenced by the instigation, *A* is not guilty at all (Section 109). I am not aware that the anomaly has ever been noticed.

LECTURE V.

"MENS REA."

Mens rea.

Mens rea or criminal intent is an essential element in every crime. There must be a mind at fault to constitute a criminal act. It is the combination of an act and an evil intent that distinguishes civil from criminal liability. There is generally nothing wrong in a mere act by which I mean a conscious movement of the body. For instance, there is nothing wrong in the mere movements that constitute an act of shooting. There is nothing wrong in shooting a rabbit or a bird. But if you shoot with the intent to kill a human being under circumstances that afford no legal justification for the act, you are guilty of murder. If you shoot a man mistaking him for a log of wood or in self-defence or if you amputate a man to save his life, there is no evil intent and no crime. The Chapter of General Exceptions in the Indian Penal Code mainly deals with matters the existence of which negative the existence of such an intent. Besides that the definition of offences generally contains ref erenceto an evil intent so as to exclude all acts where such an intent is not present. Even where the definition is silent regarding intent, it has been held that on general principles an evil intent must be imported into the definition of all strictly criminal offences. In India the matter is above controversy by reason of the provisions of Chapter IV, which govern all offences under the Code and also offences under special and local laws. *Actus non facit reum nisi mens sit rea*, "the act itself does not make a man guilty unless his intention were so," is a doctrine as old as criminal law itself. It is not an artificial principle grafted on any particular system of laws, but is a doctrine of universal application based on man's moral sense. Take a case of exception on the ground of compulsion. A strong man pushes a weaker man from behind and throws him on you, you feel resentment against the stronger man but not against the weaker man; the weaker man in such a case is a mere instrument in the hands of the other. It is a natural feeling which has found expression in the doctrine *actus me invito factus non est mens actus*, "an act done by me against my will is not my act." From this point of view the irresponsibility in such a case is independent of the doctrine of *mens rea* which may be said to proceed on the assumption of a voluntary act. For logically you cannot affirm or disaffirm the existence of an evil intent with reference to an act in which intention plays no part. What is true of acts done under compulsion is also true of other acts such as those of a sleeping man or a somnambulist. The cases which present any difficulty and round which discussions regarding the application of the doctrine have centred are cases of voluntary acts, where the evil intent, or malice as it is technically called, is negatived by reason of any mistake regarding the actual state of facts or other grounds of a like mature. A man shoots a jackal, you are behind a bush concealed from his view and you are hit by accident. You may be angry at first, but in your cooler moments you will not think of retribution. You may have such a feeling, though in a smaller degree, if you believe the act was done rashly or negligently. Your feelings would be very different against the man who shoots at you deliberately. The act is the same, the consequence is the same, the only difference lies in the intention. Similarly you feel no resentment against the surgeon who amputates your legs to cure you of a disease. If an insane person or a child abuses you, you are amused, but if an adult person in his proper senses does it, you feel inclined to knock him down. If a Judge in the discharge of his duties sends one to jail, no reasonable man will feel any resentment against him personally. These and a hundred other cases of the same kind would go to show that the nature of the man of average intelligence does not cry for retributive justice against unintentional acts and after all what are laws, but the expression of man's moral nature. What is an evil intent for one kind of offence is not an evil intent for another. For instance, the evil intent in offences against property is wholly different from what it is in offences against the human body. There is, however, one common factor in every case, and that is an intent to injure.

Volition, Will, Intention, Motive. Every movement is a weariness of the flesh. We do not move unless we *will* it, and we do not will a movement unless we have a *motive* for willing it. Intermediate between the motive and the will is the intention to cause a particular consequence by a particular act. The motive is either near or remote. Motive does not play the same important part in the determination of criminal liability as intention does, for a motive may be perfectly innocent, and yet one may adopt improper means for its attainment. Besides, though motive like intention is confined to the mind and is often difficult to discover, intention is more easily disclosed by the act itself. Sometimes the act and the evil consequence combined are not sufficient to constitute an offence and both may appear innocent in themselves, and what makes them harmful is the relation of certain other facts with the consequence intended or caused. In these cases the knowledge of those facts is essential and the existence of such knowledge makes harmful the intent which may otherwise be harmless. Cases of bigamy and receiving stolen property will explain what I mean. Before going further into these details, it will be helpful to have a clear conception of the meaning of some of the words which are used in the Code to indicate the different kinds of evil intent necessary to constitute a particular offence. We have first to understand the meaning of the words Will, Volition, Intention and Motive.

If we examine the mental condition that precedes a conscious act, we find that the bodily motions which constitute the act, are preceded by a desire for those motions. This desire working through the nervous system produces the motions. This desire may be called the volition, and when such desire for motion is not produced by fear or compulsion the act desired is called a voluntary act. The word 'voluntary' is, however, used in the Penal Code in a somewhat different sense which I shall notice hereafter. Volition.

The desire itself is in most cases preceded by a longing for the attainment of some object towards which the motions themselves are directed and related as means to an end. In adopting the motions as means, we rely upon universal experience and knowledge, which raise in the mind the expectation that the motion or the series of related motions, will be followed by the objects which we long to attain. This desire for the motions, as I have said, constitutes the volition. The longing for the object which sets the volition in motion is the motive, the expectation present in the mind that the desired motions will lead to certain consequences is the intention. Thus intention is not a desire, whilst motive is. Motive has a 'dynamical' whilst intention has a 'telescopic aspect.' The one impels the act, the other sees beyond it. Motive according to Bentham is anything which by influencing the will of a sensitive being is supposed to serve as a means of determining him to act upon any occasion. Thus where a person wishing to strike another brings his hand or a stick that is in his hand into contact with this other's body, he does the act voluntarily. If, on the other hand, another person compels him, by force or through fear, to do a similar act, he cannot be said to have acted voluntarily. The word 'voluntary' has, therefore, reference to the will that directs the motion. Most conscious and voluntary acts are directed towards a particular result or consequence, and when you act to produce a particular consequence you are said to do the act with that intention, that is, you do it intentionally. If the consequence, however, is not looked for, the act may be voluntary but not intentional. You *will* the act, but *intend* the

Intention, distinct from motive.

consequence. Intention is sometimes loosely used as synonymous with motive, but motive is different from intention. As I have said, we intend a certain consequence, by which I mean the result necessarily flowing from a particular act. But the desire for the consequence may be due to some further and more ulterior object. That is what we call a *motive*. Intention has relation to the immediate and motive to the distant object of our acts.

According to Austin "bodily movements obey wills. They move when we *will* they should. The wish is volition and the consequent movements are acts. Besides the volition and act, it is supposed there is a will which is the author of both. The desire is called an act of the will. When I will a movement I wish it, and when I conceive the wish I expect that the movement wished will follow. The wishes followed by the act wished, are only wishes which attain their ends without external means. Our desires of acts, which immediately follow our desires of them, are volitions. The act I will, the consequence I intend. This imaginary will is determined to action by motives."

According to Holland the only immediate result of a volition is a muscular movement on the part of the person willing, but certain further results are always present to his mind as likely to follow the muscular movement which alone he can directly control. Those among them to the attainment of which the act is directed are said to be "intended."

"Will," says Sir Fitz-James Stephen, "is often used as being synonymous with the act of Will.

volition, as the proper name of the internal crisis which precedes or accompanies voluntary action. This meaning of the word is narrow and special. A more important and commoner way of using the word "will" is to use it as if it denoted a man, so to speak, within the man, being capable of freedom or restraint, virtue and vice, independent action or inactivity on its own account and apart from other mental and bodily functions. This way of thinking and speaking appears to me radically false. When I speak of "will," I mean by the word either the particular act of volition which I have already described, and which is a stage in voluntary action; or a permanent judgment of the reason that some particular course of conduct is desirable, coupled with an intention to pursue it, which issues from time to time in a greater or less number of particular volitions."

Intention. "Intention," says the same learned author, "is the result of deliberation upon motives, and is the object aimed at by the action caused or accompanied by the act of volition."

"Intention is an operation of the will directing an overt act; motive is the feeling which prompts the operation of the will, the ulterior object of the person willing, *e.g.*, if a person kills another, the intention directs the act which causes death, the motive is the object which the person had in view, *e.g.*, the satisfaction of some desire, such as revenge, etc." (See Stephen's History of the Criminal Law, Vol. II.)

Motive. I have explained to you that the motive is the desire for the object we long to attain for its own sake. The ultimate motive which is at the back of all our desires is to secure our own happiness. That is the distant goal towards which all human activities are directed. Paradoxical as it may appear the ascetic who foregoes all wordly pleasures seeks his happiness in his apparent disregard and contempt for it. Ordinarily we seek pleasure or happiness—

(1) by causing pain to our enemies,
(2) by increasing such of our earthly possessions as are calculated to bring us comfort,
(3) by satisfying our natural desires.

An analysis of the various offences would show that a desire to secure happiness in a manner that is opposed to the well being of society and is inconsistent with the rights of others is at the root of all of them. There are certain limits within which we are allowed to interfere with the happiness of others or to secure our own. But if we go beyond those limits, then the intent to harm others or the knowledge of it or the desire to secure gain for ourselves constitutes an evil intent. We inflict suffering on our enemies by causing them either physical or mental pain. The desire to cause physical pain leads us to the commission of offences against the human body. The desire to cause mental pain prompts us to harm our enemies in respect of their property, their reputation or with regard to their domestic relations. Origin of offences.

Often more than one desire combine to constitute the motive for a particular crime. More frequently the direct motive for a crime is not the desire to harm an enemy, but a desire to secure ease and comfort for ourselves. Our happiness largely depends on our earthly possessions, on accumulation of wealth and property generally. The right of property which at the beginning was only a right of possession is now jealously guarded by law. No one is allowed to deprive a man of his property, which is often the fruit of his labours, except by his consent. To acquire property in any of these ways often entails a great deal of trouble, and even with trouble it is sometimes difficult to attain. A desire for a short cut to happiness often induces us to adopt illegal means for acquiring property. Theft and other offences against property owe their origin to this desire. As I have said, sometimes both the motives, *viz.*, the desire to harm others and the desire to do good to oneself combine and supply the incentive for committing an offence. Except in the case of those suffering from mental aberration, seldom is an offence committed for which there is no motive. But proof of the existence of a motive is not necessary for a conviction for any offence. But where the motive is proved it is evidence of the evil intent and is also relevant to show that the person who had the motive to commit a crime actually committed it, although such evidence alone would not ordinarily be sufficient.

Section 8, Evidence Act.

Under Section 8 of the Evidence Act any fact is relevant which shows or constitutes a motive or preparation for any fact in issue or relevant fact. Although in all strictly criminal prosecutions innocence of intention is a defence, innocence

Innocence of motive no defence.

of motive is no defence. An act which is unlawful cannot in law be defended on the ground that it was committed from a good and laudable motive. A man who kills his children to save them from starvation cannot escape punishment for murder. Men also seek pleasure in the satisfaction of natural lust. This furnishes the motive for adultery, rape and other offences of the same kind. It will be seen that though the remote motive for all criminal acts is perhaps the same, the nearer, the immediate motives for different offences vary widely. These motives for the commission of crimes create and bring into being the intention which constitutes the *mens rea* for most of the offences. Intention is a mere mental condition and is often difficult of direct proof. We infer the intention often from the act itself.

"In all the graver class of crimes a particular intent or state of mind is a necessary ingredient of the offence, and must be averred in the indictment and proved by the prosecution.

"When an act which is of itself indifferent becomes criminal if done with a particular intent, the intent must be proved. But when the act is unequivocal, the proof that it was done may of itself be evidence of the intention which the nature of the act conveys. In such case there is a presumption of law that the person accused intended the probable consequences of his act." (Hals. Laws of England, Vol. 9, Art. 504).

The knowledge that a certain consequence would follow a particular act is distinct from the intention to cause it. This knowledge, where it exists, is sufficient to supply the place of intention. A man knows that his servant has an enlarged spleen. He knows also that a kick is likely to rupture the spleen and that such rupture may cause death. With all this knowledge if he causes the death of his servant by kicking him, he cannot escape liability for murder, by showing that it was not his intention to cause death. If you refer to the definition of culpable homicide, you will find that it not only covers acts done with the intention of causing death, but also covers acts done with the knowledge that death is likely to be caused by such act, and so also the definition of hurt.

Definitions of offences in the Indian Penal Code.

The general doctrine of *mens rea* is not of very great importance where, as in India, the law is codified and offences are carefully defined so as to include the *mens rea* in the definition itself. The definitions in the Indian Penal Code along with the Chapter of General Exceptions are perhaps sufficient to exclude all cases to which a *mens rea* cannot be attributed. Where neither the definition nor the Chapter of General Exceptions exclude a case of this kind—I doubt if such a case exists—the general doctrine would be, I presume, of no great help. The Indian Penal Code defines offences with great care and precision and the Chapter of General Exceptions is very comprehensive. However, even where the law is codified, the application of the doctrine may sometimes be found useful in remedying defective and incomplete definitions or at any rate in interpreting them.

In speaking of *mens rea* as the essential ingredient of a crime, I only speak of crimes properly so called. I do not include in the term, offences against municipal or fiscal laws which are sometimes punished without reference to any intention or knowledge.

The question as to whether a criminal intent must be imported into every crime defined in the Statute, even where it is not expressly mentioned as an ingredient has been very fully discussed in two English cases—*Reg.* v. *Prince* and *Queen* v. *Tolson.* They are important as elucidating an important question of principle.

Reg. vs. Prince.

In *Reg.* v. *Prince* (L. R. 2 C. C. R. 154) Henry Prince was tried upon the charge framed under S. 55 of 24 and 25 Vict., C. 100, which makes it an offence unlawfully to take or cause to be taken any unmarried girl, being under the age of sixteen years, out of the possession and against the will of her father or mother, or of any other person having the lawful care or charge of her.

All the facts necessary to support a conviction existed, except that the girl Annie Phillips, though proved by her father to be fourteen years old, looked very much older than sixteen, and the jury found upon evidence that before the defendant took her away she had told him that she was eighteen, and that the defendant *bona fide* believed that statement, and that such belief was reasonable. It was contended that although the Statute did not insist on the knowledge on the part of the prisoner that the girl was under sixteen as necessary to constitute the offence, the common law doctrine of *mens rea* should nevertheless be applied, and that there could be no conviction in the absence of a criminal mind. It was, however, held that the prisoner's belief that the girl was eighteen years old was no defence.

A distinction was drawn between acts that were in themselves innocent but made punishable by Statute (*malum prohibitum*) and acts that were intrinsically wrong or immoral (*malum in se*). In the former a belief, a reasonable belief, in the existence of facts which, if true, would take the case out of the mischief of the Statute, would be a good defence, but in the latter case such a belief was immaterial unless of course the law made it otherwise. The man who acted under such erroneous belief took the risk and should suffer the consequence. The distinction between the two classes of cases would appear from the following observations of Bramwel J.—

" The same principle applies in other cases. A man was held liable for assaulting a police officer in the execution of his duty, though he did not know he was a police officer. Why? because the act was wrong in itself. So, also, in the case of burglary, could a person charged claim an acquittal on the ground that he believed it was past six when he entered, or in house-breaking, that he did not know the place broken into was a house? Take, also, the case of libel, published when the publisher thought the occasion privileged, or that he had a defence under Lord Campbell's Act, but was wrong; he could not be entitled to acquittal, because there was no *mens rea*. Why? because the act of publishing written defamation is wrong where there is no lawful cause.

" As to the case of the marine stores, it was held properly that there was no *mens rea* where the person charged with the possession of naval stores with the Admiralty mark did not know the stores he had bore the mark: (*Reg.* vs. *Sleep*); because there is nothing *prima facie* wrong or immoral in having naval stores unless they are so marked. But suppose his servant had told him that there was a mark, and he had said he would chance whether or not it was the Admiralty mark? So in the case of the carrier with game in his possession; unless he knows he had it, there would be nothing done or permitted by him, no intentional act or omission. So of the vitriol senders; there was nothing wrong in sending such packages as were sent unless they contained vitriol."

Reg. vs. Tolson.

In the later case of *Reg.* vs. *Tolson* (23 Q. B. D. 168) a similar question arose, but this time in connection with an act which by itself was neither wrongful nor immoral. Under the Statute 24 and 25 Vict., C. 100, Section 57, "whoever being married, shall marry any other person during the life of the former husband or wife shall be guilty of felony, etc., etc." Upon the words of the Statute it is apparently immaterial whether the parties or either of them knew or did not know that the former wife or husband, as the case may be, was or was not alive. The question arose whether a *mens rea* did by implication form part of the definition. If the case had arisen under the Indian Penal Code the difficulty would not have arisen for Section 79 would have given protection to the prisoner. Considering, however, the important principles discussed in that case, I should like to read to you certain passages from the very instructive judgment of Mr. Justice Wills. It will help you to a thorough understanding of the doctrine of *mens rea*, and will also enable you to see clearly how the doctrine has been kept in view in the definition of offences under the Indian Penal Code.

"Although *prima facie* and as a general rule there must be a mind at fault before there can be a crime, it is not an inflexible rule, and a Statute may relate to such a subject-matter and may be so framed as to make an act criminal whether there has been any intention to break the law, or otherwise to do wrong or not. There is a large body of municipal law in the present day which is so conceived. Bye-laws are constantly made regulating the width of thoroughfares, the height of buildings, the thickness of walls, and a variety of other matters necessary for the general welfare, health or convenience, and such bye-laws are enforced by the sanction of penalties, and the breach of them constitutes an offence and is a criminal matter. In such cases it would, generally speaking, be no answer to proceedings for infringement of the bye-law, that the person committing it had *bona fide* made an accidental miscalculation or an erroneous measurement. The acts are properly construed as imposing the penalty when the act is done, no matter how innocently, and in such a case the substance of the enactment is that a man shall take care that the statutory direction is obeyed, and that if he fails to do so he does it at his peril. Whether an enactment is to be construed in this sense or with the qualification ordinarily imported into the construction of criminal statutes, that there must be a guilty mind, must, I think, depend upon the subject-matter of the enactment, and the various circumstances that may make the one construction or the other reasonable or unreasonable."

* * * * * *

"Assistance must be sought *aliunde*, and all circumstances must be taken into consideration which tend to show that the one construction or the other is reasonable, and amongst such circumstances it is impossible to discard the consequences. This is a consideration entitled to little weight, if the words be incapable of more than one construction; but I think I have abundantly shown that there is nothing in the mere form of words used in the enactment now under consideration, to prevent the application of what is certainly normal rule of construction in the case of a Statute constituting an offence entailing severe and degrading punishment. If the words are not conclusive in themselves, the reasonableness or otherwise of the construction contended for, has always been recognised as a matter fairly to be taken into account."

After referring to the case of a woman indicted for having in her possession, without a proper certificate, Government stores, in which it was contended that having regard to the terms of the Statute, the possession of the certificate was the sole justification that could be pleaded—a contention which was overruled by Foster J.—Mr. Justice Wills continued :—

"*Prima facie* the Statute was satisfied when the case was brought within its terms, and it then lay upon the defendant to prove that the violation of the law, which had taken place, had been committed accidentally or innocently, so far as he was concerned. Suppose a man had taken up by mistake one of two baskets exactly alike and of similar weight, one of which contained innocent articles belonging to himself, and the other marked 'Government stores;' and was caught with the wrong basket in his hand, he would, by his own act, have brought himself within the very words of the Statute. Who would think of convicting him? And yet what defence could there be except that his mind was innocent, and that he had not intended to do the thing forbidden by the Statute?"

Referring again to the case before him His Lordship proceeded:—" It seems to me to be a case to which it would not be improper to apply the language of Lord Kenyon, when dealing with a Statute which liberally interpreted led to what he considered an equally preposterous result, 'I would adopt any construction of the Statute that the words will bear in order to avoid such monstrous consequences.' Again the nature and extent of the penalty attached to the offence may reasonably be considered. There is nothing that need shock any mind in the payment of a small pecuniary penalty by a person who has unwittingly done something detrimental to the public interest. To subject him, when, what he has done, has been nothing, but what any well-disposed man would have been very likely to do under the circumstances, to the forfeiture of all his goods and chattels, which would have been one consequence of a conviction at the date of the Act of 24 and 25 Vict., to the loss of civil rights, to imprisonment with hard labour, or even to penal servitude, is a very different matter; and such a fate seems properly reserved for those who have transgressed morally, as well as unintentionally done something prohibited by law."

Commonwealth vs. Presby.

In an American case (*The Commonwealth* vs. *Presby*, 14 Gray 65), this doctrine was fully recognised and read into the Statute, although upon the definition of the offence no question of an evil intent at all arose. The defendant, a police officer, had arrested one Harford for being found intoxicated in a public place. He was indicted for the wrongful arrest. The Statute gave the power of arrest in respect of intoxicated persons only, and it was argued that if the man arrested was not intoxicated, a mere belief, however well founded, that the man was intoxicated could not be pleaded as a defence to the indictment. Hoar J. disallowed the contention. After stating the general doctrine that where there is no will to commit an offence there can be no transgression, and the hardship that any other interpretation would involve, concluded as follows:—

"Now the fact of intoxication, though usually easy to ascertain, is not in most cases a fact capable of demonstration with absolute certainty. Suppose a watchman to find a man in the gutter stupified and smelling very strongly of spirituous liquors. The man may have fallen in a fit; and some person may have tried to relieve him by the application of a stimulant, and then have left in search of assistance. Or, in another case, the person arrested may, for purposes of amusement or mischief, have been simulating the appearance and conduct of drunkenness. Is the officer to be held criminal, if, using his best judgment and discretion and all the means of information in his power, in a case where he is called upon to act, he makes a mistake of fact and comes to a wrong conclusion? It would be singular, indeed, if a man, deficient in reason, should be protected from criminal responsibility, but another, who was obliged to decide upon the evidence before him, and used in good faith all the reason and faculties which he had, should be held guilty. We, therefore, feel bound to decide that if the defendant acted in good faith, upon reasonable and probable cause of belief, without rashness or negligence, he is not to be regarded as a criminal because he is found to have been mistaken."

Doctrine of *mens rea* in relation to Municipal laws.

I have told you that *mens rea* is essential in all strictly criminal offences. As pointed out by Mr. Justice Wills, there is a large body of Municipal law so framed as to make an act criminal whether there is any intention to break the law or not. Cases of this kind are generally of a civil nature, but for special reasons have been included in the category of offences. That they are not criminal offences in the strict sense of the term may also be gathered from the fact that the punishment for these offences is generally a fine. Instances of such cases will be found in Halsbury's Laws of England, Vol. 9, page 235.

In cases of this kind the ordinary doctrine of criminal law, that a master or principal cannot be held liable for the act of his servant or agent, because the condition of mind of such servant or agent cannot be imputed to him does not apply. These are instances which go to show that though technically offences, they are not really so, and are not governed by the general principles applicable to really criminal cases. I may observe that the Chapter of General Exceptions would apply to all such cases by reason of the definition of an offence contained in Section 40, whereby it is made to include offences under any special or local law as defined in Sections 41 and 42 of the Act for the purposes of the application of that Chapter.

The doctrine laid down in *Reg.* vs. *Prince* cannot be pushed so far as to make a child or a lunatic personally responsible for an infringement, even though the offence may be complete without a *mens rea*, the act being a *malum in se.* I am sure, if the prisoner in that case had been a lunatic there would have been no conviction.

The distinction between an act that is *malum in se* and an act that is *malum prohibitum* has been fully recognised in America where Crimes have been divided according to their nature into crimes *mala in se* and crimes *mala prohibita*, the former class comprising those acts which are immoral or wrong in themselves, such as murder, rape, arson, burglary and larceny, breach of the peace, forgery, and the like, the latter class comprising those acts to which, in the absence of Statute, no moralt urpitude attaches, and which are crimes only because they have been prohibited by Statute.

The distinction, though in many ways convenient and even just, is open to the objection that there is no clear line of demarcation between the two classes of acts and it is not always easy to say whether a particular act, lies on one side of the line or the other. Our ideas of right and wrong are often the result of early training and environments. Acts are often singled out for punishment on mere considerations of policy which may vary in different countries and at different times. The Spartans anxious to rear up a race of heroes, the old Rajputs with their peculiar notions about caste and purity of blood saw nothing wrong even in infanticide. Compare again the wide gulf that separates the Christians from the Mahomedans and the Hindu Kulins in respect of their views relating to polygamy. It has been truly said that there is nothing absolutely good and nothing absolutely bad in this world.

Analysis of Offences as defined in the Code.

I have already told you that the Indian Penal Code gives full effect to the doctrine of *mens rea*, and that it does so in two ways. In the first place the Chapter of General Exceptions which controls all the offences defined in the Code as well as all offences under special and local laws, deals with the general conditions which negative *mens rea*, and thereby exclude criminal responsibility. Under Section 6, "throughout this Code every definition of an offence, every penal provision and every illustration of every such definition or penal provision, shall be understood subject to the exceptions contained in the chapter entitled 'General Exceptions,' though those exceptions are not repeated in such definition, penal provision or illustration."

A large number of cases having thus been excluded from the category of crimes, every offence is carefully defined so as to include in the definition the precise evil intent which is the essence of a particular offence, as well as the other necessary elements of it. If these definitions are analysed they generally comprise the following principal elements :—

Analysis of definitions in the Indian Penal Code.

(*a*) A human being.

(*b*) An intention on the part of such a human being to cause a certain consequence considered injurious to individuals or to society, and which for the sake of brevity we call an evil intent.

(*c*) The act willed.

(*d*) The resultant evil consequence.

In cases where the intended consequence is not injurious by itself, but is injurious in conjunction with certain other facts, a further element is added, *viz.*—

(*e*) A knowledge of the existence of such facts.

Human being.

As to (*a*)—a human being—it is indicated by the use of the word 'whoever' with which the definition of every offence begins.

Evil intent.

Words used in the definitions to denote evil intent.

As to (*b*)—the evil intent—it is indicated generally by the use of such words as intentionally—voluntarily—fraudulently—dishonestly—malignantly—wantonly—maliciously, etc. I have already told you that intention has reference to consequences of acts rather than to acts themselves. You will naturally ask, how is it then that these words denoting different intentions are generally used as adverbs qualifying verbs which are supposed to indicate acts. We read of intentionally joining an unlawful assembly (Section 142), intentionally preventing service of summons (Section 173), intentionally omitting to attend in obedience to summons (Section 174), intentionally omitting to produce a document (Section 175), intentionally obstructing sale of property (Section 184), intentionally omitting to assist a public servant (Section 187), intentionally giving false evidence (Section 193), intentionally omitting to give information of an offence (Section 202), intentionally omitting to apprehend an offender (Sections 221 and 222), intentionally offering resistance to lawful apprehension (Sections 224, 225, 225A and 225B), intentionally offering insult (Section 228), intentionally causing to be returned as a juryman (Section 229). This mode of expression at first creates the impression that 'intentionally,' 'dishonestly' and other words of the same class have not been used as they ought to be, to refer to consequences of acts. This impression is mainly due to the fact that we are accustomed to regard verbs as indicating merely acts. But most verbs whilst indicating acts also indicate the consequences of those acts. Transitive verbs from their very nature cannot be confined to mere acts, for they are defined to be verbs expressing actions which pass from the agent to an object. To explain what I have said: obstructing sale of property, intentionally offering insult, is equivalent to doing an act with the intention of causing the consequence indicated by the words 'obstruction' or 'insult.' Intentionally causing hurt is to do an act, the effect of which is to cause hurt. Intentionally to kill a person is to do an act, the effect of which is to cause death. Death is, therefore, the consequence of that act. It is hardly necessary to multiply these instances. Intentionally joining an unlawful assembly, intentionally omitting to attend in obedience to summons, intentionally omitting to assist a public servant, intentionally giving false evidence are all susceptible of the same explanation.

Offences sometimes defined without any reference to intention.

There are a few cases where words indicating intention are not used in defining an offence. But these are either cases where the acts with their consequences are so hurtful to the State or to society that it has been deemed just and expedient to punish them irrespective of any intention to cause those consequences, or cases where the acts themselves are of such a character that they raise a violent presumption that whoever willed the act must have intended the consequences. Waging war against the Queen (Section 121), sedition (Section 124A), kidnapping and abduction (Sections 359—363) are examples of the former, counterfeiting Queen's coin (Section 232) is an example of the latter.

There is, I have told you, between the intention and the act a will which determines the movements that constitute the act. It is a subconscious mental process assumed in every definition, and in most cases a necessary inference from the act itself. The inference is only negatived where the act is shown to be caused by force, compulsion or accident, or under other circumstances indicating the absence of this will and these special cases are among others excluded by the provisions of the Chapter of General Exceptions, and are consequently not repeated in the definition.

The act willed. As to (*c*)—the act willed—it is an essential element in every offence even where it is an incomplete offence such as an attempt. It is with the commencement of the act that the offence emerges from mind to matter. If the act willed has not taken place completely or partially there is no offence, for, as I have already told you, the law does not punish a mere evil intent so long as it has not led to some overt act. Whilst it is an offence to hurt a person or to forge a document, it is not an offence merely to intend to cause hurt or to commit forgery. There are, however, some offences which do not seem to contemplate any particular acts but merely punish an existing state of things, but these are special cases, and if closely examined are not exceptions to the general rule. The existing state of things in such cases only indicates an antecedent criminal act where we reason from effect to cause, *e.g.*, possession of an instrument for counterfeiting coin or possession of stolen articles all indicate an antecedent criminal act.

The consequence. As to (*d*)—the resultant consequence—it is not always necessary that the intended consequence should take place. Sections 216A, 217 and 263 are instances in point. The man who harbours a robber or dacoit with the intention of facilitating the commission of a robbery or dacoity (Section 216A) cannot plead in defence, that as a matter of fact, no robbery or dacoity took place or that his action did not facilitate such robbery or dacoity. Where, however, the happening of the intended consequence is an essence of an offence, the non-happening of it would reduce the offence to a mere attempt to commit it. This matter I have already discussed under another head.

The intended consequence is sometimes innocent by itself and becomes nocent only by reason of the existence of other circumstances. Sometimes the existence of these other circumstances only aggravates the offence. In these cases the definition after describing the act adds 'knowing or having reason to believe, etc.' These special cases bring in the element I have referred to under (*e*).

Sometimes the immediate consequence of an act is either not harmful or is less harmful than the remote consequence, and the happening of the latter is either a necessary condition of an offence or is only an aggravation.

I have tried, in this chapter, to give you a general analysis of the definition of crimes in the Indian Penal Code. I do not pretend that the analysis is applicable to all the definitions in the Code, but I believe it will be found correct in a very large number of them, and will help you to a better appreciation of all their component parts.

LECTURE VI.

WORDS USED IN THE CODE TO DENOTE *MENS REA*.

I shall now proceed to explain to you the meaning of the various words used in the Code to denote the *mens rea*. I have already referred to these words in a general way.

VOLUNTARILY.

'Voluntarily' as used in the Indian Penal Code.

Ordinarily a voluntary act is opposed to a compulsory act and means an act done in the exercise of volition or an act done willingly without being influenced or compelled. It is also opposed to an act done accidentally or negligently. This, however, is not the sense in which the word has been used in the Code. 'Voluntarily' has been used with reference to the consequence of acts for which 'intentionally' would perhaps have been the more appropriate word, but 'voluntarily,' as defined in Section 39 of the Code, has a more extended meaning than 'intentionally.' A person is said to cause an effect voluntarily when he causes it by means whereby he intended to cause it or by means which at the time of employing those means he knew or had reason to believe to be likely to cause it. The illustration to Section 39 makes the matter clear.

> '*A* sets fire, by night, to an inhabited house in a large town, for the purpose of facilitating robbery, and thus causes the death of a person. Here, *A* may not have intended to cause death, and may even be sorry that death has been caused by his act: Yet, if he knew that he was likely

to cause death, he has caused death voluntarily.'

A person is said to have reason to believe a thing if he has sufficient cause to believe that thing but not otherwise (Section 26). Belief is somewhat weaker than knowledge, but a well grounded belief that a certain consequence will follow a certain act is ordinarily as good as knowledge. 'Knowledge,' says Locke, 'is the highest degree of the speculative faculties and consists in the perception of the truth of affirmative or negative propositions.' To know a thing is to have mental cognition of it. To believe a thing is to assent to a proposition or affirmation, or to accept a fact as real, or certain, without immediate personal knowledge. A man whom you know to be poor, brings to you for sale a valuable gold ornament and offers it to you for one-tenth of its real price. He comes to you at night under suspicious circumstances, you may not know that the article is stolen, but you have good reason to believe that it is so. In the illustration to Section 39 the man setting fire to the house might not have the knowledge that the house was inhabited, but if he had grounds for belief that the house was inhabited, this belief is sufficient without the knowledge or the intention. There are, however, cases where the mere belief is considered insufficient. The word 'voluntarily,' as explained in Sections 321 and 322, however, do not seem to cover cases of mere reasonable belief, but seem to insist on intention or knowledge. It is, however, not clear to me why reasonable grounds of belief should be excluded in these cases. Though generally where a knowledge of facts is considered

Belief and knowledge.

essential, a reasonable ground of belief is given the same effect, and the words 'knows or has reason to believe' are offen used together, in some cases mere belief has not been considered to be sufficient but culpable and actual knowledge has been insisted on as an essential element to constitute a crime. Take, for instance, an offence under Section 181. A false statement on oath is an offence when the statement is false, and which the offender either knows to be false or believes to be false or does not believe to be true. Section 188, however, insists on higher certainty and makes it penal for any one to disobey the order of a public servant only when he knows that the order has been promulgated by such a person.

There are very good reasons why knowledge or reasonable grounds of belief should in most cases supply the place of intention. Intention is purely an operation of the mind and is often difficult to prove. The act itself generally furnishes the evidence of intention, for it is a self-evident proposition that every man is supposed to intend the natural consequences of his own act. What is the natural consequence of an act depends in some cases on knowledge and in others on mere belief both based on past experience. Where by personal experience you find that an act invariably leads to a particular consequence it is a matter of knowledge, but in many matters we have no personal experience but have to rely on the knowledge or experience of others. In cases of personal knowledge, the degree of certainty is much greater than where we act upon the experience or knowledge of others. In such cases we act on mere belief. There are also cases in which a particular act invariably leads to a particular consequence and cases where a consequence generally follows but not invariably. Thus, inferences are sometimes based on certainty and sometimes on different degrees of probability. Where an inference is more or less certain it is knowledge, where it is only probable it is belief. In many cases a reasonable ground of belief is for all practical purposes as good as knowledge.

There are also cases where a knowledge of consequence insisted upon is in no way inferable from the act itself, and in those cases knowledge has to be positively proved and has to be insisted on as part of the definition. Every sane person, for instance, knows that shooting a man causes death, and if a man shoots another, it is presumed that he intended to kill him. In such cases knowledge of a consequence is enough to prove the intention to produce such a consequence, and the definition is complete if it makes only the knowledge a necessary ingredient in the crime and omits any reference to intention.

I have already told you that 'voluntarily' is a compendious term which covers intention, knowledge and reasonable grounds of belief.

'Intentionally' and 'Voluntarily.'

Although there is, as I have explained, a distinction between doing a thing intentionally and doing it voluntarily, sometimes it is difficult to discover the reason for choosing one word rather than the other. Take, for instance, Sections 184 and 186. The first makes it penal for any one to intentionally obstruct the sale of property offered for sale by the lawful authority of any public servant as such, the second makes it penal to voluntarily obstruct a public servant in the discharge of his public functions. The only apparent difference is that the first refers to obstruction to an act and the second to obstruction to an individual. But this is only an apparent difference. Where we speak of obstructing a person, we really mean obstructing some act by such a person.

FRAUDULENTLY—DISHONESTLY.

'Fraudulently' and 'dishonestly' are two words of most common occurrence in the Code.

Dishonestly. 'Dishonestly' has been very clearly defined in the Code. "Whoever does anything with the intention of causing wrongful gain to one person or wrongful loss to another person is said to do that thing dishonestly" (Section 24). Wrongful gain is defined to be gain by unlawful means of property to which the person gaining it is not legally entitled. Wrongful loss, on the other hand, is loss by unlawful means of property to which the person losing it is legally entitled.

Wrongful gain includes wrongful retention as well as wrongful acquisition and wrongful loss includes wrongfully keeping out any person of any property as well as wrongfully depriving him of it (Section 23).

Fraudulently. The word 'fraudulently' has also been defined, but the definition is vague and has been a fruitful source of conflicting decisions. A person is said to do a thing fraudulently if he does that thing with intent to defraud, but not otherwise (Section 25). The definition or rather the explanation is not very helpful. What is an intention to defraud ? To defraud is to commit fraud. Fraud has not been defined, and eminent Judges have refused to commit themselves to any definition, by reason of the fact that vicious human ingenuity contrives to give such different complexions to fraud that an exhaustive definition likely to cover all cases has been considered well nigh impossible. Every fraud involves deception but is every deception a fraud ? It is essential that in order to amount to legal fraud, besides deception, there must be an intention to cause injury or an infraction of a legal right. Deception like falsehood is merely a moral wrong. The law does not ordinarily punish a falsehood unless it is calculated to injure some one else. In the same way a mere deception is not punishable unless it has a similar effect. The world, one might think, would be happier if a falsehood or a deception were made punishable, irrespective of consequences, but punishment has not always helped in hastening the millennium and experience has shown that it is not always conducive to the well being of society to create offences of mere moral wrongs, by which I mean wrongs which do not tend directly to the injury of others. Take the case of a person who brings a present to his wife and magnifies its value. There is undoubted deception, but the wife is none the worse for it and is perhaps happier for the falsehood, and the act is not an offence. In the same way you often tell a patient, pronounced hopeless by the doctor, that he is going to recover soon. This is deception but not fraud. " An intent to deceive the public or particular persons," says Sir Fitz James Stephen in his Digest of Criminal Law, "but not to commit a particular fraud or specific wrong upon any particular person, is not an intent to defraud within the meaning of this Article" (*i.e.*, Article 384 which defines forgery). So far as I can see there is no section in the Code which makes a mere act of deception punishable irrespective of an intention to injure. Although wherever the word 'fraudulently' is used in defining an offence an intention to cause injury is implied by the word itself, the framers of the Code however were not content to rely on the implication alone and in many cases they have expressly insisted on the presence of an intention to cause a particular injury as a necessary ingredient of the offence. For instance, Section 206 which makes fraudulent removal or concealment of property an offence insists that besides the fraudulent removal, there must be an intention to prevent the property from being taken in execution of a decree or other intention of the same nature. Similar intention to injure rights of others will be found present in the definition of most other offences concerned with fraudulent acts, but where such specific intention does not expressly form part of the definition, the nature of the act itself is such that it has been considered essential as a matter of public policy to punish it, without reference to any specific intention to injure, the act itself being of such a character as to give rise to a violent presumption that something more than mere deception must have been contemplated. As an instance you may refer to Section 208 which makes it punishable to cause or suffer a decree to be passed for a sum not due or for a larger sum than is due. It is clear that anyone who does such an act not only intends to deceive, but also contemplates some material injury to others, and it is also a part of public policy not to allow any abuse of the processes of Courts of Justice. This question has arisen more pointedly in connection with the definition of forgery, and the question has been asked whether fraudulent execution of a document by a person with the intention of causing it to be believed that such document was executed by another person who in fact did not execute it involves necessarily an intention to cause injury to some body. You will observe that the making of a false document with intent to commit fraud amounts to forgery (Section 463). Leaving aside the clumsiness of the definition and the tautology that is involved in speaking of fraudulent execution of a document with intent to commit fraud, for that is what it comes to referentially, the definition makes no mention of any intention to injure, and this is to be read into the definition by holding that 'fraudulently' or 'intent to commit fraud' includes, besides deception, an intention to injure. This view is supported by the fact that in England an intention to injure is an essential part of forgery which is a common law offence. For an authority it would be enough for me to point out that it was distinctly laid down in *Reg.* vs. *Hodgson* (D & B 3, 1856) that a person who forged a diploma of the College of Surgeons with the object of inducing a belief that the document was genuine and that he was a member of the College of Surgeons, and then showed it to two persons with intent to induce that belief in them did not intend to defraud, though he intended to deceive. The correctness of the decision was not questioned, and it led to the passing of the Medical Act which made the act punishable for the first time. Blackstone defined forgery as the fraudulent making or altering of a writing *to the prejudice of another's right.* In 1865, however, Cockburn C.J. declared that forgery by universal acceptation is understood to mean 'the making or altering a writing so as to make the alteration purport to be the act of some other person which it is not' (*In re Windsor*, 10 Cox C. C. 118). If this was correct mere intention to deceive would have sufficed for a conviction. The definition, as pointed out by Wharton, was soon found too scant, and Kelly C.B., with the concurrence of his colleagues, laid down, four years later (*R.* vs. *Ritson*, L.R., 1 C. C. 200), that the offence consists in the fraudulent making of an instrument, in words purporting to be what they are not, to the *prejudice of* another's right, thus going back to the definition given by Blackstone. I may lastly quote the definition in Stephen's Digest which may be taken as crystallising the decisions of the English Courts on the subject. "Forgery is making a false document as defined in Article 385 with intent to defraud." The learned author then proceeds to explain what fraud means: "Whenever the words 'fraud' or 'intent to defraud' or 'fraudulently' occur in the definition of a crime two elements at least are essential to the commission of the crime, namely first, deceit or an intention to deceive or in some cases, mere secrecy; and, secondly, either actual

Forgery involves injury.

injury or possible injury or an intent to expose some person either to actual injury, or to a risk of possible injury, by means of that deceit or secrecy. A practically conclusive test as to the fraudulent character of a deception for criminal purposes is this: Did the author of the deceit derive any advantage from it which he could not have had if the truth had been known? If so, it is hardly possible that that advantage should not have had an equivalent in loss, or risk of loss, to some one else; and if so, there was fraud. In practice, people hardly ever intentionally deceive each other in matters of business for a purpose which is not fraudulent." As an illustration the learned author refers to the case of *Reg.* vs. *Hodgson* to which I have already drawn your attention. It is fairly certain that forgery, as defined in the Code, was not intended to be different from forgery as understood in England. This view of the case is strengthened by a reference to the illustrations under Section 464, where the intention to defraud is apparently intended to cover not only an intention to deceive, but also an intention to cause injury. Illustration (*a*) runs as follows:—

> "*A* has a letter of credit upon *B* for Rs. 10,000 written by *Z*. *A* in order to defraud *B*, adds a cipher to 10,000, and makes the sum 1,00,000, intending that it may be believed by *B* that *Z* so wrote the letter. *A* has committed forgery."

If then 'fraudulently' in Sections 463 and 464 includes an intention to injure, you are forced by the operation of Section 7 to hold that wherever 'fraudulently' is used, it not only involves the idea of deception, but also the idea of injury to others. This view finds support from the decisions of the Indian High Courts, where it has been held, for instance, that a person who fabricated a document merely to obtain payment of money, justly due to him, which was being illegally withheld, was not guilty of forgery (*Queen-Empress* vs. *Syed Hussain*, 7 All. 403). The decision is perhaps open to criticism that one may cause injury to another even if he only wants to get what is his own. However that need not be considered here. It may be said that the intention to cause an injury being an essential part of the meaning of the word 'fraud,' the distinction between a fraudulent and a dishonest act practically disappears. But this is not so, and there still remains a clear distinction between the meaning of the two words. The points of difference between the two may be stated thus:—

Distinction between fraud and dishonesty.

(*a*) 'Fraud' necessarily involves deception, 'dishonesty' does not. This is clear and requires no further explanation.

(*b*) 'Dishonesty' necessarily involves the idea of injury to *property*, 'fraud' covers injury to property as well as injury of every other kind. Although 'dishonesty' includes wrongful gain as well as wrongful loss of property, there can hardly be a wrongful gain without a corresponding loss to somebody else. The illustrations to Section 464 may, at first, create the impression that the injury involved in forgery is injury to property only, but this is not so. In *Reg.* vs. *Harris* (1 Moody 393, 1833) it was held to be forgery to forge an order from a Magistrate for the discharge of a prisoner, and it has been generally accepted from the earliest days of English Common Law that the forgery of any matter of judicial or executive record is indictable.

(*c*) A dishonest intention is intention to cause loss of specified property, actually belonging to a definite individual, known or unknown and it must be property actually belonging to an individual at the time of the act described as dishonest. This is fairly clear from the words of Section 24. 'Fraudulently,' on the other hand, even where it implies injury to property, may refer to injury in respect of unspecified property, to unknown and unascertained individuals.

The observations of Norris and Beverley JJ. in Haradhan's case (19 Cal. 380) that in construing Sections 24 and 25, Indian Penal Code, the primary and not the more remote intention must be looked at is perhaps correct as regards Section 24, but is perhaps not correct in their application to Section 25. The distinction I have suggested is to a great extent borne out by the following provision of the New York Code, which lays down that where an intention to defraud constitutes a part of the crime it is not necessary to aver or to prove an intent to defraud any particular person. It has, for instance, been held to be an offence, to forge—

(*a*) a certificate of character to induce the Trinity House to enable a seaman to act as Master—*R.* vs. *Toshack* (1 Den. 492, S. C. 4 Cox 38, 1849).

(*b*) testimonials whereby the offender obtained an appointment as a Police Constable—*R.* vs. *Moah* (D. and B. 550, 1856).

(*c*) the like with intent to obtain the office of a Parish School Master—*R.* vs. *Sharman* (Dears, C.C. 285, 1854).

(*d*) a certificate that a liberated convict was gaining his living honestly, to obtain an allowance—*R.* vs. *Mitchell*, 2 F. & F., 44, 1860).

With reference to these cases it may be contended that they do not show any tendency to prejudice the right of others. But, as Wharton points out, in most cases of forged writs, the officer issuing the writ, if it were genuine, would be liable for misconduct in an action on the case and in cases of forgery of records, there is usually a party to be injured by the falsification, and that in any view the prejudice to others is enough, even if it be contingent and remote. As regards the case of forgery of the writ for the discharge of a prisoner, I would justify it on the ground that it is an injury to the State. In the other cases an injury to some one else in respect of property is the ultimate consequence. For instance, obtaining employment or permission to sit for an examination by means of forged certificates has the effect of excluding others from employment, and, as such, involves injury to property to the persons so excluded.

The views, I have expressed, are perhaps somewhat inconsistent with the statement in Stephen's Digest that an intent to deceive the public or particular persons, but not to commit a particular fraud or specific wrong upon any particular person, is not an intent to defraud. It is, however, not clear to what class of cases the learned author refers. The illustrations to Article 384 of his Digest do not make the matter clear.

Before leaving this subject I should like to draw your attention to a few Indian cases, in which the meaning of the two terms 'fraudulently' and 'dishonestly' has been discussed and differentiated.

Judicial decisions explaining 'fraudulently.'

In *Lolit Mohan Sen* vs. *Queen-Empress* (22 Cal. 313) it was contended that a person who had altered certain *chalans* with the intention of concealing past acts of fraud and dishonesty could not be said to have done so dishonestly or fraudulently within the meaning of Section 464, inasmuch as there was no intention to cause any wrongful gain or wrongful loss in future. In overruling this plea the learned Judges observed: "We think the word 'fraudulently' must mean something different from 'dishonestly.' It must be taken to mean, as defined in Section 25 of the Code, 'with intent to defraud,' and this was the view taken by the Bombay High Court in the case of *Queen-Empress* vs. *Vithal Narain Joshi* (13 Bom. 515, note)." The intention to defraud in the above passage apparently means an intention to deceive to the prejudice of somebody. In support of this view the Judges cited the case of *Queen-Empress* vs. *Sabapati* (11 Mad. 411) and declined to follow two earlier cases—*Empress of India* vs. *Jivanand* (5 All. 221) and *Queen-Empress* vs. *Girdharilal* (8 All. 653). In a later case *Queen-Empress* vs. *Abbas Ali* (25 Cal. 512) a Full Bench of the Calcutta High Court took the same view of the difference between 'fraudulently' and 'dishonestly.' That was a case where a man had forged a certificate in order to qualify himself as a candidate for the examination of engine driver under Act 7 of 1884. The decision of the Full Bench was that 'dishonestly' and 'fraudulently' do not cover the same ground and that an intention to defraud does not necessarily involve deprivation of property actual or intended. The learned Judges supported this view by a reference to *Reg.* vs. *Toshack* (4 Cox 38) and overruled *Queen-Empress* vs. *Haradhan* (19 Cal. 380). In the latter case Norris and Beverley JJ. had held that the fabrication of a false certificate in order to get permission to sit for an examination was not fraudulent. This is in conflict with the English cases I have cited and the distinction I have tried to draw between fraudulent and dishonest acts. Abbas Ali's case has subsequently been followed in *Kedar Nath Chatterji* vs. *King-Emperor* (5 C. W. N. 897).

What constitutes an intention to defraud was discussed in *Babu Ray* vs. *The Emperor* (9 C. W. N. 807). In this case the Collector was withholding payment of money which Babu Ray was entitled to draw and was subsequently induced to make the payment on the basis of false receipts alleged to have been signed by two others on whose signature the Collector was unnecessarily insisting, apparently under a wrong view of the law. It was held that the trick by which the Collector was induced to deliver up property which he was erroneously retaining, did not constitute fraud, and was, therefore, not an offence under Section 415 of the Code. Reference was made to the case of *Reg.* vs. *Duthibeva* (2 B. L. R., Cr. 1, 25) where one Kumari after having executed a conveyance had sent another person to register the document by personating her. It was held that there had been no offence under Section 415 of the Code, as the false personation did not disclose an intention either to defraud or to cause injury to anyone. In the first of these cases there is also reference to a Madras case (*Reg.* vs. *Longhurst*) which however was decided before the Penal Code came into force and is not therefore a direct authority on the question. In this case a person was indicted for obtaining a carriage from the prosecutor by a false pretence. The defence was that the prosecutor owed him money and he got the carriage in order to compel payment. In charging the jury for an acquittal Bittleston J. said : "If you think the accused did not obtain the carriage with the intention of keeping it, but of putting a screw upon the prosecutor then I think he is not guilty of the offence." These cases, specially the first two, leave the law in a very unsatisfactory condition although regarding the particular question arising in the second case the defect has been remedied by legislation (Section 82 of the Registration Act).

I now turn to some of the more important cases in which the meaning of the word 'dishonestly' has been discussed. Judicial decisions explaining 'dishonestly.'

In the case of *Emperor* vs. *Nabi Bukhsh* (25 Cal. 416) where the accused had removed his master's box to a cowshed and kept it concealed there in order, as he said, to give a lesson to his master, it was held that this did not amount to wrongful loss. "Of course," said the Judges, "when the owner is kept out of possession with the object of depriving him of the benefit arising from the possession even temporarily, the case will come within the definition. But where the owner is kept out of possession temporarily, not with any such intention, but only with the object of causing him trouble, in the sense of mere mental anxiety, and with the ultimate intention of restoring the thing to him without exacting or expecting any recompense, it is difficult to say that the detention amounts to causing wrongful loss in any sense. In the case of *Prasanna Kumar Patra* vs. *Udaysant* (22 Cal. 660) it was held that gaining possession of property for a temporary purpose by a creditor in order to coerce the debtor to pay his debt was not taking dishonestly. The cases for and against this view will be found fully discussed in the judgment of the learned Judges (Petheram C.J. and Beverley J.) which show considerable divergence in the decisions of the various Courts in India. This case came up for discussion in the case of Sree Churn Changa (22 Cal. 1017), and was overruled. Reliance was placed on the words of Section 23 and the learned Judges quoted with approval the following passage in Mayne's Penal Code :—

"It is sufficient to show an intention to take dishonestly the property out of any person's possession without his consent, and that it was moved for that purpose. If the dishonest intention, the absence of consent, and the moving, are established, the offence will be complete however temporary may have been the proposed retention."

You will observe that a mere intention to defraud without any intention to cause wrongful gain to one person or wrongful loss to another is sufficient for offences under Sections 206, 207, 208, 210, 239, 240, 242, 243, 250, 251, 252, 253, 261, 262, 263, 264, 265, 482 and 488, but the latter intention is essential to constitute the offence of theft, extortion, criminal misappropriation, criminal breach of trust, receiving stolen property and other similar offences, and either intention would suffice to constitute offences under Sections 209, 246, 247, 415, 421, 422, 423, 424 and 477. An examination of these sections would further elucidate the difference between the two terms.

Corruptly—Malignantly—Wantonly.

'Corruptly' occurs in Sections 219 and 220 only and requires no explanation. **Corruptly.**

'Malignantly' occurs only in Sections 153 and 270. It is synonymous with 'maliciously' which occurs in Sections 219, 220 and 270. A thing is done maliciously if it is done wickedly, or in a depraved, perverse or malignant spirit or in a spirit regardless of social duty and deliberately bent on mischief. Any formed design of doing mischief may be called malice. This is the explanation given of the word by Russell. Sir Fitz James Stephen calls it a vague general term introduced into the law without much perception of its vagueness and gradually **Malignantly.**

reduced to a greater or less degree of certainty in reference to particular offences by a series of judicial decisions. The judicial decisions are, however, wanting in India as the word is not used more than about three times in the Code. 'Malice' in its ordinary non-technical sense means any wicked or mischievous intention of the mind, a depraved inclination to mischief, a wanton disregard of the rights or safety of others. In the absence of any definition we may take it that the word has been used in its plain dictionary meaning. The word is apparently very comprehensive in its nature and would cover all wicked mischievous or perverse acts.

Wantonly. 'Wantonly' occurs in Section 153 and means doing a thing recklessly, that is, without regard to consequences.

RASHLY—NEGLIGENTLY.

Rashly, Negligently. The words 'rashly' and 'negligently' have not been explained in the Code. They are used in the definition of offences not to denote a positive evil intent, but to denote that want of care with which reasonable people are expected to act and the want of which is considered culpable. These words were explained by Mr. Justice Holway in the case of Nidamarti Nagabhushanam (7 Mad. H. C. R. 119) and was quoted with approval in the case of *Empress* vs. *Kitabdi Mandal* (I. L. R., 4 Cal. 764). Mr. Justice Holway says: "Culpable rashness is acting with the consciousness that mischievous and illegal consequences may follow, but with the hope that they will not, and often with the belief that the actor has taken sufficient precautions to prevent their happening.

"The imputability arises from acting despite of the consciousness.

"Culpable negligence is acting without the consciousness that illegal or mischievous effects will follow, but in circumstances which show that the actor has not exercised the caution incumbent on him, and that if he had, he would have had the consciousness.

"The imputability arises from the neglect of the civic duty of circumspection.

"It is manifest that personal injury, consciously and intentionally caused, cannot fall within either of these categories, which are wholly inapplicable to the case of an act or series of acts, themselves intended, which are the producers of death."

The English law on the subject of culpable negligence is thus stated in Stephen's Digest of Criminal Law, Art. 232:—

"Everyone upon whom the law imposes any duty, or who has by contract or by any wrongful act taken upon himself any duty, tending to the preservation of life, and who neglects to perform that duty, and thereby causes the death of any person, commits the same offence as if he had caused the same effect by an act done in the state of mind, as to intent or otherwise, which accompanied the neglect of duty:

"Provided, that no one is deemed to have committed a crime only because he has caused the death of or bodily injury to another by negligence which is not culpable. What amount of negligence can be called culpable is a question of degree for the jury, depending on the circumstances of each particular case. An intentional omission to discharge legal duty always constitutes culpable negligence.

"Provided also that no one is deemed to have committed a crime by reason of the negligence of any servant or agent employed by him.

"Provided also that it must be shown that death not only follows but is also caused by the neglect of duty."

The following illustrations given by the same learned author based on the decisions of English Courts will help to elucidate the statement of law quoted above :—

> "(1) It is *A's* duty, by contract, as the banksman of a colliery shaft, to put a stage on the mouth of the shaft in order to prevent loaded trucks from falling down it. *A* omits to do so, either carelessly or intentionally. A truck falls down the shaft and kills *B*. *A* is in the same position as if he had pushed the truck down the shaft carelessly or intentionally.
>
> "(2) *A*, acting as a surgeon, physician, or midwife, causes the death of a patient by improper treatment, arising from ignorance or inattention. *A* is not criminally responsible, unless his ignorance, or inattention, or rashness is of such a nature that the jury regard it as culpable under all the circumstances of the case. It makes no difference

whether *A* is or is not a properly qualified practitioner."

Gross negligence.

The expression 'gross negligence' has not been used in the Code. It, however, makes no difference for, as has been observed by an eminent Judge, it is the same thing as negligence with the addition of a vituperative epithet. Rash and negligent acts have been made penal where they affect the safety of the public such as rash driving or riding on a public way (Section 279), rash navigation of vessels (Section 280), negligently conveying for hire any person by water in a vessel (Section 282), negligent conduct with respect to—

(*a*) poisonous substances, Section 284,
(*b*) fire or any combustible matter, Section 285,
(*c*) any explosive substance, Section 286,
(*d*) machinery, Section 287,
(*e*) animals, Section 289,

and generally rash and negligent acts endangering life or personal safety of others. It has also been made penal by rash or negligent act to cause hurt (Section 337), to cause grevious hurt (Section 338), to cause death (Section 304A).

HEEDLESSLY.

Heedlessly.

'Heedlessly' has not been used in the Code, but has nearly the same meaning. It means the doing of a thing without due regard to consequences.

LECTURE VII.

CONDITIONS OF NON-IMPUTABILITY.

Grounds of exemption.

Having dwelt at some length upon *mens rea* as a necessary condition of criminality and discussed with reference to the Indian Penal Code the precise meaning to be attached to the more important words used in the definition of offences to indicate the evil intent essential to constitute the different offences, I shall now proceed briefly to explain the general conditions of non-imputability. Strictly speaking these are rules of evidence carrying either conclusive or rebuttable presumptions. The basis of these exemptions are from their very nature subjective. Whatever may be the form in which these conditions are enunciated, when carefully examined they will be found to deal with circumstances which preclude the existence of *mens rea*, and are therefore mere enumeration of the circumstances that are incompatible with its existence. I have already told you that to constitute a crime there must be a voluntary act, and that this act must be the outcome of an intent to cause an evil consequence. It follows as a corollary to the above that the actor must possess—

Essential conditions of responsibility.

(*a*) Free will.

(*b*) Intelligence to distinguish between good and evil.

(*c*) Knowledge of facts upon which the good and evil of an act may depend. (This includes besides the knowledge of existing facts also the knowledge that a particular act may cause a prohibited evil consequence).

(*d*) Knowledge that the act is prohibited by law. (This, however, is excluded on grounds of expediency as I shall show hereafter).

Where any one of these elements is wanting, responsibility is negatived, for the true basis of responsibility is to be found in the fact that man is a rational animal, that he has intelligence to know what is right and what is wrong, and this intelligence coupled with the freedom of will enables him to choose the one and avoid the other. If man were to act by instinct which is a blind tendency to act in a particular way, instead of acting by reason, there would have been no more justification for punishing him than for punishing a vicious wild beast. It would be an act of senseless cruelty to punish in such cases for mere retaliation or even for making an example of him. In fact the line that divides human beings from the lower animals is exactly the line that divides responsibility from irresponsibility. There are certain rules of evidence which help us in the application of these principles. For instance, in case of infants up to a certain age the presumption is absolute that he is not possessed of the intelligence or knowledge referred to above, and consequently is incapable of committing a criminal act.

As to (*a*) *i.e.*, the possession of a free will, every human being is presumed to be free to act as he likes unless such freedom of will is taken away by physical force or mental compulsion. Mental compulsion again may be the result of threat of Free Will.

injury to person or property or may be the outcome of a diseased mind. Mental compulsion arising from threat of injury is only recognised as a valid excuse for a crime when it is a threat reasonably causing the apprehension that instant death would otherwise be the consequence (Section 94). The other form of mental compulsion is not clearly recognised in the Indian Penal Code, but is recognised in various other systems of law. This compulsion arising from a diseased state of the mind is known as irresistible impulse and is treated as part of the law of insanity.

Intelligence. As to (*b*) *i.e.*, possession of intelligence to discriminate between good and evil, the presumption is conclusive that every human being has sufficient intelligence to distinguish between what is right and what is wrong, and the law will not allow an enquiry as to the sufficiency of a person's intelligence for the purpose of making such a distinction except in certain special cases, such as infancy (Section 83), insanity (Section 84), or involuntary drunkenness (Section 85).

I now come to (*c*) and (*d*) which relate respectively to ignorance of fact and ignorance of law. Ignorance of fact is always an excuse unless it is the result of carelessness or negligence. It includes both ignorance of existing facts perceptible by the senses or inferable from other facts so perceptible, as well as ignorance of another kind, *viz.*, ignorance of the relation of one fact to

Knowledge. another, a knowledge of which we gain by experience. However, in whatever form it may occur, ignorance of fact excuses criminal responsibility

(Section 79), but when it is due to carelessness it is no excuse (Section 52).

Ignorance of law and of fact.

On principle, ignorance of law should be as good a defence as ignorance of fact, for the one is as effective in negativing *mens rea* as the other. Both are knowable. If it is difficult for a man in a crowded thoroughfare to avoid treading on another's toes, it is no less difficult for every man to acquaint himself with the laws of the country in which he lives. Why then exclude the one and include the other? The only justification for the distinction is, that it would be difficult to administer the criminal law if it were open for a man who has broken it to set up the plea that he was not aware that the act was prohibited. There is much force in this argument but it has its weak points. If a man, for instance, killed another or stole his purse or forged his name, no court would believe that the offender did not know that murder, theft or forgery was by law punishable, and there is no real danger in allowing the plea to be raised. On the other hand there are offences of which a man may truly say that he was not aware of them. Take the case of a person who shortly after the enactment of the Code gave a beating to a person whom he caught stealing in his house. It was customary in those days to give a beating to a thief when caught. The change introduced by the Penal Code may not have become sufficiently known at the time, the plea of ignorance may be a just and a true plea in such a case. Or take the more recent example of the amendment of Section 375 I.P.C. by the Act known as the Age of Consent Act. In a remote village it might take years for the information to filter down. Should in such cases the plea of ignorance be shut out? Thus there are considerations both for and against the view that ignorance of law should be no excuse. The best solution is perhaps to recognise the distinction between a *malum in se* and a *malum prohibitum*, and to lay down that when by consensus of public opinion an act is considered wrongful no one should be allowed to plead that he was not aware that the law had penalised the act. Where, however, such is not the case and a new offence is created by the legislature, it ought to be open to a person to plead ignorance of the Statute. But in the Code, as in most systems of law, no such distinction is recognised, obviously because it is considered expedient to insist that every man must know the law of the land in which he lives. This doctrine is carried to such an extreme that it is not relaxed even in cases where the acquisition of such knowledge is an impossibility. How far this is defensible I shall discuss later. The presumption is conclusive except where the existence of such knowledge is negatived by immaturity of age by the existence of a diseased mind or by involuntary drunkenness.

The presumption that everybody knows the law, that everybody whatever his intelligence or upbringing, has the capacity to distinguish between the right and wrong of every phase of human conduct may have no foundation in fact, but the rule is based on balance of convenience, and the rigour of the law is softened in all such cases by the discretion which every modern system of law allows to Judges to pass lenient sentences. But this is not enough for the brand of criminality remains.

But apart from the mere theoretic responsibility of individuals for criminal acts, there are other considerations besides those already indicated which enter largely into the consideration of the question of punishment. According to more advanced juridical notions, the mere liability for a wrongful act is not enough to justify punishment. Punishment is not to be inflicted for the mere sake of punishment. It must have an objective. The aims and objects of punishment must therefore largely influence the question of exemption. I shall here refer very briefly to this subject.

Objects of punishment a necessary consideration.

Discussions on this question have sometimes proceeded on the wrong assumption that there is only one object of punishment, with the result that different writers have advanced different theories, and none has been found entirely satisfactory to explain the trend of criminal legislation in modern times in regard to punishments. Legislation regarding punishment of crimes has been influenced by the requirements of particular times and particular countries, but of the various recognised objects of punishment none has been wholly ignored, though the importance to be attached to any particular object has varied. The most important aim of punishment, recognised from the earliest times, is the satisfaction of the desire of human beings, both in their individual and their corporate capacity, for retribution. The feeling is natural and the world must grow considerably older before human nature is so changed that the ordinary man will, when struck on the one cheek, turn the

Retribution.

other. It exists even among the lower animals. The cow turns on you when you strike her calf. Does it do so to make an example of you or to teach you a lesson for future good behaviour? It is the instinctive demand for retribution. The idea of retribution gave birth to the *Rex Talionis* of the Roman law following the old Mosaic law of a tooth for a tooth and an eye for an eye. Whatever theoretical objections there may exist to effect being given to a feeling of this kind, we cannot shut our eyes to its existence and to its intensity so long as human sentiment remains as it is. The strength of this demand for retribution has, however, been gradually diminishing with the growth of culture and ideas of humanity, and we may congratulate ourselves on having attained a plane of thought and culture when we are able to confine this demand for retribution to deliberate acts and against rational beings only, and have not only ceased punishing bulls, pigs, asses and horses not to speak of axes and stones which were not spared even by civilised Athenians, but have also ceased punishing purely accidental acts. The demand for retribution is gradually diminishing but has not disappeared.

Prevention. Another object of punishment is prevention. This is aimed at mainly in three ways :—

(*a*) By depriving the criminal of the opportunity of committing crimes.

(*b*) By reforming him.

(*c*) By making an example of him.

Reform. The reform of the criminal, as an object of punishment, is gradually acquiring more importance and there are many who think that this is the only legitimate object of punishment. We must, they say, respect the man even in the criminal and refuse to sacrifice him merely for making an example.

This reform is attempted in various ways. Juvenile offenders are sent to reformatories, others are taught useful crafts to enable them when out of jails to earn an honest living.

The infliction of bodily and mental pain is another way of reforming the criminal. The painful experience of the past serves as a warning for the future.

The various forms of punishment with which we are familiar have one or more of these objects in view.

A death sentence is mainly retributive. And as retribution is losing its importance as an object of punishment, in some countries in Europe death sentences have been abolished. **Death sentence.**

In old days when the making of an example was one of the most important aims of punishment, the heads of criminals after execution were often exhibited at the city gate to strike terror. We had similar examples in England. We read, for instance, of Moore's head being exhibited on the London Bridge.

Long terms of imprisonment are mainly preventive but like whipping, fine, and similar other punishments also serve the double purpose of causing mental and bodily pain as well as of warning others.

There were some forms of punishment now obsolete which obtained in India even under the British rule which had the effect not only of **Certain obsolete forms of punishment.**

causing mental pain to the criminal, but was also most effective as an example to others.

In India, punishment by public exposure (*Tashhir*), as by carrying the delinquent through the town on the back of a donkey with his face blackened as a special punishment for perjury, was common during the Mahomedan period, and was recognised in Bengal Regulation II of 1807, but was abolished by Act II of 1849. A confirmed perjurer had the word *Darogh-go* (liar) tattooed on his forehead. We also find amusing instances of the same kind of punishment in the laws of *Manu*.

In ancient and mediæval periods there was a tendency to punish a criminal by depriving him of the particular member of the body with which a particular offence was committed. We find examples of it in *Manu* and also in Mahomedan law. "With whatever limb," says *Manu*, "the thief sins, even of that the King shall deprive him." A common instance is cutting off the hands of thieves. These have now fallen into disuse.

With these general observations I proceed to consider the provisions of the Chapter of General Exceptions in the Code. In dealing with the provisions of this Chapter, I think, it would be convenient to discuss them in the order in which they are stated in the Code. Sections 76 and 79 may, however, be conveniently considered together.

Chapter IV, I. P. C.—General Exceptions. Section 76.

Section 76.—'Nothing is an offence which is done by a person who is, or who, by reason of a mistake of fact, and not by reason of a mistake of law, in good faith believes himself to be, bound by law to do it.'

Illustrations.

(*a*) *A*, a soldier, fires on a mob by the order of his superior officer, in conformity with the commands of the law. *A* has committed no offence.

(*b*) *A*, an officer of a Court of Justice, being ordered by that Court to arrest *Y*, and, after due enquiry, believing *Z* to be *Y*, arrests *Z*. *A* has committed no offence.

Section 79.—'Nothing is an offence which is done by any person who is justified by law, or who by reason of a mistake of fact and not by reason of a mistake of law in good faith, believes himself to be justified by law in doing it.' Section 79, I. P. C.

Illustration.

A sees *Z* commit what appears to *A* to be a murder. *A*, in the exercise, to the best of his judgment, exerted in good faith, of the power which the law gives to all persons of apprehending murderers in the fact, seizes *Z*, in order to bring *Z* before the proper authorities. *A* has committed no offence, though it may turn out that *Z* was acting in self-defence.

Ignorantia facti excusat is a well known maxim of criminal law and follows from the doctrine of *mens rea*. Ignorance of fact to be an excuse must be ignorance in respect of a material fact; *i.e.*, a fact which is essential to constitute a particular offence. Such ignorance alone absolves which negatives the evil intent necessary to constitute the offence. "The guilt of the accused," says Ignorance of fact.

Baron Parke, "must depend on circumstances as they appear to him." The doctrine is subject to certain reservations which, it is important, you should bear in mind. In the first place no one is allowed to plead ignorance of fact where responsible enquiry would have elicited the true facts. Where a person shuts his eyes to true facts he cannot plead such voluntary ignorance as an excuse. A woman hears a rumour that her husband is dead. She makes no enquiries whether the rumour is true or false and marries again. It is afterwards found that the man was alive. The belief carelessly entertained cannot be pleaded as an excuse in an indictment for bigamy.

A takes away *B*, a girl under the age of sixteen years, out of the keeping of her lawful guardian without his consent. He believes that the girl is above that age, but does so without making any enquiry, and basing his belief on the mere appearance of the girl which as we know is often deceptive. He is guilty of kidnapping from lawful guardianship under Section 361 of the Code and his belief will not avail him.

Good faith. Section 52 of the Code lays down that nothing is said to be done or believed in good faith, which is done or believed without due care and attention. Reference may also be made to Section 26 which says, that a person is said to have reason to believe a thing if he has sufficient cause to believe that thing, but not otherwise. Whether in any particular case the belief of a person in the existence of a certain state of facts is based on reasonable grounds or is the result of negligence or carelessness is a question of fact to be decided by the jury in each case. It may be argued that every fact is knowable and a mistake of fact may in all cases be attributed to negligence. Such a view, however, will render the doctrine wholly nugatory. Life would be too short and intolerable if everyone was obliged to scrutinise every fact and take nothing on trust. It is true men often lie, but even the greatest liar speaks the truth in ninety cases out of a hundred. A man sells a watch to you. He tells you that the watch is his. Unless there are any circumstances arousing your suspicion you would be perfectly justified in trusting him, and no one can say you are guilty of negligence, because you did not enter into an enquiry into the history of the watch. Law-givers with the best of reasons take the world as it is, and do not insist on men doing more than they are accustomed to do in the daily transactions of human life. When you do less you are guilty of negligence. In the case of the watch if you believe the watch to belong to the man who brought it to you, you cannot be guilty of being the receiver of stolen property. Take another instance, that of a police officer, who goes with a warrant of arrest against *A*. *B* points out *C* to the police officer as *A*, and the officer without any further enquiry and believing *C* to be *A* arrests *C*. He can plead the mistake of fact as a good defence, and no one would blame him for apprehending the wrong man. The amount of care which the law insists upon, is the care which a reasonable man would ordinarily take and act upon. *A* marries *B*, a young girl, living with her parents in India. She is treated by everybody as an unmarried girl, and *A* has no reason to suspect that she is otherwise. It afterwards transpires that whilst in England she had secretly married *C* and had deserted him. No reasonable man in *A's* position would think it his duty to make enquiries in England for the mere chance of finding that *B* was a married woman. In such a case very little enquiry would be expected. But suppose *A* knew that *B* was married to *C* and *B* told him that she had been divorced, and he acts entirely on *B's* statement, it is very doubtful if his ignorance will not be considered as due to negligence. Similarly in the case of a libel where truth is a justification, the accused will not be allowed to give evidence that there was a rumour floating which he carelessly believed and upon which he acted.

As regards the degree of enquiry it is perhaps permissible to make a distinction between acts that are *malum in se* and those that are merely *malum prohibitum*. You may remember that the distinction between *Reg.* v. *Prince* and *Reg.* v. *Tolson* was based on the view that in the case of an immoral act a man who acts under a mistaken belief takes the risk of punishment if it is found that his belief was wrong in fact, even if there were reasonable grounds for such belief; and that in the case of a *malum prohibitum* such a ground of belief is quite sufficient. The Indian Penal Code, as you will see, makes no such distinction. But all the same, I think, if those two cases had been decided under the Code the result would probably have been the same, but the reasons might have been different. In the case of a man charged with having enticed away a girl below the age of sixteen, the jury would expect a much greater degree of care and caution for the belief that the girl is over that age than in the case of a person who openly enters into a marriage relation with a woman in the belief that she had not a husband living. In the case of enticement it would be expected of the man who commits such an act that he should not feel satisfied with the mere look of the girl, nor should he rely merely upon the girl's statement regarding her age. Whereas in the case of *Reg.* v. *Tolson* the amount of enquiry upon which the prisoner believed that her husband was dead was held to be sufficient, and would have been so held in this country on a similar charge under Section 494 of the Code, I doubt if a person charged with an offence under Section 497 could successfully defend himself by alleging that upon the same materials he honestly believed that the woman had not a husband living. It seems only just that a man who under a mistaken belief as to facts does an act which is at least morally wrong must, in order to avoid punishment, satisfy the Court that his belief was not based on hasty deductions.

"Justified by law", meaning of.

Having regard to the very general terms of Section 79 it is fairly obvious that there is very little room for the distinction made in English and American cases between *malum in se* and *malum prohibitum*. Such a distinction would have no foundation on anything expressed or implied in the Code, unless it is held that the words 'justified by law' mean approved by law or as just or conformable to right and justice. If this is the meaning of the words 'justified by law' the taking away of a girl over the age of sixteen as in the case of *Reg.* v. *Prince* would not be an act justified by law, but would only be an act not prohibited by law, and as such not covered by the words of Section 79. In the case of bigamy, however, not only the law does not punish marriage, but approves of it and encourages it in various ways. If this interpretation of the word 'justified' were admissible, the distinction between '*malum in se*' and '*malum prohibitum*' would arise here also. But if we adopt such an interpretation, we will be confronted with this difficulty that many acts which are innocent, and which the law neither approves nor disapproves would not come within the words of the section. Take for instance the case of a person who shoots a human being in a jungle believing that he was shooting a jackal, under circumstances that would render such a belief reasonable. You cannot say that the law approves or disapproves shooting. Therefore the words 'justified by law' must be taken to mean 'not prohibited by law.' If the distinction between *malum in se* and *malum prohibitum* is thus wiped off, the only way to arrive at the same result as in *Reg.* v. *Prince* and *Reg.* v. *Tolson* would be to insist on greater care and scrutiny in the one case than in the other. It may be noted that in neither kidnapping nor bigamy as defined in the Code, a knowledge of the true age in one case or a knowledge of the existence of a husband or wife in the other, is an essential part of the definition. So that, except in so far as the question may be affected by the provisions of Section 79, there is no distinction between the English Statute and the provisions of the Indian Penal Code. It may also be urged that there is nothing which is absolutely good and nothing absolutely bad in this world, and very often the distinction instead of influencing legislation is influenced and even created by it. All the same, there are certain prevalent ideas among intelligent and cultured people by which we judge human acts and divide them into good and evil, and this standard is quite enough for making a selection between acts innocent in themselves but which for reasons of state have been made punishable, and wrongs which by reason of their evil tendency are worthy of condemnation and have been made penal on that account.

Distinction between Sections 76 and 79, I. P. C.

The distinction between Sections 76 and 79 consists in this : Section 76 deals with cases where by reason of a mistake of fact the person under a mistake considers himself *bound by law* to act in a particular way, although on the true state of facts his act is an offence. Section 79, on the other hand, deals with cases where by reason of a mistake of fact the person under such mistake considers himself simply *justified* by law to act in a particular way. The antithesis between the two cases is involved in the words 'bound by law' in Section 76 and 'justified by law' in Section 79. To punish an act done under a mistake of fact would neither be justified by the principle of retaliation nor by the theory of prevention. You can never guard against committing mistakes and punishment would not prevent their occurrence.

Besides cases of mistake, both these sections also provide for cases which have nothing to do with mistakes, cases which fall within the definition of an offence but are excepted from punishment, because of legal compulsion or legal justification. Illustration (*a*) of Section 76 belongs to this class. Probably it would have been more logical if one of these sections had dealt with mistakes, and another with cases of legal compulsion or legal justification, without bringing in the question of mistake at all. You have seen that both Sections 76 and 79, whilst admitting the validity of an excuse based on ignorance of fact, exclude expressly an excuse when based on ignorance of law. *Ignorantio legis non excusat* is an equally well known principle of law. The doctrine is based on the fiction that every citizen knows or at any rate ought to know the law under which he lives and by which his actions are governed. It is, as we know, a fiction, but, as many other legal fictions are supposed to be, it is a creature of imperative necessity or expediency. The presumption that every one knows the law is a conclusive presumption, and will be enforced even where it could be shown that it was impossible for the accused to have known the law. In *Reg.* v. *Bailey* (R. & R. 1) the prisoner was indicted for an offence under the

Ignorance of law.

Act of the 39, Geo. III, C. 37, and was convicted, although it was found that the Act received Royal assent on the 10th of May 1799, that the fact charged in the indictment happened on the 27th of June, that the ship *Langley* of which the prisoner was the Captain, was at that time upon the coast of Africa and could not possibly know that any such Act had existed. Lord Eldon told the jury that the prisoner was in strict law guilty, though he could not then know that the Act had been passed. The prisoner was, however, pardoned on the recommendation of the Judges. Even if a penal statute is ambiguously worded it is no defence that the accused tried to ascertain the law and was misled by advising counsel. If an offence is committed in England by a foreigner he cannot be excused, because he did not know the English law, and in his country it was no offence. (Barronet's case, 1 E. & B. 1).

Reasons for the distinction between ignorance of fact and ignorance of law.

The validity of the reasons for distinguishing ignorance of fact from ignorance of law has been the subject of some controversy. I have already referred to it but would like to state mere fully the arguments put forward in support of the distinction.

That every man knows or ought to know the law is no doubt a fiction, but a very necessary fiction. Law has to be based not only on theoretic principles but expediency must always play a very large part in the legislation of every country. Theoretically, of course, ignorance of fact being an excuse, equally well should ignorance of law be an excuse, for both negative the existence of a guilty mind. But there are cogent considerations for maintaining such a fiction. The fiction rests on the broad foundations of public policy. Without it justice cannot be administered. For if ignorance of law is admitted to be an excuse in every case, it will be open to an accused to allege that he was not cognisant of the law under which he is arraigned. It is pointed out by Judge Hunt of the United States, with reference to this doctrine, that no system of criminal jurisprudence can be sustained on any other principle. The question of policy is thus discussed by Austin:

"Now to affirm 'that every person may know the law' is to affirm the thing which is not. And to say 'that his ignorance should not excuse him *because* he is *bound* to know,' is simply to assign the rule as a reason for itself. Being bound to know the law, he cannot effectually allege his ignorance of the law as a ground of exemption from the law. But *why* is he bound to know the law? or *why* is it presumed, *juris et de jure*, that he knew the law"?

"The only *sufficient* reason for the rule in question seems to be this: that if ignorance of law were admitted as a ground of exemption, the Courts would be involved in questions which it were scarcely possible to solve, and which would render the administration of justice next to impracticable. If ignorance of law were admitted as a ground of exemption, ignorance of law would always be alleged by the party, and the Court, in every case, would be bound to decide the point."

Ignorance of fact according to Austin is either evitable or inevitable. Inevitable ignorance is such ignorance as no amount of attention *practicable under the circumstances* could remove. As an instance, he quotes the case of a man who intending to kill a burgler, who has broken into his house, strikes in the dark and kills his own servant. In such a case if the man had good reasons to suppose that it was the burgler and not his own servant, he would not be guilty of murder or even manslaughter. The same distinction may perhaps with advantage be imported into cases of ignorance of law. Every man can know the law and it would be right to hold, that he must know the law if he can. Therefore ignorance of law under ordinary circumstances would not be inevitable; but it would be an inevitable mistake of law where it is impossible for a person to have such knowledge. Take the case of a person who lives in the interior of the Darjeeling district and who breaks the law the day after the law is passed and published in Calcutta. To guard against ignorance of this kind, in some countries the law wisely provides that no act of the legislature shall take effect until a certain time has elapsed from the date of its passing unless there be special provision to the contrary. Sometimes in Indian statutes also a date is fixed on which the statute takes effect. The General Clauses Act provides that where any Act of the Governor General in Council is not expressed to come into operation on a particular day, then it shall come into operation on the day on which it receives the assent of the Governor General.

Evitable and inevitable ignorance.

If this distinction between evitable and inevitable mistakes were adopted the difficulty that arose in the case of *Reg.* v. *Bailey* would have been avoided and the law would have been placed on a more rational basis. It is better that hard cases like these should be excluded from the operation of criminal law instead of their being left to executive clemency.

The effect of ignorance both of law and fact is not the same in respect of civil and criminal liability, and naturally so, for in the case of civil law the end is not punishment but *reparation* and civil liability generally arises without reference to intention, and it is considered just and equitable that 'he by whose act a civil injury has been occasioned should ultimately sustain the loss that has accrued rather than another.'

Uncertainty of the law and its effect on the doctrine.

Another hardship that the application of the doctrine often involves is due to the uncertainty of the law. The Bengal creditor who after the decision of the High Court in the case of *Prasanno Kumar Patra* v. *Udai Santa* (22 Cal. 669) walked away with his debtor's cattle in order to compel the latter to pay his debt, when convicted, would have a real grievance, and I think in all such cases where a man acts *bona fide* upon legal advice, he should get the benefit of his mistake in the same way as he gets the benefit of a doubt arising upon facts. In all such cases, as I have already said, the hardship may, to a great extent, be met by imposing a nominal sentence, and this is what was done in the Full Bench case of *Empress* v. *Srichurn* (22 Cal. 1017) that overruled the earlier decision. But in such cases it would be much better to recognise the inevitable nature of the ignorance and to acquit the accused than to brand him as a thief for having followed the interpretation of law given by two learned Judges of the highest court in the land. These hard cases are, however, of rare occurrence and cogent arguments may be put forward in support of the universal application of the doctrine. Taking first the strictly penal offences with *mens rea* as an essential element, such as are defined in the Indian Penal Code, most of these would be looked upon as deserving of punishment in any state of society and under any system of law however primitive, and the Penal Code may be said to have only defined, systematised and consolidated them. Most offences defined in the Code existed before our criminal laws were codified. That these acts are wrongful is realised by every man of average intelligence, for laws are often mere expressions of the moral sentiments of a people or the ideal to which the law-giver desires to conduct them. Most of the offences under the Indian Penal Code will be found in the breast of every man who has the sense to distinguish right from wrong. A few doubtful cases may arise, but these are indeed very few. As regards municipal and fiscal laws which do not insist on a *mens rea* ignorance of law or fact are on principle both immaterial. The reasons for this special treatment are, as you have seen, fully explained in *Reg.* v. *Tolson*.

The chapter of general exceptions comes into play only when an act is otherwise included in the definition of an offence. It gives the accused a plea of avoidance, the onus of the proof of which lies on him. Before the plea of avoidance becomes material there must be proof of facts to constitute the offence, and if it is the essence of the offence that there must be proof of a particular evil intent, it will, I apprehend, be held in India as it has been held under other systems, that ignorance of law may be proved to rebut the positive evidence regarding the existence of *mens rea.* Take for instance a case of theft. It is not open to one, accused of theft, to get rid of his liability by saying that he was not aware of the law which made theft punishable. But ignorance of law may be pleaded for a collateral purpose. For example, to bring a case within the definition of theft, it must be shown that there was dishonest taking; a *bonâ fide* claim of right if proved, would therefore take the case out of the definition of theft, and it would be immaterial that such claim was based on a view of law that was erroneous. To illustrate what I mean: suppose a Mahomedan dies, leaving an illegitimate son and daughters. The son removes some of his properties without the knowledge and consent of the heirs in the honest but mistaken belief that he also had a share in the estate of the deceased. This ignorance of law may be admissible to negative *mens rea.* So also in a case of criminal trespass the existence of a similar ignorance on point of law may be pleaded to negative the existence of an intention to annoy.

It was held in an American case that it was no defence to an indictment for bigamy that the defendants believed that the female defendant, her husband being married again, could lawfully marry and that they were so advised by the Magistrate who married them, they relying upon such opinion in good faith. (*State* v. *Goodenow*, 65, Me, 30, 1874). Under the Indian law also a *bonâ fide* belief like this, having regard to the language of Section 494, I. P. C., will not be a defence, for the definition does not require any particular state of mind to constitute the offence. The case of adultery is on a different footing, for Section 497 requires as an essential condition a knowledge or reasonable belief that the woman is another's wife. It has accordingly been held that where a prisoner accused of adultery set up in defence a *Natra* contracted with the woman with whom he was alleged to have committed adultery, in accordance with the custom of his caste, the question the Court had to determine was, whether or not, the accused honestly believed, at the time of contracting the *Natra* that the woman was the wife of another man. (Manchar, 5 Bom. H. C. R. 17). However it will not be sufficient to show that the accused believed that the husband could not complain of the adultery, but it must be shown that the accused believed that the woman was no longer the wife of the complainant.

Take another case. A Mahomedan husband divorces his wife and another person believing that the divorce is valid marries her. Should he be convicted of bigamy because the divorce turns out to be ineffectual under the Mahomedan law?

It is well established, that a mistake regarding a mixed question of law and fact is on the same footing as a mistake of fact pure and simple.

Sections 77 and 78 may be taken together.

Sections 77 and 78, I. P. C.

Section 77.—Nothing is an offence which is done by a Judge when acting judicially in the exercise of any power which is, or which in good faith he believes to be, given to him by law.

Section 78.—Nothing which is done in pursuance of, or which is warranted by the judgment or order of a Court of Justice, if done whilst such judgment or order remains in force is an offence, notwithstanding the Court may have had no jurisdiction to pass such judgment or order, provided the person doing the act in good faith believes that the Court had such jurisdiction.

Sections 76 and 79, so far as they give protection to a person acting under the erroneous belief that he is either bound by law or justified by law to do a particular act, would cover a portion of the ground covered by Sections 77 and 78, but not the whole of it. For instance, neither of these sections (76 and 79) would protect a Judge from criminal prosecution if he convicted a person upon a mistaken view of the law, and yet it is essential that a Judge should be protected against all such mistakes. The necessity for giving special protection to Judges is thus obvious and this protection is given by Sections 77 and 78.

Judges and those carrying out their orders are exempt from civil liability by the operation of the Judicial Officers Protection Act (Act XVIII of 1850), which enacts:—

Judicial Officers Protection Act.

"No Judge, Magistrate, Justice of the Peace, Collector, or other person acting judicially, shall be liable to be sued in any Civil Court, for any act done or ordered to be done by him in the discharge of his judicial duty, whether or not within the limits of his jurisdiction: provided that he at the time, in good faith, believed himself to have jurisdiction to do or order the act complained of: and no officer of any Court or other person bound to execute the lawful warrants or orders of any such Judge, Magistrate, Justice of the Peace, Collector, or other person acting judicially, shall be liable to be sued in any Civil Court, for the execution of any warrant or order, which he would be bound to execute, if within the jurisdiction of the person issuing the same."

Sections 77 and 78 give the same immunity from criminal prosecutions. The propriety of the rule is obvious and need not be discussed at any length. As observed by Crompton J. in *Fray* v. *Blackburn* (3 B. and S. 576 at p. 578), the rule exists for the benefit of the public and was established in order to secure the independence of the Judges and prevent their being harassed by vexatious actions. The question of good faith only arises when there is no jurisdiction. When there is jurisdiction the immunity extends even to acts which constitute an abuse of it. Lord Esher laid down in *Anderson* v. *Gorrie* (L. R., Q. B., 1895, p. 668) that no action lay against a Judge of a Court of Record in respect of any act done by him in his judicial capacity, even though he acted oppressively and maliciously, to the prejudice of the plaintiff and to the perversion of justice. Referring to the observations of Chief Justice Cockburn in *Thomas* v. *Churton*, he said: "I am reluctant to decide, and will not do so until the question comes before me, that if a Judge abuses his judicial office, by using slanderous words maliciously and without reasonable and probable cause, he

Immunity of Judges.

Malice.

is not to be liable to an action" Lord Esher observed: "All I can say is, that I am convinced that had the question come before that learned Judge he must and would, after considering the previous authorities, have decided that the action would not lie. That case was decided in 1862, and there are subsequent cases that confirm the principle which I have stated to be derived from the common law." The same rule was laid down in *Meghraj* v. *Zakir* (1 All. p. 280) in which it was laid down that no person acting judicially is liable for an act done or ordered to be done by him in the discharge of his judicial duty within the limits of his jurisdiction. In such a case the question whether he acted in good faith does not arise. See also 2 M. H. C. 396; 2 M. H. C. 443; 3 B. H. C., A. C. 36; 4 B. L. R., A. C. 37; 4 B. H. C., A. C. 150; 14 B. L. R. 254; 21 W. R. 126.

Meaning of 'Judge.'

Section 19 of the Code explains that the word "Judge" denotes not only every person who is officially designated to be a Judge, but also every person who is empowered by law to give in any legal proceeding, civil or criminal, a definitive judgment or a judgment which, if not appealed against, would be definitive, or a judgment which, if confirmed by some other authority, would be definitive or who is one of a body of persons, which body of persons is empowered by law to give such a judgment.

Thus as the illustrations show:—

What it includes.

(*a*) A Collector exercising jurisdiction in a suit under Act X of 1859, is a Judge.

(*b*) A Magistrate exercising jurisdiction in respect of a charge on which he has power to sentence to fine or imprisonment, with or without appeal, is a Judge.

(*c*) A member of a *panchayat* which has power, under Regulation VII, 1816, of the Madras Code, to try and determine suits, is a Judge.

(*d*) A Magistrate exercising jurisdiction in respect of a charge on which he has power only to commit for trial to another Court, is not a Judge.

A definitive judgment means a final judgment. According to this definition a Magistrate holding an enquiry or trial preliminary to commitment, is not a Judge within the meaning of Section 19 of the Indian Penal Code, because he is not empowered to give any definitive judgment or any judgment at all. But although such a person does not come within the exemption, no difficulty would seem to arise, for his powers are extremely limited, and it is inconceivable that any such person would by mistake do an act which would bring his act within the definition of an offence defined in the Indian Penal Code. The necessity for protection may however arise in connection with the exercise of the power to grant or refuse bail. It will also appear from the definition that it makes no difference that a judgment is subject to appeal or revision or that, as for instance, in the case of a capital sentence, the judgment is subject to confirmation by the High Court.

A judgment is defined in the Civil Procedure Code to be the statement given by the Judge of the grounds of a decree or order. In criminal law, however, it means the sentence of the law pronounced by the Courts upon the matter contained in the record. Ordinarily a judgment in a criminal case has to contain the point or points for determination, the decision thereon and the reasons for the decision (Section 367, Criminal Procedure Code).

In England a distinction is made between a Judge of an inferior Court and a Judge of a Court of Record. In *Calder* v. *Halket* (2 Moo. I. A. 293), Baron Parke, dealing with the question as to what constitutes a Court of Record, referred with approval to the decision in *Dr. Grenville* v. *The College of Physicians*, 12 Mod. 388, in which it was laid down that wherever there is power *de novo* created by Parliament to convict and fire and imprison, either of those two makes it a Court of Record.

Privilege confined to judicial acts.

It is not every act of a Judge that comes within the exemption. If a Judge, for instance, assaults or abuses his peon, he cannot claim privilege which only extends to judicial acts. The immunity, however, is not confined to acts done in open Court and may extend to acts done in the Judge's private room. Nor is it confined to what are generally called Courts of Justice, but to all other Tribunals discharging similar functions.

Court.

The largest statement of this immunity is to be found in the judgment of the Exchequer Chamber in *Dawkins* v. *Lord Rokeby*, 8 Q. B. 255, where it was laid down that no action for libel or slander lay, whether against Judges, Counsel, witnesses or parties, for words written or spoken in the ordinary course of any proceeding before any Court or Tribunal recognised by law. Lord Justice Fry in *Royal Aquarium* v. *Parkinson* (1 Q. B., 1892,

p. 431, at 452) "accepted" that proposition with this qualification. "I doubt," he said, "whether the word 'Tribunal' does not really rather embarrass the matter; because that word has not, like the word 'Court,' an ascertainable meaning in English law. Moreover, the judgment of the Exchequer Chamber appears to me to proceed upon the hypothesis that the word is really equivalent to the word 'Court,' because it proceeds to inquire into the nature of the particular Court there in question, and comes to the conclusion that a Military Court of Inquiry, 'though not a Court of Record, nor a Court of Law, nor coming within the definition of a Court of Justice, is nevertheless a Court duly and legally constituted and recognised in the articles of War and many Acts of Parliament.' I do not desire to attempt any definition of a 'Court.' It is obvious that, according to our law, a Court may perform various functions. Parliament is a Court. Its duties as a whole are deliberative and legislative: the duties of a part of it only are judicial. It is nevertheless a Court. There are many other Courts which, though not Courts of Justice, are nevertheless Courts according to our law. There are, for instance, Courts of Investigation, like the Coroner's Court. In my judgment therefore, the existence of the immunity claimed does not depend upon the question whether the subject-matter of consideration is a Court of Justice, but whether it is a Court in law. Wherever you find a Court in law, to that the law attaches certain privileges, among which is the immunity in question."

The ground of the rule is public policy. It is applicable to all kinds of Courts of Justice, but is not confined to these Courts alone and the doctrine has been carried further; it seems that this immunity applies wherever there is an authorised inquiry, which though not before a Court of Justice, is before a Tribunal which has similar attributes. In the case of *Dawkins* v. *Lord Rokeby* the doctrine was extended to a Military Court of Inquiry. It was so extended on the ground that the case was one of an authorised inquiry before a Tribunal acting judicially, that is to say, in a manner as nearly as possible similar to that in which a Court of Justice acts in respect of an inquiry before it. Referring to the case before him in which defendant a member of the London County Council claimed immunity against an action for damages for having made defamatory statements against the plaintiff Company, Lord Esher observed: "This doctrine has never been extended further than to Courts of Justice and Tribunals acting in a manner similar to that in which such Courts act. Then can it be said that a meeting of the County Council, when engaged in considering applications for licenses for music and dancing, is such a Tribunal? It is difficult to say who are to be considered as Judges acting judicially in such a case. The manner in which the business of such a meeting is conducted does not appear to present any analogy to a judicial inquiry. Again, there is another consideration. It is argued for the plaintiffs that this function of granting licenses, which has been transferred from the Justices to the County Council, is not judicial but merely administrative. The Justices had two distinct and separate duties. They had judicial duties. They had to try criminal cases, and in respect of that duty they would be entitled to the absolute immunity which I have mentioned. They had also administrative duties, one of which was this duty of granting licenses, and for the purpose of performing these they held consultations among themselves. In the case of duties properly administrative, such as that of granting licenses, their action was consultative, for the purpose of administration and not judicial. When such duties are transferred to the County Council, what they do in respect of them is likewise consultative for the purpose of performing an administrative duty, it is not judicial. That consideration also appears to me to show clearly that the case does not come within the doctrine of absolute immunity applicable to Tribunals similar to Courts of Justice."

This point was further elucidated by Lopes L.J., who observed :—" The word 'Judicial' has two meanings. It may refer to the discharge of duties exercisable by a Judge, by Justices in Court, or to administrative duties which need not be performed in Court, but in respect of which it is necessary to bring to bear a judicial mind—that is, a mind to determine what is fair and just in respect of the matters under consideration. Justices, for instance, act judicially when administering the law in Court, and they also act judicially when determining in their private room what is right and fair in some administrative matter brought before them, for instance, levying a rate."

Meaning of 'Judicial.'

Good Faith. I have already told you that the question of good faith does not arise when a Judge acts within the limits of his jurisdiction, but it arises when those limits are exceeded. It appears from some of the authorities that the question of good faith is controlled by the legal fiction that every person knows the law of his own country, so that it is not open to a Judge to plead that he assumed jurisdiction on an erroneous view of the law, although he can plead that by reason of a mistake of fact he acted under the wrong belief that he had jurisdiction. The distinction between these two classes of mistakes was pointed out and fully discussed in *Houlden* v. *Smith*, 14 Q. B. 841. Defendant, a Judge of the County Court, summoned the plaintiff

Jurisdiction. who lived outside the jurisdiction of the Court to appear and show cause why he had not paid a judgment-debt, and on his failure to attend he was committed for contempt for 12 days in jail. Neither was the debtor at the time living within the jurisdiction of the Court from which the summons

Want of jurisdiction. was issued, nor was the jail in which the debtor was confined within the jurisdiction of the Court. In delivering the judgment of the Court in an action for trespass and false imprisonment, Patterson J. held that the "commitment was without jurisdiction, that the defendant ordered it under the mistake of the law and not of the facts, that although as laid down in *Lowther* v. *Earl Rudnor*, 8 East. 113, and *Gwinn* v. *Pool*, 2 Lut. W. 935, where the facts of the case, although subsequently proved to be false, were such as, if true, would give jurisdiction, the question as to jurisdiction or not, must depend on the state of facts as they appear to the

Magistrate or Judge, but that mistaking the law as applying to the facts cannot give even a *prima facie* jurisdiction or semblance, if any. "Although it is clear," said the learned Judge, "that the Judge of a Court of Record is not answerable at common law in an action for erroneous judgment or for the act of any officer of the Court wrongfully done, not in pursuance of, though under colour of a judgment of the Court, yet we have found no authority for saying that he is not answerable in an action for an act done by his command and authority when he has no jurisdiction," and it was held that the defendant Judge was not protected from liability at common law.

I have told you on the authority of *Houlden* v. *Smith* that where jurisdiction is assumed on a wrong view of law it is not a valid defence. The matter, however, is not free from doubt and it seems quite clear to me that if this is correct law, the immunity does not go far enough. We constantly come across cases where jurisdiction is assumed by Magistrates on erroneous reading of the law, and it seems to me it would be dangerous to lay down that in such cases even if the Magistrate acts in perfect good faith he is liable to action, civil or criminal. Such a view of the law would make the position of Magistrates one of difficulty. It is true, as pointed out by Sir Francis Maclean in *Brojendra Kishore* v. *Clarke* (13 C. W. N. 458) "it is of the highest importance, in the interest of the public, that, when executive officers are invested with statutory powers of a special and drastic nature, they ought to be very cautious, before exercising those powers, in satisfying themselves that they have strictly complied with the provisions of the Act which created them." But giving due weight to the argument I am not convinced that an honest and *bona fide* error of law should not be a good defence under Sections 77 and 78 I. P. C. or under the Judicial Officers Protection Act. Of course, if jurisdiction is assumed without due care and caution, having regard to the definition of good faith, such a mistake will not avail.

As laid down by Lord Esher M.R. and Lopes L.J. in *Royal Acquarium* v. *Parkinson*, 1 Q. B. 431, in an action for slander where the occasion is privileged, the defence of privilege may be rebutted by showing, that from some indirect motive, such as anger or gross and unreasoning prejudice with regard to a particular subject-matter, the defendant stated what he did not know to be true, reckless whether it was true or false.

Want of jurisdiction may arise under different circumstances. A Judge may have no general jurisdiction to act in a certain matter at all or he may have jurisdiction but only under certain conditions or though having general jurisdiction to deal with a matter, he may not have jurisdiction to act in a particular manner. In some cases the plea has been upheld that where general jurisdiction exists, the absence of the conditions by which it may be limited or the exercise of it in a particular way not authorised by law, does not take away the privilege. The distinction was referred to but not decided in *Calder* v. *Halket* as upon the facts found the question did not arise. Baron Parke said " it is unnecessary to determine, whether, if distinct notice had been given by the plaintiff to the defendant, or proof brought forward that the defendant was well acquainted with the fact of his being British-born, the defendant would have been protected in this case, as being in the nature of a Judge of record, acting irregularly within his general jurisdiction, or liable to an action of trespass, as acting by virtue of a special and limited authority, given by the statute, which was not complied with, and therefore altogether without jurisdiction."

Jurisdiction and error of law.

In *Spooner* v. *Juddow* (4 M. I. A., p. 353) the validity of a defence based on error of law was recognised and the law was laid down in these terms. "Assuming now that the act complained of was a judicial act and not within the power given by law, the section requires that it should be further done in good faith and *in the belief that it was sanctioned by law.* These two requisites are the necessary pre-requisites for exoneration from criminal responsibility of all persons empowered to act under the direction of law. Law extends its protection only to a person who *bona fide* and not absurdly believes that he is acting in pursuance of his legal power." This question was discussed in *Teyen* v. *Ramlal* (12 All., 115) where the law was laid down thus:

"Under Act XVIII of 1850, where an act done or ordered to be done by a judicial officer in the discharge of his judicial duties is within the limits of his jurisdiction, he is protected whether or not he has discharged those duties erroneously, irregularly or even illegally or without believing in good faith that he had jurisdiction to do the act complained of. Where the act done or ordered to be done in the discharge of judicial duties is without the limits of the officer's jurisdiction, he is protected if, at the time of doing or ordering it, he in good faith believed himself to have jurisdiction to do or order it.

"The word 'jurisdiction' is used in Act XVIII of 1850 in the sense in which it was used by the Privy Council in *Calder* v. *Halket* (2 Moo. I. A. 293). It means authority or power to act in a matter, and not authority or power to do an act in a particular manner or form. A judicial officer who in the discharge of his judicial duties issues a warrant which he has authority to issue, though the particular form or manner in which he issues it is contrary to law, acts within and not without the limits of his jurisdiction in this sense.

"Where a Magistrate of the first class having sentenced an accused person to three years' rigorous imprisonment and Rs. 500 fine under Sections 379 and 411 of the Penal Code, and having issued a warrant purporting to act under Section 386 of the Criminal Procedure Code, for the levy of the fine by distress and sale of cattle belonging to the accused, sold such cattle before the date fixed for the sale, and in contravention of Form 37, Schedule V, and Section 554 of the Code, and Form D in Chapter V of the Circular Orders of the High Court, he was acting in the discharge of his judicial duty within his jurisdiction as a Magistrate of the first class; under such circumstances, it was immaterial that he did not in good faith believe himself to have jurisdiction to sell the property in the manner he did; and the fact that he acted with gross and culpable irregularity did not deprive him of the protection afforded by Act XVIII of 1850."

Clarke v. *Brojendra Kishore* is an authority for the proposition that where jurisdiction is given under certain conditions the existence of those conditions must be proved before immunity can be claimed, and it is not enough that the existence of jurisdiction was believed in good faith (16 C. W. N., p. 865). The plaintiff, a Zemindar in the District of Mymensingh, sued the Magistrate of that District for damages for a trespass alleged to have been committed by the latter in searching the plaintiff's cutchery on the allegation that the search was not authorised by law and the defendant acted maliciously and without reasonable and probable cause. The allegation of malice was not established. The defence was that the search was justified both under the provisions of the Arms Act, as well as of the Criminal Procedure Code, and that in any case the Magistrate was protected from liability under Act XVIII of 1850. It was held by Maclean C.J. and Harington J. (Brett J. dissenting)—(1) that the defendant had no jurisdiction to issue the search warrant under the Code of Criminal Procedure, inasmuch as under Section 96 only a Court is authorised to issue such warrant, and as there was no proceeding under the Code initiated before him he was not acting as a Court, but was acting in his administrative and executive capacity; (2) that the search was not authorised under the Arms Act inasmuch as the Magistrate did not comply with the requirements of the Act, *viz.*, that the Magistrate did not, before causing a search, record the grounds of his belief that the plaintiff was in possession of arms for an unlawful purpose, etc., that the case, thecefo re, fell within the rule that when a statute creates a special right but certain formalities have to be complied with, antecedent to the exercise of that right, a strict observance of the formalities is essential to the acquisition of the right; (3) that the defendant not having acted in his judicial capacity in issuing the search warrant, he could not rely on the provisions of Act XVIII of 1850. Their Lordships of the Judicial Committee, however, held that the word "Court" in Section 96 includes every Magistrate, and every Magistrate has the power to issue search warrants and make searches, though the proceeding in connection with which the search is made, may not yet have been instituted. Upon this view of the case their Lordships held that the search was authorised, and it was not necessary for the defendant to claim the protection of Act XVIII of 1850, but if it were necessary he might have done so. Their Lordships, however, expressed their concurrence with the view of the law taken by the High Court on the second point. Their Lordships said that Mr. Clarke not having complied with the preliminary condition prescribed by the Arms Act cannot defend his action under that Statute. On the other hand, they had no doubt that Mr. Clarke, in directing a general search of the plaintiff's cutchery in view of an enquiry under the Code of Criminal Procedure, was acting in the discharge of his judicial functions, and they thought that if it had been necessary he might have appealed for protection to the Act No. XVIII of 1850.

In *Kemp* v. *Neville* [10 C. B. (H. S.) (1861) 523] the plaintiff having sued the defendant, Vice-Chancellor of the University of Cambridge, for false imprisonment, it was pleaded in defence that the Charter of the University empowered them by their officers to make search in the town for common women, and to punish by imprisonment or otherwise as the Chancellor or the Vice-Chancellor should seem fit, all persons as they should upon search find guilty or suspected of evil. The plaintiff was found in company with some scholars under conditions that led to the suspicion that they were there for disorderly and immoral purposes. The proctors thereupon brought her before the Vice-Chancellor who after examining the plaintiff caused her to be punished by imprisonment. Plaintiff, however, denied that she was there for any disorderly purpose and alleged certain irregularities in the procedure. The jury found that the proctors had reasonable grounds for suspicion, that the defendant did hear and examine the plaintiff, but had not made due inquiry into her character. It was held, first, that the Vice-Chancellor in the exercise of the jurisdiction given to him was a Judge of a Court of Record. Secondly, that the jurisdiction attached when the proctors brought the plaintiff before him; and that as the Charter defined no form of proceeding either for the hearing or the determination, no action of trespass lay against the defendant for the imprisonment complained of. On the general question of exemption of Judges from liability Earle C.J., in the course of his judgment, affirmed the rule that a judicial officer cannot be sued for an adjudication according to the best of his judgment upon a matter within his jurisdiction, and also the rule that a matter of fact so adjudicated by him cannot be put in issue, in an action against him. Reference was made to the earlier cases of *Gwinn* v. *Pool*, *Floyd* v. *Barker* (12 Rep. 23), *Hammond* v. *Howell*, *Cave* v. *Mountain*, *Metcalfe* v. *Hodson* (Hut 120), *Garnett* v. *Ferrand*, *Tozer* v. *Child*, *Calder* v. *Halket*, *Houlden* v. *Smith*, *Taaffe* v. *Lord Downes*, and *Dr. Grenville* v. *The College of Physicians*.

It may be useful to reproduce a summary of those cases as given in the judgment of this case. In *Gwinn* v. *Pool* the defendant was held not to be liable in trespass, although as Judge of inferior Court he had caused the plaintiff to be arrested in an action where the cause of action arose, because although there were certain irregularities in the procedure, yet he was held justified because he acted as a Judge in a matter over which he had reasons to believe that he had jurisdiction. In *Floyd* v. *Barker* (12 Rep. 23) it was held that the Judge and the Grand Jury were not liable to be sued in the Star Chamber for a conspiracy, in respect of their action in Court, in convicting of felony. In *Hammond* v. *Howell* the Judge who committed for an alleged contempt, under a warrant showing that in truth no contempt had been committed, was held not liable in trespass, because he had jurisdiction over the question, and his mistaken judgment, was no cause of action. In *Cave* v. *Mountain* the Justice who committed the plaintiff on an information that contained no legal evidence either of any offence or of the plaintiff's participation in that which was supposed to be an offence, was held not liable in trespass, because the information was considered to be directed against an offence over which the Justice had jurisdiction if there had been any proof thereof. In *Metcalfe* v. *Hodson* (Hut 120) the defendant was held not liable for taking insufficient bail in a cause in a local Court, because in that Court it was a judicial act by him. In *Garnett* v. *Ferrand* the Coroner, who removed the plaintiff from the place of an inquest, was held not liable for trespass, as the removal was ordered by him in a judicial capacity. In *Tozer* v. *Child* the churchwarden was held not liable for refusing a lawful vote in a vestry, because, although he was acting partly in a ministerial capacity in receiving the votes, yet he was also acting partly in a judicial capacity in refusing a vote, and in that capacity he was not liable for a mistake if he acted according to the best of his judgment.

Calder v. *Halket* was a case in which the defendant, a Magistrate of the Foujdari Court at Nadia, was sued for having ordered the arrest of the defendant for being concerned in a riot. Under the authority of that order the defendant was arrested and kept under surveillance. On these facts an action of trespass was commenced in the Supreme Court at Calcutta against the defendant for assault and false imprisonment. It was alleged that the defendant had no jurisdiction over the plaintiff who was a British subject. Baron Parke, in delivering the judgment of the Court, said "it is clear, therefore, that a Judge is not liable in trespass for want of jurisdiction, unless he knew, or ought to have known, of the defect ; and it lies on the plaintiff, in every such case, to prove that fact. In the case now under consideration, it does not appear from the evidence in the case that the defendant was at any time informed of the European character of the plaintiff, or knew it before, or had such information as to make it incumbent on him to ascertain that fact. The point, therefore, which is contended for by the plaintiff does not arise."

In *Houlden* v. *Smith* the Judge of the County Court was held liable in trespass, because he was within the exception thus laid down ; and had the means of knowing that he had no jurisdiction. In *Taaffe* v. *Lord Downes* (3 Moo. P. C. 36) the Judge was justified by a plea in trespass showing a warrant issued by him in his capacity of Judge, although the plea did not show that the warrant was lawful, but was purposely confined to the right of a Judge to protection : see the judgment of Fox J., p. 50.

Throughout these cases among others the vital importance of securing independence for every judicial mind was recognised.

It will be seen that in dealing with Sections 77 and 78 I have quoted freely from cases dealing with the question of civil liability. I have done so, because the law as regards both is practically the same, so far at least as Section 77 is concerned. As regards Section 78 which deals with the immunity of ministerial officers there seems to be some difference between it and the Judicial Officers Protection Act. It has been said by Mayne that the scope of the latter is wider than that of the former.

The learned author points out that for purposes of civil liability the warrant is an absolute protection to the officer so long as he obeys it, whether it was lawful or unlawful and whether it was issued with or without jurisdiction. Under Section 78 where the Court had no jurisdiction to issue the order, it is necessary further to show that the officer acting upon the order in good faith believed that the Court had jurisdiction. This is true as far as it goes, but it may be observed that under Section 78 all that is necessary is to show that the act done was done *in pursuance of an order* of a Court of Justice or *warranted* by such an order. The *obligation* to carry out the order is not essential. Whereas in the case of civil liability the order must be one which an officer is *bound* to execute, so that in some respect there is a larger protection to ministerial officers under Section 78 than under the Act of 1850.

In the case of *Thacoordass Nundee* v. *Shunkur Roy* (3 W. R. Cr., p. 53) it was held that a Civil Court peon who in contravention of the provisions of the Civil Procedure Code arrested under civil process a judgment-debtor going to a Court in obedience to a citation to give evidence within the precincts of that Court cannot claim the protection of Section 78. The question of good faith does not appear from the report to have been raised. A similar view was taken in another case reported in 7 W. R. Cr., p. 12. In that case a bailiff, in executing a process against the moveable property of a judgment-debtor, broke open a gate which, it was held, he had no authority to do. He was convicted and the conviction was upheld.

Before leaving the subject I may refer incidentally to a question that arose in *Pulin Behary Das* v. *King-Emperor* (16 C. W. N., p. 1105) as to whether the validity of the initial appointment of a Judge can be questioned in order to support a plea of the want of jurisdiction on his part to try a case. Mr. Justice Mukerjee, in an elaborate judgment relying on a number of English and American authorities, held that the acts of one who, although not the *de jure* holder of a legal office, was actually in possession of it under some colour of title or under such conditions as indicated the acquiescence of the public in his actions, could not be impeached in any proceeding to which such person was not a party. In other words, to put it shortly, the title of *de facto* judicial officers was held not to be collaterally assailable.

Accident. Section 80, I.P.C.

Section 80.—Nothing is an offence which is done by accident or misfortune, and without any criminal intention or knowledge in the doing of a lawful act in a lawful manner by lawful means and with proper care and caution.

ILLUSTRATION.

A is at a work with a hatchet; the head flies off and kills a man who is standing by. Here, if there was no want of proper caution on the part *A*, his act is excusable and not an offence.

According to Stephen an effect is accidental, when the act by which it is caused is not done with the intention of causing it, and when its occurrence as a consequence of such act is not so probable that a person of ordinary prudence ought, under the circumstances in which it is done, to take reasonable precautions against it. It would be useless and cruel to punish an act that no human forethought or care could prevent. When a consequence is caused by an accidental act it is not possible to impute any evil intent to the agent. Strictly speaking the accidental act is not his act at all. He neither wills the act nor the consequence. The illustration to Section 80 makes the matter clear. The man at work could not foresee that the head of the hatchet would fly off, he did not will it nor did he intend the death that was caused. The matter is self-evident and requires no elaboration. In all these cases there must be no negligence.

Some difficulty may arise in interpreting the words "doing of a lawful act in a lawful manner by lawful means." Suppose *A* is in possession of an unlicensed gun with which he shoots a jackal in a jungle; by accident he hurts a person who had concealed himself in that jungle, and there is no want of proper care and caution. Would the fact of the want of a license preclude him from claiming the protection of Section 80? I think not, for shooting is a lawful act and killing a jackal with a gun is killing it in a lawful manner by lawful means. The fact that the possession of the gun was unlawful and constituted an offence ought not to deprive a man of the protection which is given to him, because the circumstances under which the act was done were such as to negative the existence of a *mens rea*. Or take the case of a person who accidentally causes the death of another as the result of a shooting in a closed area or in a close season. By shooting under those circumstances the person may be guilty under the special law, for the breach of that law, but the existence of the prohibition should not to my mind render the act or the manner or the means unlawful.

The law in England relating to accidental acts is on a more satisfactory footing. In Stephen's Digest it is explained that an effect is accidental when the act by which it is caused is not done with the intention of causing it, and when its occurrence as a consequence of such act is not so probable that a person of ordinary prudence ought, under the circumstances in which it is done, to take reasonable precautions against it. A similar explanation is to be found in the Tenth Parliamentary Report wherein it is provided that an injury is said to be accidentally caused whensoever it is neither wilfully nor negligently caused. Nothing corresponding to this Section is to be found in Macaulay's original draft. His views are to be found in the following note :—

> "It will be admitted that when an act is in itself innocent, to punish the person who does it because bad consequences, which no human wisdom could have foreseen, have followed from it would be in the highest degree barbarous and absurd.
>
> A pilot is navigating the Hooghly with the utmost care and skill: he directs the vessel against a sand-bank which has been recently formed, and of which the existence was altogether unkown till disaster. Several of his passengers are consequently drowned. To hang the pilot as a murderer on account of

this misfortune would be universally allowed to be an act of atrocious injustice. But if the voyage of the pilot be itself a high offence, ought that circumstance alone to turn his misfortune into a murder? Suppose that he is engaged in conveying an offender beyond the reach of justice; that he has kidnapped some natives, and is carrying them to a ship which is to convey them to some foreign slave-colony; that he is violating the laws of quarantine at a time when it is of the highest importance that those laws should be strictly observed; that he is carrying supplies, deserters and intelligence to the enemies of the State. The offence of such a pilot ought, undoubtedly, to be severely punished. But to pronounce him guilty of one offence because a misfortune befell him while he was committing another offence,—to pronounce him the murderer of people whose lives he never meant to endanger, whom he was doing his best to carry safe to their destination, and whose death has been purely accidental, is surely to confound all the boundaries of crime.

* * * * * * For example, hundreds of persons in some great cities are in the habit of picking pockets. They know that they are guilty of great offence; but it has never occurred to one of them, nor would it occur to any rational man, that they are guilty of an offence which endangers life. Unhappily one of these hundreds attempts to take the purse of a gentleman who has a

loaded pistol in his pocket. The thief touches the trigger, the pistol goes off, the gentleman is shot dead. To treat the case of this pick-pocket differently from that of the numerous pick-pockets who steal under exactly the same circumstances, with exactly the same intentions, with no less risk of causing death, with no greater care to avoid causing death; to send them to the house of correction as thieves, and him to the gallows as a murderer, appears to us an unreasonable course. If the punishment of stealing from the person be too light, let it be increased, and let the increase fall alike on all the offenders. Surely the worst mode of increasing the punishment of an offence is to provide that, besides the ordinary punishment, every offender shall run an exceedingly small risk of being hanged. The more nearly the amount of punishment can be reduced to a certainty the better; but if chance is to be admitted, there are better ways of admitting it. It would be a less capricious, and therefore a more salutary course, to provide that every fifteenth or every hundredth thief selected by lot should be hanged, than to provide that every thief should be hanged who, while engaged in stealing, should meet with an unforseen misfortune, such as might have befallen the most virtuous man while performing the most virtuous action.

We trust that his Lordship in Council will think that we have judged correctly in proposing that when a person engaged in the commission of an offence causes death by pure accident, he shall suffer only the punishment of his offence, without any addition on account of such accidental death."

This view seems to be in accord with the law in England as well as in the Continent. The Prussian law, as quoted by Hamilton in his Penal Code, makes the matter perfectly clear. It lays down that 'if the act which had the accidental result were in itself unlawful, yet cannot the result itself be held to be a crime.'

The question, however, is not of any great importance in so far at least as offences under the Indian Penal Code are concerned ; for the definition of offences in the Code, with rare exceptions, includes as a necessary ingredient, an intention to cause a particular injury. An accidental act is necessarily unintentional and such an act would not generally fall within the definition of an offence even apart from the provisions of Section 80 of the Code. Even if the act is negligent it cannot be said to be purely accidental. The omission of any provision similar to Section 80 in Macaulay's original draft is no doubt due to this.

Accident is, however, not a defence when the defendant *meaning* to strike one person and unintentionally strikes another person. Thus if one of two persons, who are fighting, strikes at the other, and hits a third person unintentionally, this is a battery, and cannot be justified on the ground that it was accidental. (Russell on Crimes p. 882.)

Section 81.—Nothing is an offence merely by reason of its being done with the knowledge that it Sec. 81, I.P.C.

is likely to cause harm, if it be done without any criminal intention to cause harm, and in good faith for the purpose of preventing or avoiding other harm to person or property.

ILLUSTRATIONS.

(*a*) *A*, the captain of a steam vessel, suddenly and without any fault or negligence on his part, finds himself in such a position that, before he can stop his vessel, he must inevitably run down a boat *B* with twenty or thirty passengers on board, unless he changes the course of his vessel, and that, by changing his course, he must incur risk of running down a boat *C* with only two passengers on board, which he may possibly clear. Here, if *A* alters his course without any intention to run down the boat *C* and in good faith for the purpose of avoiding the danger to the passenger in the boat *B*, he is not guilty of an offence, though he may run down the boat *C* by doing an act which he knew was likely to cause that effect, if it be found as a matter of fact that the danger which he intended to avoid was such as to excuse him in incurring the risk of running down *C*.

(*b*) *A* in a great fire pulls down houses in order to prevent the conflagration from spreading. He does this with the intention in good faith of saving human life or property. Here if it be found that the harm to be prevented was of such a nature and so imminent as to excuse *A's* act, *A* is not guilty of the offence.

This section covers three different kinds of cases, *i.e.*, cases in which injury is done to one man in order to prevent greater injury to another, cases in which a smaller injury is done to a man in order to prevent greater injury to himself, and also cases in which to prevent injury to a person he is put to the risk of an equal or greater injury.

The motive, however, must be the prevention and not the causing of injury. Illustration (*a*) to Section 81 is an instance of the first kind. Illustration (*b*) is of the second kind, and the third class of cases may be illustrated as follows :—

You see a tiger attacking a man and you feel sure the tiger will be on him in a minute, you shoot the tiger fully knowing that the man and the tiger are so close that you might kill the man and not the tiger. In all these cases you are guilty of no offence. No evil intent can be imputed in any of these cases.

INFANCY.

Section 82.—Nothing is an offence which is done by a child under seven years of age. **Infancy. Secs. 82, 83, I.P.C.**

Section 83.—Nothing is an offence which is done by a child above seven years of age and under twelve, who has not attained sufficient maturity of understanding to judge of the nature and consequences of his conduct on that occasion.

The question whether a criminal intent can be negatived in any given case by reason of tender age of the agent, and subsequent immaturity of intellect, depends upon a variety of circumstances. The age at which a person may be said to have acquired sufficient intelligence to judge of the nature and consequences of his acts varies with climatic condition, education, precocity, etc. Up to a certain age, however, the presumption of innocence is conclusive. Both according to English as well as Indian Law a child under seven is *doli incapax*, and against this presumption no averment can be received. An infant above the age of seven and below the age of twelve is according to Indian Law not responsible for his acts, if he has not attained sufficient maturity of understanding to judge of their nature and consequence. Nothing is said in the Code as to whether the onus to prove want of mature understanding is on the infant or whether it is on the prosecution to prove affirmatively the existence of sufficient mental capacity to fasten upon him the responsibility for the criminal act. Having regard, however, to the provisions of the Indian Evidence Act, which places the burden of proving the existence of grounds of exemption upon the party alleging the same, it is clear that the law starts with the presumption of criminality until the negative conditions are established.

Onus of proof.

In *Queen* v. *Lukhini Agradanini* (22 W. R. Cr. 27) it was held that the non-attainment of sufficient maturity of understanding would have to be specially pleaded and proved. That the onus is on the person who claims the benefit of a general exception to prove the circumstances which entitle him to the exemption. But observed the Judges: "Looking at the matter from a practical point of view, it seems that the cases of infants such as we are at present considering have not been adequately provided for by the legislature. It may be said and indeed it has been held that where the accused is under twelve years of age it is the imperative duty of the trial Judge to find whether he is possessed of sufficient maturity of understanding. But the question of onus of proof seems to be upon defendant."

In this case a girl of over seven and under twelve years of age was placed on her trial on a charge of arson. On the preliminary objection to the trial under Section 83 the jury found that the prisoner was aware of the nature of her act, *i.e.*, she was aware that it would do damage, but that she was not aware that she would be imprisoned in consequence. The Sessions Judge referred the case to the High Court expressing the opinion that if a person be aware of the nature of his or her act, *i.e.*, whether it is right or wrong, that person may, even if he or she does not know that punishment will follow, be considered capable of committing an offence. The High Court (Jackson and McDonald, JJ.) held that the words "consequences of his conduct" in Section 83 do not refer to the penal consequences to the offender, but the natural consequences which flow from a voluntary act, such for instance as that when fire is applied to an inflammable substance it will burn.

According to the English law, however, children above the age of seven and under the age of fourteen are presumed not to possess the degree of knowledge essential to criminality, though this presumption is rubuttable by strong evidence of a mischievous discretion. Sir Fitz James Stephen is of opinion that the limit of age of absolute irresponsiblity should be raised to twelve, and that the stage of rebuttable presumption should be done away with. Whatever view may be held of the precocity of Indian children, to start with a presumption of responsibility against a child of eight years seems unreasonable, and no Judge with any idea of responsibility is likely to hold a child of that age criminally responsible without fully satisfying himself that the child had sufficient maturity of understanding to judge of the nature and consequence of his acts. According to German law an infant up to the age of twelve is considered wholly irresponsible, after which age, and until he has completed the age of eighteen, proof of the absence of requisite intelligence may rebut the presumption.

After the full age of responsibility has been attained, youth may be a ground of extenuation but not of exemption.

LECTURE VIII.

CONDITIONS OF NON-IMPUTABILITY—*continued.*

INSANITY—GENERAL.

The condition of non-imputability based on the existence of a diseased mind is ordinarily dealt with under the head of insanity which is meant to include both mental derangement and imbecility. The word 'insanity' does not occur anywhere in the Code and the rule of exemption regarding it is laid down in very general terms in Section 84, which runs as follows :— **Insanity. Sec. 84, I.P.C.**

> "Nothing is an offence which is done by a person who at the time of doing it, is, by reason of unsoundness of mind, incapable of knowing the nature of the act, or that he is doing what is either wrong or contrary to law."

The use of the more comprehensive term 'unsoundness of mind' has the advantage of doing away with the necessity of defining insanity and of artificially bringing within its scope various conditions and affections of the mind which ordinarily do not come within its meaning, but which none the less stand on the same footing in regard to exemption from criminal liability. It would interest you to know that in Macaulay's draft the law was stated thus :—

> *Section 66.*—Nothing is an offence which is done by a person in a state of idiocy;
>
> *Section 67.*—Nothing is an offence which a person does in consequence of being mad or delirious at the time of doing it.

The wider expression 'unsoundness of mind' covers mental defects both congenital and post natal, such as idiocy, madness, delirium, melancholia, mania, hypochondria, dementia, hallucination and every other possible form of mental affection known to medical science by whatever name designated. I shall, however, in dealing with the subject, use the more familiar, though less precise expression 'insanity' as an equivalent for 'unsoundness of mind 'used in the Code.

General observations.

In dealing with the legal aspect of the question we are only concerned with the effect insanity has on the mind and with special reference to the question whether the sufferer has that minimum of knowledge and intelligence and that freedom of will which are at once the basis of responsibility and the justification for punishment. You will observe that one of the elements I have mentioned, namely, freedom of will has no place in Section 84. This is a point I shall discuss later when dealing with that particular form of insanity now recognised both in England and America and known 'as irresistible impulse.'

The subject of insanity is one of the most difficult in the whole range of the Law of Crimes and has given rise to endless discussions and controversies. An examination of the inner working of that complicated machinery called the human mind is always difficult, and the difficulty is greatly enhanced when that mind is not normal. In carrying our investigations into the regions of psychology we have to rely almost entirely on an examination of the working of our own mind, but we cannot argue from a sane to an insane mind, and that again with reference to matters which represent not what is common between the two, but what the one excludes and the other includes. Unfortunately the insane cannot help us in our investigations. A great deal of difficulty in the treatment of the subject has been due to an anxiety to bring all the different phases of insanity under one common denominator and to apply one common test to all. The right and wrong test of which you will hear more later on, has been adopted as a measure of legal responsibility in the same way as a yard stick is taken as a measure of length. The mental condition of two insane persons often differ as widely as sanity from insanity, and this greatly enhances the difficulty of laying down general rules which can be satisfactorily applied to all its forms.

In dealing with the subject I do not propose to confine myself to the limited question of what the law in India actually is, which reduces itself to the question of the interpretation of Section 84 of the Code which I have already quoted, but would like to discuss, as many other text-writers have done, the larger question which is this : what ought to be the law relating to insanity. That law even in England has never been authoritatively laid down in spite of the pronouncement of the Judges in McNaghten's case. In India Section 84 contains the barest skeleton of the law of insanity, and in interpreting the section the question of what the law ought to be is as important as the question what the law is. The law has wisely refrained from going into details, and it is not possible that a subject which a great American writer has discussed in a book of nearly thousand pages, could be squeezed into a section of thirty-nine words. The question of what the law ought to be is certainly not less important even in India than the question of what the law is. In dealing with the former question it is of the utmost importance to bear in mind what I have said regarding—

(*a*) The basis of criminal responsibility and

(*b*) The object of punishment.

What the law ought to be, according Mr. Mercier, depends on what appears to be fair and just to the ordinary man when the matter is explained to him, in other words, to the common sense of the jury and not that which commends itself as equitable and right to the faddist, the pedant, or the enthusiat. I venture to think that law cannot be left entirely to the judgment of the man in the street nor does it appear that the learned author meant it. The reference to the explanation itself brings in all the considerations based on theories of law and those considerations can never be discarded.

The danger of leaving cases entirely to the common sense of the jury which results practically to leaving them to their sympathies, is illustrated by the result of recent sensational cases in France and America ; cases which resulted in acquittals in absolute disregard of the clear provisions of law. Madame Cailaux's case in France and White's case in America are the most recent instances of that danger. In England in numerous trials the verdicts in cases of insanity have been guided not by the directions given by the presiding Judge regarding the law of insanity, but by the answer which the jury in their common sense have thought fit to give to the question "should the prisoner at the bar be punished for the act he has done," and their verdict in most cases, though in disregard of Judge's directions, has been what to the layman must appear eminently just. The reason is to be found in the fact that the law, as laid down in McNaghten's case, is too narrow and even harsh, and the verdict of the jury in many cases represents a revolt against the law so laid down. When the law, as laid down in that case, has not met with popular approval, it is necessary to move out of the narrow groove into which Judges have often found themselves and to go out in search of a test that would conform to well-established theories of legislation, and yet would not be too fine for the common sense of the jury.

Basis of exemption from ability.

There is no charm in the word insanity and a person suffering from a mental disease is no more entitled to exemption from liability by the mere fact of the disease than a person suffering from fever or any other ailment. Irresponsibility can only be claimed when the disease has affected the judgment in a particular way or in the words of the Indian Penal Code, when it has rendered the sufferer incapable of knowing the nature of the act or that he is doing what is either wrong or contrary to law. Exemption in the case of the insane is based on grounds similar to those applying to infants specially those who are outside the age of absolute exemption, *i.e.*, such want of the reasoning faculty as renders a person incapable of distinguishing right from wrong. Lord Hale accepted as his standard of responsibility the intelligence of a child of fourteen. "The best measure," says he, "is this: such a person as labouring under melancholy distemper hath yet ordinarily as great understanding as ordinarily a child of fourteen years hath, is such a person as may be guilty of treason or felony." Sir Fitz James Stephen can find no analogy between healthy immaturity and diseased maturity. The question, however, is not one of maturity or immaturity of intellect, but of the level of intelligence in which a person may be found at a certain point of time. One often comes to the same point from opposite directions. You pass the same spot in ascending up a hill as in descending down it, and the position is the same whichever way you arrive at it. Shakespeare's second childhood is in many respects similar to the first and real childhood. The absence of a certain degree of intelligence is the point of importance, and it is immaterial whether this is due to one cause or another.

Lord Hale's analogy, however, is not quite complete, and there is this difference between the two cases that in the case of children below a certain age the exemption is absolute and is no way dependent upon the degree of intelligence possessed by such a child, whereas insanity is never an absolute ground of exemption, for the very obvious reason that insanity affects the mind in various ways and in different degrees of intensity, and there is no justification for extending the exemption to a person, simply because medical men would call him insane, if his intellect, though diseased, has not been deranged to an extent that would negative the existence of intelligence justifying responsibility. As I have told you the grounds of exemption in cases of infancy are not materially different from those of insanity, such differences as exist are not differences of principle but of policy. Whereas it is safe to lay down that within certain age limits a child is incapale of distinguishing right from wrong and must be given absolute immunity from punishment, it is not possible to lay down any such general proposition in cases of insanity. Cases of insanity have thus greater analogy with the case of children between the age of 7 and 12, whose exemption as you have seen is dependent on proof in each case of the absence of sufficient maturity of understanding to judge of the nature and consequence of the act constituting the offence charged. In judging of the sufficiency of understanding in all such cases regard must be had to the simplicity or complexity, as the case may be, of the elements constituting the offence charged. Unsoundness of mind may deprive a person of the understanding that it is wrong to make a defamatory statement, even though the statement be true, and yet such a person may have sufficient sense to know that it is wrong to steal his neighbour's horse.

Views of differront schools of thought.

So far it seems simple enough to arrive at the principles upon which exemption in the case of the insane is to be determined. However, the conflicts and controversies, and these have been endless, which have ranged round the subject are largely due to the existence of two schools of thought which have diverged very considerably and have influenced legislation in different countries. One school which I shall call the logical school look upon insanity as merely a source of intellectual error vitiating the judgment, and generally influencing the mental attitude of the insane towards a criminal act or as destroying the free-will which is the fundamental basis of responsibility. Accordingly they limit exemption on the ground of insanity only in so far as it has been productive of such intellectual error as would, if existing in the mind of a sane person, afford grounds for exemption, or has to the same extent interfered with his freedom of will. To understand this school and to carry their arguments to their logical conclusions, it would be necessary once again to advert shortly to the basis of criminal responsibility and to the theory of punishment. The first essential of responsibility, as you have already seen, is the existence of a free-will, and where this is negatived as in the case of compulsion, there is no crime and the insane, besides being entitled to the benefit of all forms of external compulsion to which the sane may be subject, have the additional advantage of being allowed to plead the existence of a species of internal compulsion, which I propose to discuss under the head of irresistible impulse. The sane are also excused if they act under a mistake of fact which may negative *mens rea*, but the mistake must not be such as could be avoided by acting with reasonable care and caution. In the case of the insane where the mistake is due to a diseased mind and not to any extraneous grounds, it would be enough to show that the mistake existed and no question of care or caution would arise. Again for the sane a mistake of law is no excuse, but it would be an excuse for an insane, because the presumption that every man knows the law cannot arise in his case. Therefore on strict principle and looking upon insanity as a mere source of intellectual error and intellectual compulsion, insanity, whether temporary or permanent, complete or partial, is excusable—

(*a*) If it overpowers the will and the sufferer ceases to be a free agent or, in other words, if it gives rise to what is known as irresistible impulse.

(*b*) If it deprives the sufferer of the knowledge that the act is either morally wrong or contrary to law.

This want of knowledge of the right and wrong of an act or of its being illegal may again be due to various causes; it may for instance be due to—

(*a*) Mental disorder leading to error regarding external objects.

(*b*) Affection of the cognitive faculties and loss of memory depriving the sufferer wholly or partially, generally or with reference to a particular matter, of the knowledge gained by past experience of the connection between different events.

This again may lead to ignorance—

(*i*) regarding the relation between two things as cause and effect;

(*ii*) regarding one's own obligation to society and consequent ignorance regarding the rights and wrongs of an act;

(*iii*) regarding the law of the country.

You will thus see that it is not difficult to theorise regarding the principles that should govern exemptions on grounds of insanity, and that these principles are in many respects not different from those which we apply in fixing the criminal character of acts done by sane and adult persons, except that the causes which bring conditions of irresponsibility into being in the case of the sane are different from those which operate in the case of the insane, and the knowledge gained by experience which we impute to the sane are not imputable to the insane. Difficulty, however, arises in the application of these principles to individual cases by reason of the difficulty that arises in determining the extent of the mental affection in a particular case. As Tracy J. told the jury in Arnold's case, (1 Collinson, Lunacy, 475; S. C. 16 St. Tr. 695,) 'it is not every kind of idle and frantic humour of a man or something unaccountable in his actions which will show him to be such a mad man as to be exempted from punishment.'

Insanity, as I have already pointed out, is not a single condition of the mind, and I propose in dealing with the subject to treat it as far as practicable under the various heads indicated above. I shall endeavour to show how these different affections give rise to different considerations upon which exemption is or at least ought to be based. You have seen that the ultimate basis of exemption in all cases is the absence of *mens rea*, and the mental conditions the existence of which enables us to predicate its absence in the case of sane persons are in many respects neither different nor less diversified than those in the case of the insane, and I hope that the method of treatment which I propose to adopt will simplify the consideration of the matter. The difficulty of laying down a rule of law that would apply to all forms of insanity was recognised by the Judges in Macnaghten's case [10 Cl. &c. F. 200] in giving their answers to the questions put to them by the House of Lords. They prefaced their answers by the following pertinent observation :—

> "They think it right in the first place to state that they have forborne entering into any particular discussion upon these questions, from the extreme and almost insuperable difficulty of applying those answers to cases in which the facts are brought judicially before them. The facts of each particular case must of necessity present themselves with endless variety, and with every shade of difference in each case. As it is their duty to declare the law upon each particular case on facts proved before them, and after hearing argument of counsel thereon, they deem it at once impracticable, and at the same time dangerous to the administration of justice if it were practicable to attempt to make minute applications of the principles involved in the answers given by them to your Lordships' questions."

This is one of those cases without which no discussion of the subject of insanity can be considered complete.

Macnaghten was tried in 1843 for causing the death of Mr. Drummond, the Private Secretary of Sir Robert Peel. The evidence was to the effect that the prisoner was suffering from morbid delusion and that persons so suffering might have a moral perception of right and wrong, but that in the case of the prisoner it was a delusion which carried him away beyond the power of his own control, and left him no such perception; and that he was not capable of exercising any control over acts which had connection with his delusion; that it was of the nature of the disease with which the prisoner was affected to go on gradually until it had reached a climax, when it burst forth with irresistible intensity; that a man might go on for years quietly, though at the same time under its influence, but would all at once break out into the most extravagant and violent paroxysms. Macnaghten's delusions were that he thought he was harassed by his enemies and that Mr. Drummond was one of them. Tindal C.J. charged the jury in the following terms:—" The question to be determined is whether, at the time the act in question was committed, the prisoner had or had not the use of his understanding so as to know that he was doing a wrong or wicked act. If the jurors should be of the opinion that the prisoner was not sensible, at the time he committed it, that he was violating the laws both of God and man, then he should be entitled to a verdict in his favour; but if, on the contrary, they were of opinion that when he committed the act he was in a sound state of mind, then their verdict must be against him."

The verdict of the jury was 'not guilty' on the ground of insanity. It was an unpopular verdict and was debated in the House of Lords and the House determined to take the opinion of the Judges on the law. Accordingly all the Judges assembled on the 19th June 1843, and various questions of law were propounded to them on the law relating to insanity. I quote below these questions and answers :—

Question I.—" What is the law respecting alleged crimes committed by persons afflicted with insane delusion in respect of one or more particular subjects or persons, as, for instance, where, at the time of the commission of the alleged crime, the accused knew he was acting contrary to law, but did the act complained of with a view, under the influence of insane delusion, of redressing or revenging some supposed grievance or injury, or of producing some supposed public benefit ? "

Answer I.—" Assuming that your Lordships' inquiries are confined to those persons who labour under such partial delusions only, and are not in other respects insane, we are of opinion that, notwithstanding the accused did the act complained of with a view, under the influence of insane delusion, of redressing or revenging some supposed grievance or injury, or of producing some public benefit, he is nevertheless punishable, according to the nature of the crime committed, if he knew at the time of committing such crime that he was acting contrary to law, by which expression we understand your Lordships to mean the law of the land."

Question II.—" What are the proper questions to be submitted to the jury when a person, afflicted with insane delusions respecting one or more particular subjects or persons, is charged with the commission of a crime (murder for instance), and insanity is set up as a defence ? "

Question III.—" In what terms ought the question to be left to the jury as to the prisoner's state of mind at the time when the act was committed ? "

Answers II and III.—" As these two questions appear to us to be more conveniently answered together, we submit our opinion to be that the jury ought to be told in all cases that every man is to be presumed to be sane, and to possess a sufficient degree of reason to be responsible for his crimes, until the contrary be proved to their satisfaction. That, to establish a defence on the ground of insanity, it must be clearly proved that at the time of committing the act the accused was labouring under such a defect of reason from disease of the mind as not to know the nature and quality of the act he was doing, or if he did know it, that he did not know he was doing what was wrong. The mode of putting the latter part of the question to the jury on these occasions has generally been, whether the accused at the time of doing the act knew the difference between right and wrong; which mode, though rarely, if ever, leading to any mistake with the jury, is not, we conceive, so accurate when put generally and in the abstract, as when put with reference to the party's knowledge of right and wrong in respect to the very act with which he is charged. If the question were to be put as to the knowledge of the accused, solely and exclusively with reference to the law of the land, it might tend to confound the jury by inducing them to believe that an actual knowledge of the law of the land was essential in order to lead to a conviction ; whereas the law is administered on the principle that every one must be taken conclusively to know it without proof that he does know it. If the accused was conscious that the act was one which he ought not to do, and if that act was at the same time contrary to the law of the land, he is punishable, and the usual course therefore has been to leave the question to the jury whether the accused had a sufficient degree of reason to know he was doing an act that was wrong ; and this course we think is correct, accompanied with such observations and corrections as the circumstances of each particular case may require."

Question IV.—" If a person under an insane delusion as to existing facts commits an offence in consequence thereof, is he thereby excused ? "

Answer IV.—" The answer must of course depend on the nature of the delusion ; but, making the same assumption as we did before, namely, that he labours under such partial delusion only, and is not in other respects insane we think he must be considered in the same situation as to responsibility as if the facts with respect to which the delusion exists were real. For example, if under the influence of his delusion he supposes another man to be in the act of attempting to take away his life, and he kills that man, as he supposes in self-defence, he would be exempt from punishment. If his delusion was that the deceased had inflicted a serious injury to his character and fortune, and he killed him in revenge for such supposed injury, he would be liable to punishment."

These answers, although they do not amount to judicial decisions, have been and are still regarded as authoritative expositions of the law relating to insanity, and I shall criticise those answers in dealing with the form of insanity to which any particular answer may relate.

The procedure by which these answers were obtained was very irregular and the prefatory remarks of the Judges which I have quoted show that they did not quite approve of the method adopted, yet, in the words of Wharton, "these answers, thus dubiously born and almost smothered from their birth in a cumbrous phraseology, have been the oracle of Anglo American Jurisprudence on insanity for sixty years."

IRRESISTIBLE IMPULSE.

Irresistible impulse.

I shall now deal with the species of insanity which affects the will. I have already told you that sane or insane, an agent is not responsible for an act done by him against his own will. To constitute criminality you must have as a first condition a voluntary act. Civil law recognises both physical and moral compulsion as affecting one's freedom of action and thereby his legal liability. Criminal law is more stringent and the only compulsion it recognises is physical compulsion. Strictly speaking what is called moral compulsion is no compulsion at all. In the case of persons with a sound mind it is a conclusive presumption that in the absence of actual physical compulsion he is free to act as he likes and internal compulsion or in other words, no mere prompting of one's own mind, however strong it may be, is recognised as constituting legal excuse for crimes. This principle has been consistently followed even in most extreme cases, one instance of which is to be found in *Reg.* v. *Dudley* (14 Q. B. D. 273), to which I have already referred. This presumption of free agency may not be applicable to a person with a deranged mind. The impulse to do a particular act, even though known to the actor to be wrongful, may be entirely due to mental disorder or such a disorder as may have weakened the power of resistance which a sane person is expected to possess.

Criminal law while punishing a man for his faults, does not punish him for his misfortunes, and it is only right that if such a state of mind exists and is due to disease it should be recognised as a valid excuse. But the mere fact that an impulse is not resisted would not show that it is irresistible. When a man, not suffering from any disease, commits a crime and then attributes it to an irresistible impulse the plea has never been admitted. In some of these cases medical experts have come forward to say that irresistible impulse itself is a disease. These experts seem to have a partiality for discovering new diseases. We read of cases under the Defence of the Realm Act being defended in England on the ground that cowardice is itself a disease. In one sense everything abnormal is a disease, but Courts of law would hardly be justified in accepting such a doctrine as it will have the effect of condonation of crime to an extent that is dangerous to society at large. Putting aside these extreme views it seems to me that the position is really this: *A* commits an offence under an impulse which he says was irresistible; in substance it only means that the impulse was not resisted, not that under no circumstances could it be resisted. If a sane person were to put forward such a plea he would be told that he was bound to resist the impulse, and that there is no impulse which a sane person cannot resist if he tries his utmost. But if a person otherwise proved to be insane puts forward such a plea he is excused, not necessarily because the impulse was irresistible but because the disease had so far weakened his power of resistance that he yielded to the impulse under circumstances in which a sane person would have been expected not to yield. I believe this would be a more correct and consistent view of the law on the subject. The plea of an irresistible impulse therefore will not by itself be a defence, but should be a good defence only where there is evidence of an antecedent unsoundness of mind.

In dealing with these cases we must try to adopt the golden mean, remembering that law is intended to be a benefit to society and not a scourge, and in settling the line of demarcation between conditions of imputability and non-imputability we must be very careful, lest in the words of Lord Hale, "on one side there be a kind of inhumanity towards the defects of human nature or on the other side too great an indulgence given to great crimes."

A habitual thief may at the sight of a valuable article feel what he would call an irresistible impulse to put the article into his pocket. The impulse would perhaps have been less irresistible if he had found a policeman near by. The irresistible impulse in such cases would be found to be due to familiarity with prison life, to a sense of security against detection, and the consequent absence of that dread of punishment which would ordinarily operate upon the mind of a first offender. Before the act, the offender has perhaps balanced the advantages and the disadvantages, the probable gain and the probable loss, and has found that the former outweighs the latter. This judgment of the mind is often arrived at by a process so quick as to be almost imperceptible. At any rate when the act is done, in nine cases out of ten, the offender will have forgotten, that before striking the balance he had gone through this process of mental arithmetic, and when he finds his calculations have gone wrong he wonders at the state of his mind and then, perhaps, honestly attributes it to the existence of what he calls an irresistible impulse. Once a plea of this kind is indiscriminately admitted, impulses will be found to have proved irresistible in many more cases than they do now. Besides, if we were to give protection to a person sane in other respects who cannot or will not control his temper, it will be difficult to withhold such protection from the fanatical *gazi*, or the American Negro who act under strong impulse undeterred by fear of legal punishment. The grant of such protection takes away all the incentive towards self-control and sets a premium to brutal murders and other offences of an aggravated kind. Both the *gazi* and the Negro after going through a few years schooling in a jail will perhaps find on their return that they could control their impulses if they wished. Even if we were to assume that there is such a thing as irresistible impulse without any other symptoms of insanity, how are we to distinguish cases in which the impulse was controllable from cases in which it was uncontrollable? It would be most impolitic to allow an issue to be raised which is incapable of satisfactory determination. The same principle which has induced the legislature to ignore the existence of motive in determining the criminal character of an act or to ignore the mere existence of a criminal intent unaccompanied by an overt act would justify our shutting out a plea of irresistible impulse except in cases of insanity. Criminal law as pointed out by Sir Fitz James Stephen is itself a system of compulsion on the widest scale. It is a collection of threats of injury to life, liberty and property if people do commit crimes, and it is necessary in order to be effective that at the moment when the impulse to commit crimes is strongest that the law should speak out most clearly and emphatically to the contrary.

The plea of irresistible impulse has been raised in many cases, specially in cases of unaccountable and motiveless murders, but I am not aware of a single case in which the sturdy common sense of an English Jury has not prevailed over specious arguments put forward in defence of bad cases. *Reg.* v. *Haynes* (1 F. and F. 666) was a case in which the prisoner had murdered an "unfortunate woman" with whom he was intimate. The plea of insanity was based upon the contention that it being impossible to assign any motive for the perpetration of the offence, the prisoner must have been acting under what is called a powerful and irresistible influence or homicidal tendency. The learned Judge Baron Bramwell, after telling the jury that mere absence of motive was not sufficient upon which they could safely infer the existence of such an influence, added—"A morbid and restless (but irresistible) thirst for blood would itself be a motive urging to such a deed for its own relief. But if an influence be so powerful as to be termed irresistible, so much the more reason there is why we should not withdraw any of the safeguards tending to counteract it. There are three powerful restraints existing, all tending to the assistance of the person who is suffering under such an influence—the restraint of religion, the restraint of conscience, and the restraint of law. But if the influence itself be held a legal excuse against rendering the crime punishable you at once withdraw a most powerful restraint, that forbidding and punishing its perpetration. We must, therefore, return to the simple question you have to determine. Did the prisoner know the nature of the act he was doing; and did he know that he was doing what was wrong?"

In *Reg.* v. *Barton* (3 Cox 275) prisoner was indicted for the wilful murder of his wife. It was proved that immediately before murdering her, he had killed his own child, and that after murdering his wife he tried to cut his own throat.

When questioned by the Surgeon he exhibited no sorrow or remorse, but stated that the trouble, dread of poverty and destitution had made him do it, fearing that his wife and child would starve while he was dead. Apparently there was no other motive. The Surgeon formed the opinion that at the time the prisoner committed the act he had not, in consequence of an uncontrollable impulse, exercised any control over his conduct. "Monomania," he said, "was an affliction which for the instant completely deprived the patient of self-control in respect of some particular subject which is the object of the disease." Baron Park told the jury that the question was whether the prisoner knew the nature and character of the deed he was committing, and if so, whether he knew he was doing wrong in so acting. As to the excuse of an irresistible impulse he expressed his concurrence with Baron Rolfe's views that the excuse of an irresistible impulse co-existing with the full possession of reasoning power might be urged in justification of every crime known to the law for every man might be said, and truly, not to commit any crime except under the influence of some irresistible impulse. Something more than this was necessary to justify an acquittal on the ground of insanity, and it would be dareful for the jury to say whether taking into consideration all that the Surgeon had said the impulse was one which altogether deprived him of the knowledge that he was doing wrong. Could he distinguish between right and wrong?

The prisoner was sentenced to death.

This was a clear case of sane motive. But having regard to the fact that the act was the result of a motive not wholly unworthy, no Court in India would have sentenced the prisoner to death in the exercise of the discretion that the law wisely allows Judges in this country, a discretion which was denied to Judges in England, where however very often the rigour of the law is softened by the intervention of the Crown in such cases. Crompton J. in *Reg.* v. *Davies* (1 F. F. 69) took the same view. 'It is not sufficient,' said the learned Judge to the jury, 'that the prisoner did the act (setting fire to a house) from being in a reckless depraved state of the mind.'

Irresistible impulse when attributable to a diseased mind seems to have been recognised as a valid excuse in some English cases.

In India we frequently hear of cases of persons running amock and murdering without any apparent motive any one coming in his way but in no case the murderer has escaped punishment on the ground of insanity or existence of an irresistible impulse. It is noticeable that the questions put to the Judges in Macnaghten's case were not specifically directed to cases of this kind, but it may be gathered from the answer to the first question that the learned Judges were of opinion that generally where there is sufficient intelligence to distinguish between right and wrong, the mere existence of an irresistible impulse would not excuse liability. One may ask why the existence of this species of insanity was not recognised. The reason is to be found in the fact that the meagre knowledge that existed in those days regarding the effect of insanity on the mind made both the Judge and the jury sceptic of the existence of such impulse, and it is perhaps owing to the same cause that the Indian Penal Code also does not clearly provide for this class of cases.

The right and wrong test can hardly be applied to cases of this kind. Where unsoundness of mind creates an uncontrollable impulse to act in a particular way, and the impulse is so powerful as to override the reason and judgment and to deprive the accused of the power to adhere to the right and avoid the wrong, the mere intellectual perception of right and wrong would not affect the question. 'Irresistible impulse,' says Wharton, 'is not a a defence in a criminal prosecution, unless it exists to such an extent as to subjugate the intellect, control the will, and render it impossible for the person to do otherwise than yield.' This irresponsibility will, however, not be extended to one who with no mental disorder acts from overmastering anger, jealousy or revenge. There must be insanity first.

In *Reg.* v. *Offord* (1831) (5 C. & P. 168), though the question does not seem to have been specifically raised, Lord Denmond in charging the jury clearly recognised the validity of such a plea. He said, persons *prima facie* must be taken to be of sound mind till the contrary is shown, but a person may commit a criminal act and yet be not responsible, if some controlling disease was in truth the acting power within him which he could not resist, then he will not be responsible. This is also the view taken by Sir Fitz James Stephen. After discussing the question at great length with reference to the answer of the Judges, the learned author observes :—

"I am of opinion that even if the answers given by the Judges in Macnaghten's case are regarded as a binding declaration of the law of England, that law as it stands, is that a man who by reason of mental disease is prevented from controlling his own conduct is not responsible for what he does."

Again observes the same learned author :—

"There are cases in which madness interferes with the power of self-control and so leaves the sufferer at the mercy of any temptation to which he may be exposed, and if this can be shown to be the case, I think the sufferer should be excused."

The law in America is much in the same state. It is specifically provided in the New York Code that a morbid propensity to commit a prohibited act existing in the mind of a person who is not shown to have been incapable of knowing the wrongfulness of such acts, forms no defence to a prosecution therefor. Although there have been some decisions to the contrary in America, it is now well settled that mere emotional insanity or temporary frenzy or passion arising from excitement or anger, although ungovernable or mere mental depravity or moral insanity, so-called, which results, not from any disease of mind, but from a perverted condition of the moral system, where the person is mentally sane, does not exempt one from responsibility for crimes committed under its influence. Care must, however, be taken to distinguish between mere moral insanity or mental depravity and irresistible impulse resulting from disease of the mind. (Cyclopædia of Law and Procedure, Vol. 12, p. 170).

It may be urged that if irresistible impulse is a good defence it ought to be so for the sane and the insane alike, but in the case of persons otherwise sane we have yet to be convinced that any impulse can really be irresistible. It may also be objected that so long as there is intelligence to judge between right and wrong, it is immaterial whether an act is committed under a sane or insane impulse. I shall in dealing with other aspects of insanity have to criticise the undue stress that has generally been laid in the discussion of this intricate problem upon this rigid standard of right and wrong. For the present I would only quote the words of an eminent Scotch Judge Lord Justice Clerk, who very pertinently said to the jury in 1874: "It is entirely imperfect and inaccurate to say that if a man has a conception intellectually of moral or legal obligations he has a sound mind. Better knowledge of the phenomenon of lunacy has corrected some loose and inaccurate language which lawyers used to apply in such cases. A man may be entirely insane and yet may know well enough that an act which he does is forbidden by law. It is not a question of knowledge but of soundness of mind. If a man have not a sane mind to apply his knowledge, the mere intellectual apprehension of an injunction or prohibition may stimulate his unsound mind to do an act, simply because it is forbidden or not to do it because it is enjoined. If a man has a sane apprehension of right and wrong, he is certainly responsible, but he may form and understand the idea of right and wrong and yet be hopelessly insane. You may discard these attempts at definition altogether. They only mislead."

The law regarding irresistible impulse may be stated thus :—

(*a*) The existence of such an impulse is not to be presumed from the mere absence of a motive for a criminal act.

(*b*) Where, however, the existence of a diseased mind is proved by other evidence, such evidence along with the evidence furnished by the act itself may suffice to prove the existence of an irresistible impulse, and when proved, is according to more recent decisions in England and America a good ground for exemption, even though there may be sufficient understanding that the act is wrong or illegal.

(*c*) Where, however, the existence of such understanding is not negatived, the mere irresistible impulse does not seem to be a ground of exemption in India :

In support of the first proposition I may refer you once again to *Reg.* v. *Haynes* and to the observations of Baron Bramwell in that case. The learned Judge said—

" It has been urged that you should acquit the prisoner on the ground that it being impossible to assign any motive for the perpetration of the offence, he must have been acting under what is called a powerful and irresistible influence, or homicidal tendency. But the circumstance of an act being apparently motiveless, is not a ground from which you can safely infer the existence of such an influence. Motives exist unknown and unknowable, which might prompt the act. A morbid and restless, but irresistible thirst for blood, would itself be a motive urging to such a deed for its own relief."

On similar ground the defence of insanity failed in *Reg.* v. *Burton* (1863, 3 F. and F. 772).

There have, however, been cases in which insanity has been inferred from the nature of the crime itself. On these cases a well-known writer on Medical Jurisprudence observes: "It is a dangerous doctrine to adduce the crime or the mode of perpetrating it as evidence of insanity, but such cases incontestably prove that there are some instances in which this is almost the only procurable evidence."

As to (*b*) the decisions are conflicting, but on the whole I think this is the better view of the law. *Reg.* v. *Brixey* was a case of this nature. In this case a quiet inoffensive maid-servant suddenly showed signs of violence of temper about trivial matters and a few days afterwards cut the throat of her master's infant child. She was perfectly conscious of the crime, and wished to know whether she would be hanged or transported. The case satisfied three of the medical tests for detecting homicidal monomonia laid down by Dr. Taylor, *viz.*, absence of motive, of any attempt to escape, and of any accomplice. She was acquitted.

As to (*c*) the words of Section 84 seem to be fairly decisive. The point was discussed in *Reg.* v. *Lakhshman Dagdu* (10 Bom. 512).

The accused in this case had killed his two young children. The learned Judges, whilst holding that the fever from which the accused was suffering had made him terrible and sensitive to sound, that his thoughts were confused, that the prisoner was very fond of his children and the reason for the murder as given by him,—*viz.*, that the children began to cry which vexed him,—was altogether insufficient and unreasonable, that there was no premeditation, no precaution, no concealment, or attempt to escape, nor sorrow nor remorse, and that according to medical writers there would be no responsibility attaching to the accused, still held the accused guilty. "It is our duty," observe the learned Judges, "to apply the principles which have received judicial recognition, and these are substantially the same here and in England. And if the legal test of responsibility, in cases of unsoundness of mind, prescribed by Section 84 of the Indian Penal Code be applied to the present case, it would be impossible for us to acquit the accused, unless we could hold that the fever from which he was suffering had caused delirium.

"The fever had certainly made him terrible and sensitive to sound. He was 'bhromest' as his wife says. His thoughts were confused ; but there is no sufficient evidence, as we have already said, to warrant our holding that he was not conscious of the nature of his act. And if he was conscious of its nature he must be presumed to have been conscious of its criminality."

Although the decision does not seem open to any criticism having regard to the words of Section 84, I do not think the learned Judges were right in saying that the law was substantially the same here and in England. The learned Judges were apparently thinking of Macnaghten's case without reference to later developments which have shaken the foundation of the right and wrong theory as the sole test of exemption.

This decision was followed in Madras in the case of *Queen-Empress* v. *Venkata Sami* (12 Mad. 459). In that case the learned Judges thus deal with the medical evidence: "The medical officer's evidence does not amount to more, in our opinion, than that there is the possibility of a sudden attack of homicidal mania; but judging the evidence by the ordinary judicial tests which we are bound to apply, we cannot say that it warrants a finding that the appellant did not know that what he was doing was wrong within the meaning of Section 84 of the Indian Penal Code. The case of *Queen-Empress* v. *Lakhshman Dagdu*, cited by the Acting Government Pleader, contains, in our opinion, the points of the law to be decided in such cases."

For exemption on the ground of insanity this case was much stronger than that of *Reg.* v. *Brixey*. For the medical evidence in this case went much further than the evidence in that case. I reproduce the evidence of the medical officer who had the prisoner under observation and who also formed his opinion upon the evidence given in his presence. It would serve to indicate the extreme rigour of the Indian law and the necessity for its modification in order to bring it on a line with the more humane view taken of such cases in other countries. The medical officer said:

"The prisoner before the Court has been under my observation in the district jail since 4th February in consequence of a requisition addressed to me from this Court. So far as my observation has gone while the prisoner was in the jail, I have no reason to believe that he is insane; but if the medical evidence is required on the whole merits of the case, this opinion might be modified.

"I have been present in Court the whole of to-day, and have heard the evidence given by the witnesses. I find from the evidence that the prisoner had been sick of fever for six days previous to the occurrence; that he had had very little food during that period; and that whilst in this enfeebled condition, he had fever on the night previous to the deed, and that during the period when he was supposed to have had fever he used words in a manner which renders it possible that he was then suffering from delirium. I consider that the abusive tendency taken by the delirium is a matter of great importance. He was evidently suffering from the opinion that some one had injured him, and I find that the prosecution offers no theory of intention whatever. It is shown that the sword or swords with which the deed was committed were in the same hut. It is also admitted that he lived affectionately with the child he killed, and that none of the abuse of the previous evening was directed towards her. It is an established fact that during and after paroxysms of intermittent fever there occasionally arises a want of mental control known as *post febrile lunacy*, I consider that the chances are that the prisoner was labouring under the impression that some one had injured him, and under this opinion and incited thereto by the fact of the sword being at hand, without in all probability knowing that this was a child, had started at unknown enemies. The fact of the goat having been wounded also helps the theory to some extent, especially if the Head Constable's theory is correct that the wound was not caused by a slash but by a thrust. A thrust would show more deliberate intention to kill what was in reality only a harmless goat. Had he slashed the goat, the theory that the Head Constable suggested that he missed the girl and hit the goat would be more tenable. The prisoner is now in feeble state of health, and has an enlarged spleen, from which I infer that he has suffered from malarial fever recently. He has also suffered from fever in jail."

The medical officer further added—" I have had no reason to suppose that the prisoner had suffered from epileptic fits ; but if he had been subject to them, it would greatly favor the theory of a homicidal impulse ; and such impulse would be greatly aggravated by the existence of fever at the time. If the prisoner had committed the deed in a state of febrile delirium, it is quite consistent that after the delirium had left him he would be aware of what he had done. It depends greatly on the degree of delirium ; but it would be quite consistent with delirium that he should know what he had done."

The same view of the law was taken in *Queen-Empress* v. *Razai Mian*. The learned Judges observed " that the unsoundness of mind must be such as would make the accused incapable of knowing the nature of the act or that he was doing what was contrary to law."

The most important case, however, so far at least as Bengal is concerned, is that of *Queen-Empress* v.

Kader Nasyer Shah (I. L. R., 23 Cal., p. 604). Prisoner was charged with having caused the death of a boy aged about 8 years.

It was found upon the evidence that the accused had been suffering from mental derangement for some months previous to the date of occurrence, and since the destruction of his house and property by fire, that on one occasion he was seen eating potsherds and that he often complained of pain in the head. It also appeared that when the enquiry preliminary to commitment was taken up he was found not to be in a fit state of mind to be able to make his defence. The murder was committed without any apparent sane motive. The evidence further showed that the accused was fond of the boy and had no quarrel with the boy's father. On the other hand it was proved that the accused observed some secrecy in committing the murder. He tried to conceal the corpse and hid himself in a jungle.

Upon these findings the learned Judges held that a ground of exemption under Section 84, Indian Penal Code, was not made out. Following Macnaghten's case their Lordships observe "it is only unsoundness of mind which materially impairs the cognitive faculties of the mind that can form a ground of exemption from criminal responsibility, the natures and extent of the unsoundness of mind required being such as would make the offender incapable of knowing the nature of the act or that he is doing what is wrong or contrary to law." The case is open to the same comments as those I have offered in the case of *Reg.* v. *Lakshman Dagdu.*

The protection on the ground of irresistible impulse cannot, however, be extended to acts which can be shown to be the result of deliberation. For, as pointed out by Mr. Mercier in his treatise on criminal responsibility, 'those acts only should be called impulsive which are undertaken without full consideration of their advantages. An act long meditated even if decided on with reckless disregard of its disadvantage would scarcely be called impulsive. By impulsive we mean suddenness not only of conception but of execution. An impulsive act then is an act suddenly conceived and instantly carried out.'

LECTURE IX.

CONDITIONS OF NON-IMPUTABILITY—*Continued.*

INSANITY (Continued)—DRUNKENNESS.

Forms of insanity universally recognised.

I now turn to the other and more common forms of insanity—perhaps, the only forms which the framers of the Indian Penal Code, have recognised as affording grounds for criminal irresponsibility. These are also the forms with which old English text-writers have mainly concerned themselves. Where this kind of insanity exists it has been universally recognised. The only difficulty in these cases has arisen in finding whether upon the facts of a particular case insanity of this description has been made out. The test by which cases of this kind are to be judged, is as laid down by the Penal Code, *viz.*, whether the unsoundness of mind in any particular case has been such as to render the sufferer incapable, by reason of such unsoundness, of knowing the nature of the act or that the act is either wrong or contrary to law. To bring a case within this rule of law three things are essential—

(1) An unsound mind.

(2) A defect in the understanding by reason of such unsoundness.

(3) A defect in the understanding to the extent mentioned in the rule.

The three conditions are interdependent and often co-exist.

The second condition excludes cases where the defect of understanding, even if it is to the extent laid down in the third condition, is due to defective education or the result of mere upbringing. The third condition contemplates three kinds of ignorance or incapacity :

(*a*) Ignorance regarding the nature of the act.
(*b*) Incapacity to judge that an act is morally wrong.
(*c*) Incapacity to judge that the act is prohibited by law.

The incapacity to judge the nature of an act may be due to the affection of the senses leading to error in the perception of external objects, but in cases of insanity it is generally due to the imagination overpowering and dominating the senses. This kind of insanity may shortly be called delusion and consists in believing in what does not exist. An insane person may, for instance, cut off a man's head thinking he is only chipping off the heads of dandelions or he may strike a human being thinking it is only an earthen jar or what more frequently happens he may see or hear things that have no existence outside his imagination. Where ignorance such as this exists the ground of exemption is perfectly clear. Similar mistake would exempt even a sane person if the existence of the mistake is made out. There is, however, this essential difference that in the case of the sane the mistake is often due to causes that are not subjective but objective, causes that exist outside the mind, and even where a mistake is made out it is necessary to show that the obligation to be circumspect and to try to avoid such mistakes has been discharged, *i.e.*, he must show that he had reasonable grounds for the

Delusion.

mistake and that he acted with reasonable care and caution. We had a recent instance of certain soldiers firing at a village chowkidar under a tree mistaking him for a jackal. The men were acquitted. Cases of insane delusion are dealt with in answer IV of the Judges given in Macnaghten's case. An insane person suffering from such a delusion is to be considered in the same situation as to responsibility as if the facts with respect to which the delusion exists were real, and they illustrate their meaning in the following way: For example, if under the influence of his delusion he supposes another man to be in the act of attempting to take away his life, and he kills that man, as he supposes in self-defence, he would be exempted from punishment. If his delusion was that the deceased had inflicted a serious injury to his character and fortune, and he killed him in revenge for such supposed injury, he would be liable to punishment.

The remarks of Lord Justice Clerk, which I have already quoted, furnish the strongest comment on the last portion of the answer. The mental machinery works in co-ordination with all its parts and the proper action of one part is dependent on the others. Is it conceivable that a man who suffers from delusions, such as are referred to in the answer, can be credited with such accurate knowledge of law as to be able to judge under what circumstance he can cause the death of another in self-defence? Can you in dealing with such a mind raise the ordinary presumption that he knows the law? If you cannot, it would be wrong to punish. Even Section 84 of the Indian Penal

The 4th answer criticised.

Code will not in a case of this nature fasten responsibility to an insane person if it is established that the prisoner by reason of insanity and of his insane delusions was not aware that the act was wrong or contrary to law. The answer so far as it goes, partially shuts out the right and the wrong tests in the case of persons suffering from insane delusions. The explanation of the 4th answer is to be found in the fact that the Judges were confining their answer to a special kind of insanity, *viz.*, cases of partial insanity where the mind is sound in every other respect and works and reasons properly in every other matter except the particular delusion the prisoner may be suffering from. It may be doubted if such a mind is found in actual practice and whether a man suffering from such a delusion is likely to possess a mind to which a perfect knowledge of the right and wrong of an act can be attributed. In such a case, such knowledge it would be dangerous to infer from the fact merely of an attempt to conceal the act or to escape from punishment. Even the cat, when discovered stealing from the pantry, skulks away with a guilty look. Is that an indication of rationality ? Such a consciousness often comes after the act is done which brings relief to the mind just as remorse or penitence follows a wrongful act done by a sane person under the influence of an overpowering passion.

Macnaghten's case has come for much adverse criticism in America.

In a case (16 American and English Encyclopædia of law, 2nd Edition, p. 620) Judge Bartlett, in dealing with the case of a poor Italian barber who killed his wife under the insane delusion that she exerted an evil spell over him, put bugs in his ear, poison in his food, sucked blood from his ear, put water and blood in his body, and contemplated eloping with a man worth ten thousand dollars, said that the law does not require that insanity must be "clearly proven" as a preponderance of evidence meets the legal requirements; moreover if the prisoner's evidence creates in the minds of the Jury a doubt as to his sanity at the time of the killing the prosecution must remove that doubt by a preponderance of evidence.

The right and wrong test must be applied in reference to the particular act in question.

It is a most unjust rule that delusion only excuses in case that facts believed by the lunatic to be true would justify the act if they really were true.

It seems to me that the safest test is that laid down by an American Judge 'was insanity the efficient cause of the act, and whether the act would not have been done but for that affection.'

In France, as in America the law regarding insanity is on a more satisfactory footing.

There it is no offence if the accused was in a state of mental alienation at the time of doing the act, or if he acted under an irresistible impulse. The word "Mental alienation" has been held by a series of decisions of the Court of Cassation, to have the widest possible meaning, and it is understood to comprise "the whole of the possible derangements of the intellect, all varieties of lunacy, and every kind of mental affection."

Delusion.

Delusion consists in believing what does not exist. Wharton defines an insane delusion to be an unreasonable and an incorrigible belief in the existence of facts which are either impossible absolutely or impossible under circumstances of the case ; a fixed belief which is contrary to universal experience and known natural laws.

As I have said ignorant and credulous people often believe in such facts without being insane. Such belief based upon reason, however defective and absurd, is not within the meaning of the rule.

The word delusion, though often losely used to cover all cases of error in the perception or cognition of external objects, has, however, a precise meaning of its own which distinguishes it from other similar forms of error such as illusion or hallucination, but the distinction for my present purposes is unnecessary.

Hadfield's case is one of the most important cases on delusional insanity. The case was decided in 1800, and was thus anterior to Macnaghten's case. It was the first revolt against the stereotyped test 'did the prisoner know that he was acting against the laws of God and man.' It was a remarkable instance of Erskin's forensic eloquence which made an English Judge for the first time to get out of the narrow groove of the right and wrong test. This case requires more than a passing notice. The trial was for high treason for shooting the King. It was established beyond doubt that, under the influence of certain delusions, the prisoner had conceived a desire to put an end to his own life, that being reluctant to commit suicide, he had fired at the King, knowing and believing that this attempt alone will be sufficient for his purpose, and that he will be hanged for the attempt. It was also shown that the man made his preparations, watched his opportunity and aimed the gun at the King, just as any sane person would do. If the favourite right-and-wrong test had been applied to this case, there could be no doubt that the man knew that he was doing an act which was punishable by law. It was argued by counsel for the prisoner that it was the case of a morbid delusion of the intellect, and if the act in question was the immediate offspring of the disease, he was entitled to a verdict in favour of the prisoner. Lord Kenyon thew off the right and wrong test and held that there was no reason for believing that the prisoner when he committed the act was a rational and accountable being, and that he ought to be acquitted. "With regard to the law," said he, "there can be no doubt upon earth; to be sure, if a man is in a deranged state of the mind at the time, he is not criminally answerable for his act; but the material part of this case is, *whether at the very time when the act was committed this man's mind was sane.* His sanity must be made out to the satisfaction of a moral man, meeting the case with fortitude of mind, knowing he has an arduous duty to discharge yet if the scales hang anything like even, throwing a certain proportion of mercy to the party." This was undoubtedly a very rational view of the matter. But at the same time it seems clear that the direction to acquit in this case, is opposed to the views expressed by Lord Lyndhurst in Offord's case and Lord Mansfield in Bellingham's case. It is also opposed to the view taken by Tindal C.J. in *Reg.* v. *Vaughan* where the prisoner's mind being unhinged by reason of some loss suffered by him, he believed that everyone was robbing him. In an indictment for stealing a cow the learned Judge told the Jury that "mere eccentricity or singularity of manner was not sufficient and that it must be shown that the prisoner had no competent use of his understanding, so as to know that he was doing a wrong thing in the particular act in question." How this could be shown except by reference to the deranged state of the prisoner's mind with reference to other matters, it is difficult to imagine. Examined by the test laid down in Macnaghten's case, there ought to have been a verdict against Hadfield.

Ignorance or error regarding the nature of an act may also cover cases of ignorance regarding its consequences. Just as an ignorant villager unacquainted with the mysteries of electricity may by careless manipulation of a live-wire cause disastrous consequences and plead his ignorance in defence; in the same way an insane person may pull the trigger of a loaned gun or throw a lighted match on a stack of hay or let loose a tiger out of its cage not realising the dangerous nature of the act, and where he acts under such ignorance his ignorance is a good defence.

An amusing instance is referred to in Sir Fitz James Stephen's book of a lunatic cutting off a man's head when asleep, so that he might enjoy the fun of seeing the headless man awaking and looking round for his lost head. A man who thinks in this way cannot be said to be a rational being.

Delusion again may be subjective or objective. Subjective delusions are those regarding one's personal duty or obligation, as for instance, a person may suppose himself to be a King and may on the strength and by reason of such belief kill another whom he may have imagined to have deserved death for committing a real or imaginary crime. An objective delusion, on the other hand, is a delusion of visual or other sensual organs. An objective delusion may exist in the case of the sane as well as of the insane; but such a delusion may be so deep rooted as to be incapable of correction and may itself be the cause of insanity.

Delusions are thus not limited to errors regarding external objects. A man may have fancied grievances against others, as for instance, in the case of *Reg.* v. *Vaughan* the prisoner fancied that every body was robbing him and similarly in the case of *Reg.* v. *Offord* the delusion was that the inhabitants of Hadleigh were continually issuing warrants against the prisoner with a view to deprive him of his liberty. A man may fancy that he hears the voice of God commanding him to do a particular act, or that he is under a religious obligation to do a certain act; such a belief would negative the knowledge that the act is morally wrong, and if due to insanity it is a valid defence.

It is impossible to exhaust the list of various kinds of delusions under which an insane person is often impelled to act. Where the existence of a delusion can be gathered from the surrounding circumstances the plea of insanity may be held to be established, and it seems too much to expect the defence to show that the prisoner did not know either that the act is morally wrong or is contrary to law.

The two important cases of this class that are to be found in the Indian Reports are those of Ghatu Paramanick (28 Cal. 613) and Dilgazi (34 Cal. 686). In the first case it was found that the act was committed when the accused was labouring under a delusion. He imagined that he saw something very wrong in the conduct of his wife, and his brother-in-law who was a young boy of eight years only, in relation to another person, and labouring under this delusion he killed the boy; but still one of the learned Judges found himself unable to say that the accused when he committed the deed was in such a state of mind as to incapacitate him from distinguishing between right and wrong, and the conduct of the accused after committing the deed was considered as indicating the absence of such incapacity. The learned Judges finding that the delusion existed fell into the groove of Macnaghten's case and found the accused guilty. The decision might have been right for the delusion in this case did not indicate the same degree of derangement as was indicated in the English cases I have referred to, for what is called a delusion in this case may be nothing more than the working of an over-suspicious mind, and may not have been evidence of insanity at all, much less of a mind incapable of distinguishing right from wrong.

In Dilgazi's case the accused was tried for the murder of his wife and there was no rational motive for the crime. The learned Judges in acquitting the accused made the following observations :

"There is no doubt that his mind was at the time unsound. He apparently had definite delusions as to dangers that threatened his wife, his disease affected his intercourse with his neighbours, and his cultivation of his crops in both of which he showed a failure of his reasoning powers. His climbing a tree in search of his pillow indicates a state of mind resembling that which is generally described as idiocy. In view of the uncertainty that always exists as to how far a diseased state of mind extends, and in view of the difficulty that is never absent from cases like this, of obtaining any trustworthy evidence, we find that the facts on the record prove that the unsoundness of his mind prevented his knowing the nature of his act, and that it was wrong."

It may be said that in this case the learned Judges took a broader and a more rational view of the law applying to cases of this class.

Incapacity to judge that an act is either morally wrong or is contrary to law, often arises from incapacity to judge of the nature and consequences of an act but not always. A man may, for instance, know that by his act he may be causing a man's death, but at the same time he may be under the delusion that he can cause a revival after death. In some cases it may be due to insane motive such as a belief that by causing a man's death he would be sent to heaven or that the salvation of the human race depended on it. At the same time the man may have full knowledge of the fact that he may be punished for the act. Sometimes ignorance regarding the morality or the legality of an act may be due to loss of memory and utter forgetfulness of lessons and experience of life as was observed by Tracey J. in Arnold's case, 'where a man is totally deprived of his understanding and memory and does not know what he is doing, any more than an infant, or a wild beast, he will properly be exempted from the punishment of the law.'

I have dwelt perhaps at more length than was necessary on the subject of insanity as a ground of exemption from criminal liability. This subject has occupied a large part in the Criminal Law of every civilised country. China was perhaps the only country which did not recognise lunacy as a ground of exemption, but even there the penalty was commuted in cases of murder to imprisonment with fetters subject to His Majesty's pleasure. The relatives of a lunatic were bound, under heavy penalties, to notify the case to the authorities, and lunatics were, in general, required to be manacled. Matters may have improved there in recent years.

The subject has lost a good deal of its importance by the legislation undertaken in England and other countries of a preventive nature against the commission of crimes by persons of unsound mind. In England the first step in this direction was taken in view of an order passed by the Judge to keep Hadfield in confinement after his acquittal. Legislation in India has also been directed towards that end, and I may refer you to the provisions of Chapter XXXIV of the Criminal Procedure Code. It is laid down in Section 464 that if a Magistrate holding a trial or an enquiry is satisfied on medical evidence that the accused is of unsound mind and is incapable of making his defence, he shall postpone further proceedings in the case. The next section provides that if any person committed before a Court of Sessions or a High Court appears to be of unsound mind and incapable of making his defence, the question of such unsoundness or incapacity shall be tried and judgment pronounced accordingly. On such finding being arrived at by a Magistrate or a Court of Sessions if the offence is bailable, the offender may be released on sufficient security being given that the prisoner shall be properly taken care of, and shall be prevented from doing injury to himself or to any other person, and for his appearance when required before the Magistrate or Court (Section 466). On failure to furnish such security or in case of non-bailable offences the case shall be reported to the Local Government who may order the accused to be confined in a lunatic asylum, jail or other suitable place of safe custody (Section 466). These provisions relate to cases of insanity at the time of the trial without reference to the question whether the unsoundness of mind existed at the time of the commission of the offence. Section 470, however, provides that when a person is acquitted on the ground of insanity the finding shall state whether he committed the act or not, and when such finding is recorded such person shall be kept in safe custody and the case shall be reported to Local Government. The Local Government may exercise all or any functions given to the Inspector-General of Prisons by the succeeding Sections 472, 473 and 474. Section 474 empowers the Inspector-General to certify that a prisoner may be discharged without danger of his doing injury to himself or any other person, and the Local Government may thereupon order him to be so discharged or to be detained in custody or to be transferred to a public lunatic asylum. By Section 475 the Local Government is authorised to deliver a lunatic to the custody of a friend or a relation willing to take care of him. In this connection you may also refer to the Lunacy Act (Act IV of 1912).

DRUNKENNESS.

It is a settled principle of law that voluntary drunkenness is no excuse. The Indian Penal Code lays down the law in Section 85.

Sec. 85, I.P.C.

"Nothing is an offence which is done by a person who at the time of doing it, is, by reason of intoxication, incapable of knowing the nature of the act, or that he is doing what is either wrong or contrary to law, provided that the thing which intoxicated him was administered without his knowledge or against his will."

If a man chooses to get drunk, it is his own voluntary act and he does so at his risk.

Drunkenness and Insanity.

It is very different from insanity which is a disease for which the sufferer is not responsible. The disease may be brought about by carelessness or misbehaviour, but that is a different matter.

Intoxication is a voluntary species of madness which is in a party's power to abstain from, and he must answer for it. If, however, the drunkenness is involuntary, as when a man is forced to drink or when any intoxicant is administered to him without his knowledge, any criminal act he may commit will be judged with reference to his mental condition at the time the act was committed. Such a case is exactly on the same footing as unsoundness of mind. The words used in Sections 84 and 85 are identical and all the considerations that arise in case of insanity also arise in cases of involuntary drunkenness.

Voluntary Drunkenness —no excuse.

There is no dispute as to any of these propositions. It was at one time supposed that drunkenness not only does not excuse an offence, but on the other hand aggravates it. Sir E. Coke tells us : " As for a drunkard who is *voluntarius dœmon*, he hath, as has been said, no privileges thereby, but what hurt or ill so ever he doth, his drunkenness doth aggravate it." It was probably this remark which induced a learned Judge in this country to tell the Jury that "drunkenness in the eye of law makes an offence the more heinous." With reference to this remark Macpherson and Anslie JJ. observed :—" There is no authority for such a proposition, and all that the Judge should have said was that drunkenness is no excuse, and that an act, which, if committed by a sober man, is an offence, is equally an offence, if committed by one when drunk, if the intoxication was voluntarily caused." (*Q.* v. *Zoolfikar*, 16 W. R. Cr. 36). Where, however, habitual drunkenness causes any mental disease, and affects the mind such disease is looked upon as insanity *pro tanto*. One of the grounds urged by some European text-writers in support of the law laid down in Section 85, Indian Penal Code, is that few violent crimes would probably be attempted without resorting to liquor, both as a stimulant and as a shield. This argument may not apply with equal force to India.

Exception in England and America

In England and in America there is an important exception to the general doctrine that voluntary drunkenness does not excuse an offence, and the exception in the language of Sir James Stephen is stated thus :—" If the existence of a specific intention is essential to the commission of a crime, the fact that an offender was drunk, when he did the act, which, if coupled with that intention, would constitute such crime, should be taken into account by the Jury in deciding whether he had that intention."

Illustrations.

The following cases will illustrate the rule of law quoted above. In an indictment for inflicting bodily injury dangerous to life with intent to murder, where it appeared that the prisoners were both very drunk at the time, Patterson J. told the Jury that "although drunkenness is no excuse for any crime whatever, yet it is often of very great importance in cases where it is a question of intention. A person may be so drunk as to be utterly unable to form any intention at all and yet he may be guilty of very great violence." (*Rex* v. *Cruse*, 8 C. & P. 541, 546). In an indictment for attempting to commit suicide it appeared that the prisoner had thrown herself into a well. It being proved that at the time the prisoner was so drunk as not to know what she was about, Jervis C.J. said: "If the prisoner was so drunk as not to know what she was about, how can you say that she intended to destroy herself?" (*R.* v. *Moore*, 3 C. & K. 319). Again, where a person was indicted for shooting with intent to murder, and it was shewn that he was intoxicated shortly before he fired the shot, it was held that the charge could not be sustained.

Where the prisoner had stabbed a person, and it was proved that he was drunk at the time, Alderson B. said, with regard to the intention, "drunkenness may perhaps be adverted to according to the nature of the instrument used. If a man uses a stick, you would not infer a malicious intent so strongly against him, if drunk when he made intemperate use of it.........But when a dangerous instrument is used, which, if used, must produce grievous bodily harm, drunkenness can have no effect on the consideration of the malicious intent of the party." (*R.* v. *Meakin*, 7 C. & P. 297).

So also drunkenness would be taken into consideration in a case where the crime is attributed to provocation or *bona fide* mistake, but not so if there is a previous determination to resent.

In a case where a man was indicted for uttering a counterfeit coin, an offence which requires specific intent to cheat, the drunkenness at the time of the offence was taken into consideration, as there was no ground to suppose that he knew the money to be counterfeit. (*Pigman* v. *State*, 15 Ohio, 555, 1846).

Drunkenness may be a defence to perjury also, but not if the false oath was intelligently taken. (*People* v. *Willey*, 2 Park C. R. 19, 1855).

The law in India.

While the above illustrations will sufficiently elucidate the law as accepted in England and America, it seems to me more than doubtful if, having regard to the terms of Section 86, Indian Penal Code, the law in India is not different from what is laid down in those cases.

The wording of the section is somewhat peculiar. It begins by laying down the law without reference to cases in which knowledge or intent is a necessary ingredient of the offence, but in the second part it speaks of knowledge only and omits any reference to intent. Assuming that the omission is intentional, the only explanation for such omission is that given by Mr. Mayne, *viz.*, that "in the majority of cases the question of intention is merely the question of knowledge." The effect of the section seems to be that the same knowledge will be attributed to a man in a state of voluntary intoxication as to a man not so intoxicated, but not necessarily the same intention. It is said that a man must know the natural consequences of his act, and if he knows what the consequences are likely to be he must be held to have intended them. This inference from knowledge to intention would not arise when a man is drunk. In each case it will be for the Jury, after having attributed the knowledge, to ask whether, having regard to the mental condition of the prisoner, the general inference can reasonably be drawn. If this is a correct interpretation of the section, in the case of the attempted suicide as in the illustration already quoted, the law will attribute to the offender, who threw himself into a well, the knowledge that such act was likely to cause death, but will not necessarily also attribute to such a person the intention which ordinarily follows from the knowledge. Where intention and not knowledge is the gravamen of an offence and intention is to be affirmatively established by evidence, what may be sufficient proof of intention in other cases may not be sufficient evidence to prove intention on the part of a man who is drunk. I shall illustrate what I have said with reference to Section 304, Indian Penal Code. *A* under provocation strikes *B* on the head with a heavy iron bar and thereby causes his death. The mere knowledge that the act was likely to cause death without the intention to cause death brings the offence within the latter part of the section. But intention to cause death aggravates the offence which falls under the first part of the section. In ordinary cases the intention, in the absence of anything to show the contrary, will flow from the knowledge itself but not in the case of a man who is drunk.

LECTURE X.

CONSENT—COMPULSION—TRIFLES.

Preliminary observations.

Volenti non fit injuria is an old maxim of the Roman Jurisprudence. This principle, like all general principles so broadly laid down, is subject to many exceptions and I propose in this lecture to examine the principle with the limitations that have been imposed on it.

Although theoretically every crime must involve injury to the body politic, an examination of the criminal law of every country would show that the large body of offences are those which are essentially private wrongs, though they may have their reflex on the well-being of the society at large. In such cases the harm to society consists merely of the general alarm to the public resulting from the harm caused to the individual and there can be no alarm from an act done to a person with his own consent. Confining ourselves to an examination of the offences under the Indian Penal Code, we may say broadly that offences against the human body (Chapter XVI) and those against property (Chapter XVII) are private wrongs or at any rate in them the element of private injury predominates.

The question of consent justifying a criminal act does not arise in connection with offences against the public. To these may be said to belong offences enumerated in Chapters VI, VII, VIII, IX, X, XI, XII, XIII, XIV, and XV.

There are certain other offences which partake of the character of both public and private offences and as to these you have to see which is the more predominating element. I shall therefore deal principally with the two main private offences already indicated, I mean offences against the human body and those against property. Broadly speaking there is no injury to any right when the act of injury is itself consented to by the owner of the right. The underlying principle is thus explained in a note on the draft Code. "It is by no means true that men always judge rightly of their own interest. But it is true that in the majority of cases they judge better of their own interest than any law-giver or any tribunal which must necessarily proceed on general principles and which cannot have within its contemplation the circumstances of particular cases and the tempers of particular individuals."

Alienable and inalienable rights.

Rights may be divided into two classes, alienable and inalienable. All offences against property are offences against alienable rights and if done with the consent of the owner, is a complete defence both to civil and criminal actions. Offences against the human body embodying the right to security of life and limb stand on a somewhat different footing. Up to a certain stage the right is an alienable right, but beyond that stage it is inalienable and no amount of consent is of any avail to the person who infringes that right. Every man has to live. It is his duty to live. It is the right of the State that he should live and be useful to the body politic of which he is a unit. It is only the outlaw of the old days, whose life was a forfeit to the State. That was an inhuman system but is happily gone, never to come back again. The right to live is therefore an inalienable right and no one can agree to give it away. If a man attempts to kill himself he is guilty of an attempt to commit suicide (Section 309).

Under the English law inalienability also extends to injuries which amount to mayhem. Mayhem is akin to the grievous hurt of the Indian Penal Code, though it does not cover exactly the same ground. According to English law a man may not maim himself nor can he consent to such an act from a friendly hand (*Rex* v. *Wright*, 1 East P. C. 306, Co. Lit. 127 *a* ; *People* v. *Clough*, 17 Wend. 351, 352). Although there is nothing in the Indian Penal Code to prevent a man from causing grievous hurt to himself in so far as others are concerned, this is also classed among inalienable rights. Beyond these there are no further restrictions to a man consenting to any injury to his body. This extension of inalienability to mayhem or grievous hurt of the Indian law is justified in English law on the ground that it makes the person less fitted to fight for his country which is a duty which everybody owes to the State. It follows that consent is a good defence to all offences against property and to all offences which do not involve the causing of death or grievous hurt. A man cannot only not consent to the causing by another of his own death, but he cannot also consent to his eyes being blinded or his legs to be amputated or other offences of the same kind which are included in the definition of grievous hurt (Section 320). Mayhem by its very definition was strictly confined to such deprivation of the limbs as rendered the man unfit for fighting. Grievous hurt of the Indian Penal Code goes beyond that and I cannot say that it does so wisely. A more restricted definition of grievous hurt might have been wiser. In English law the dislocation of the front tooth amounted to mayhem but not of the others. This was perhaps on military considerations as in old days walls had to be scaled by means of ropes in which the front teeth were useful. In modern warfare the teeth are of little use. In some cases this is justified on the ground that the loss of the front teeth weakens a man as he cannot eat meat without them. Similarly I doubt that there was any necessity of bringing within the meaning of grievous hurt the destruction of a finger, for instance, or the permanent disfiguration of the head or face. Under the English law the cutting off of the nose is not mayhem. These might have been classed as minor offences to which at any rate consent might have been permitted to furnish a defence. Macaulay in his note on the draft Penal Code said rightly that if *Z* chose to sell his teeth to a dentist and permitted the dentist to pull them out the dentist ought not to be punished for injuring his person, and yet under the law as enacted such an act would amount to grievous hurt and the dentist would be punished in spite of the consent. Common sense would suggest a different view. The existence of the consideration would be immaterial for the benefit spoken of in Section 88 is not pecuniary benefit (Baboolun Hijrah, 5 W. R. Cr. 7). The wisdom of the law in not giving effect to consent to the causing of mayhem or grievous hurt of the more serious type except under exceptional circumstances seems obvious. Any law of conscription might be rendered ineffective, if a man could be allowed to have his legs amputated to escape joining the army.

Sections 87, 88 and 89 of the Chapter of General Exceptions in the Indian Penal Code deal with the law of consent in criminal cases. Consent does not justify causing of death or grievous hurt. As to the first, the restriction is absolute and unconditional, except that by statutory provision in some cases consent has the effect of reducing the gravity of the offence. For instance, the fifth exception to Section 300 provides that "culpable homicide is not murder when the person whose death is caused being above the age of eighteen years suffers death or takes the risk of death with his own consent." Section 314 furnishes another example of the same kind. As to the second it is removed under certain conditions. The law does not recognise that death, though it may be a relief in many cases, can be under any circumstances a benefit to a man. A man suffering from extreme or unbearable torture or pain may prefer death to his suffering and may implore another to shoot him, but if that other does shoot him he will be held guilty, though under exception to Section 300 the offence will be reduced from murder to culpable homicide not amounting to murder. I should like before proceeding further to explain to you that Sections 87, 88 and 89 do not refer to offences against property. The reason is obvious. The very definition of those offences excludes the existence of a consent. It is an element which enters into the definition of all such offences that there should be intention to cause wrongful loss to one or wrongful gain to another. There is no wrongful loss or wrongful gain when the act is assented to by the owner of the property himself, and even where instead of the word 'dishonestly,' the word 'fraudulently,' is used to denote the *mens rea* of an offence the same result follows. I have already explained to you that fraud implies besides deception an injury. Therefore want of consent is implied in all offences against property, and apart from this such offences against property as involve extortion or theft in all its aggravated forms, necessarily exclude consent, because extortion is inconsistent with consent, and theft by its definition involves removal of property without the consent of the person in possession. Sections 87, 88 and 89, in speaking of 'harm' done to another, refer apparently to bodily harm and not to 'injury' in its wider sense. The operation of consent mentioned in those sections thus relate to offences against human body with the restriction provided by Section 91.

Secs. 87, 88 and 89, I. P. C., explained.

I shall now proceed to discuss the provisions of Sections 87, 88 and 89. Section 87 gives immunity to a person who causes harm to another who takes the risk of it or gives consent to it, provided the act is not known to be likely to cause death or grievous hurt. The next section extends the operation of consent to all offences short of causing death intentionally, provided the act is done *for the benefit of the person* who has given such consent. The words in italics mark the main distinction between Sections 87 and 88. An agreement for fencing as an amusement comes under the former, whereas a surgical operation performed for the benefit of a person with his consent falls within the latter section. There is also this difference between Sections 87 and 88. The mere likelihood of causing death does not exclude the operation of consent to acts falling within Section 88, but it is enough that there was no intention to cause death. Section 89 extends the provisions of Section 88 to cases of infants under 12 years of age and to persons of unsound mind when consent is given by their guardians, with these following restrictions. If an act is *likely* to cause death or grievous hurt consent of the guardian would not justify it when done for any purpose other than the prevention of death or grievous hurt or the curing of any grievous disease.

At the risk of repetition I would state the position to be this—

(*a*) A man may not consent to an *intentional* causing of death under any circumstances.

(*b*) He may not consent to *intentional* causing of grievous hurt or to any act likely to cause death unless the act is for his benefit. In such a case the law does not stop to consider the extent of the benefit to be derived from the act.

(*c*) If he is the guardian of a minor he may not consent to an act intended to cause death or which is an attempt to cause death under any circumstances. He may not also consent to an act likely to cause death or intended to cause grievous hurt or which is an attempt to cause grievous hurt even for the benefit of the minor, unless the benefit be to the extent mentioned in the section, *viz.*, the prevention of death or grievous hurt or the curing of any grievous disease or infirmity.

(*d*) Where the consent of a guardian is insufficient to justify an act it is also insufficient to justify the abetment of such an act.

It would seem that in the case of an adult person there is no restriction to consent to acts, whatever their nature, if they only amount to attempts or abetments, and the restriction regarding attempts or abetments only apply to consent by guardians.

Consent explained.

In order to appreciate the effect of the provisions of the Code relating to consent it is necessary to explain to you what consent means and what are the general limitations to its applicability. 'Consent' is not defined in the Code but you all understand its meaning, and I do not think the legal meaning of that expression is materially different from its meaning as used in ordinary language. To consent is to agree to a thing being done. In law it is an agreement to the invasion of a right appertaining to the person so agreeing. Story explains consent to be an act of reason accompanied with deliberation of mind, weighing, as in a balance, the good and evil on each side. The explanation makes it clear that consent is a positive operation of the mind and is therefore distinguishable from mere submission, want of dissent or acquiescence, although these may be in proper cases very strong evidence of a consent.

'There is a difference,' said Coleridge J. in *R.* v. *Day* (9 C. & P. 722), 'between consent and submission; every consent involves a submission; but it by no means follows that a mere submission involves consent; it would be too much to say that an adult submitting quietly to an outrage was not consenting; on the other hand, the mere submission of a child when in the power of a strong man and most probably acted upon by fear, can by no means be taken to be such a consent as would justify the prisoner in the point of law.'

Consent is also distinct from mere approbation. Subsequent approval does not supply the place of consent.

In *R.* v. *Flattery* (2 Q. B. D. 410) it was also argued that submission was equivalent to consent, but the plea was overruled. It was held in *R.* v. *Nichol* (R. & R. 130) that if a master take indecent liberties with a female scholar without her consent, though she does not resist, he may be convicted of a common assault.

Section 90 of the Indian Penal Code explains what legal consent is and that controls the meaning of consent referred to in the three previous sections, as well as of consent which expressly or impliedly enters into the definition of offences under the Code.

Sec. 90, I.P.C. Legal consent.

The section provides as follows:—A consent is not such a consent as is intended by any section of this Code, if the consent is given by a person under fear of injury, or under a misconception of fact, and if the person doing the act knows, or has reason to believe, that the consent was given in consequence of such fear or misconception; or if the consent is given by a person who, from unsoundness of mind or intoxication, is unable to understand the nature and consequence of that to which he gives his consent; or unless the contrary appears from the context, if the consent is given by a person who is under twelve years of age.

The rest of this lecture would be practically confined to an elucidation of the provisions of this section. I can deal with the matter only briefly, but if you desire to study the subject more fully I would refer you to Mr. Hukm Chand's exhaustive treatment of the subject in his book on the Law of Consent which is a master-piece of research and study.

Consent in Civil and Criminal cases distinguished.

You will notice that the language used in Section 90 is not the usual language in which the law regarding consent is dealt with in connection with laws relating to civil injuries. For instance, *free* consent is the word used in the Indian Contract Act as an essential element in all contracts (Section 10), and this is explained as meaning consent not caused by—

(1) coercion, as defined in Section 15, or
(2) undue influence, as defined in Section 16, or
(3) fraud, as defined in Section 17, or
(4) misrepresentation, as defined in Section 18, or
(5) mistake subject to the provisions of Sections 20, 21 and 22,

Consent under fear of injury.

In criminal law it has a less restricted meaning. The word free consent is advisedly avoided. 'Fear of injury' used in Section 90 of the Code would vitiate a consent. These words would include most cases of coercion as explained in Section 15 of the Indian Contract Act, but consent would not be vitiated by undue influence for instance, nor by all kinds of fraud, misrepresentation or mistake. Some of these would, no doubt, be included in the words 'misconception of fact' but not all. But if there is misconception of fact and the offender knows or has reason to believe that consent was given by reason of such misconception, the consent has no value. To explain more fully what I mean, suppose a man takes undue liberties with a woman having obtained her consent by a promise to pay money which he never intended to fulfil. The consent was obtained by fraud, but none the less it is consent. The misconception of fact used in the section refers to misconception regarding the true nature of the act or regarding the effect or consequences of the acts.

Misconception of fact.

As regards the degree of misconception which would invalidate a consent, the practical test that a Jury may be asked to apply is this :—Would the consent have been given had the misconception not existed ? In *Sukaroo Kobiraj* v. *The Empress* (14 Cal. 566) the accused, a Kaviraj by profession, was convicted under Section 304A for having caused the death of a patient by operating on him for internal piles by cutting them out with an ordinary knife. It was held that the prisoner being admittedly uneducated in matters of surgery cannot be said to have acted in good faith and that the consent was of no avail in the absence of anything to show that the deceased knew the risk he was running in consenting to the operation.

Difficulty has arisen in dealing with case of consent obtained by fraud or misrepresentation or by suppression of material facts. In *R.* v. *Flattery* (2 Q. B. D. 410) in which under the pretext of performing a surgical operation prisoner had carnal connection with the prosecutrix, she submitting to what was done under the belief that he was treating her medically, the prisoner was held guilty. In this case there was misconception regarding the nature of the act. Mellor J. pointed out that submission was not to carnal connection, but to something else and quoted with approval the words of Wilde C.J. in *R.* v. *Case.* "She consented to one thing, he did another materially different, in which she had been prevented by his fraud from exercising her judgment and will." In an earlier case, *R.* v. *Barrow* (L. R. 1 C. C. 156), a somewhat different view was taken and the learned Judges felt doubtful as to the correctness of that decision. **Consent under misconception**

When, however, consent was obtained to a precise act complained of, though such consent was fraudulently obtained it was held that consent so obtained was a sufficient defence to a charge of rape. A woman about 42 years old consented to an act of sexual connection under the belief that the prisoner was a doctor and was making a medical examination of her. Ridley J. adopted the opinion expressed in Stephen's Digest of Criminal Law that rape is overcoming a woman by force, and that, if a woman gives conscious permission to the act of connection, the act does not amount to rape, though such permission may have been obtained by fraud, and although the woman may **Fraud.**

not have been aware of the nature of the act—*R.* v. *O'Shay* (19 Cox 76).

In *R.* v. *Bennett* (4 F. & F. 1105) it was laid down that an indecent assault is within the rule that fraud vitiates consent, and that a person suffering from a foul disease who induced a girl ignorant of his condition to consent to a connection with him might be convicted of an indecent assault. Here there was misconception regarding the effect of the act. There are numerous cases of rape in which the effect of fraud on consent has been considered, but in judging of the effect of these cases you will bear in mind that cases of rape stand apart from the rest. Under the definition, consent is an answer to the charge, except where it has been obtained by putting the woman in fear of death or of hurt or when consent is given under the belief that the man having connection with her, was her husband, or when the party consenting is under twelve years of age. It will thus be seen that mere fraud will not vitiate consent in a charge of rape by the mere operation of the words of the definition. But notwithstanding the definition Section 90 so far as it is not inconsistent with the definition will, I suppose, operate. With reference to offences in which consent is not expressly limited as in rape, misconception such as is referred to in the English cases which I have cited, would be sufficient to invalidate a consent.

Consent of lunatics and infants.

I now proceed to consider the effect of unsoundness of mind on consent. There is in this matter a great difference between Civil and Criminal law. In a Civil case the degree of unsoundness need not be so great as is insisted on in Criminal cases. The language of the section shows that to vitiate a consent by a person of unsound mind the degree of unsoundness must be the same as would furnish a defence to a criminal charge on the ground of insanity.

It has been held in cases of rape that if the connection was with a woman of weak intellect, incapable of distinguishing right from wrong, and the Jury found that she was incapable of giving consent, or of exercising any judgment upon the matter, and that (though she made no resistance) the defendant had carnal knowledge of her by force, and *without her consent*, that is a rape. *R.* v. *Fletcher* (1859), Bell, 63; 28 L. J. (M. C.) 85; 8 Cox, 131. It was, however, afterwards held that the mere fact of connection with an idiot girl who was capable of recognizing and describing the prisoner, and who was a fully developed woman, who, notwithstanding her imbecile condition, might have strong animal instincts, is not sufficient evidence of rape to be left to a Jury. (*Q.* v. *Barratt*, 2 C. C. R. 81; *R.* v. *Fletcher* (1866), L. R. 1 C. C. R. 39 explained and distinguished.)

In England the law is now settled and by 48 and 49 Vict., s. 5, sub-s. 2, connection, or an attempt to have connection, with "any female idiot or imbecile woman or girl, under circumstances which do not amount to rape, but which prove that the offender knew at the time of the commission of the offence that this woman or girl was an idiot or imbecile," is a misdemeanor punishable with two years' imprisonment.

Revocation of consent.

Consent given can always be revoked but before the act consented to has commenced. A surgeon, for instance, after he has begun a surgical operation, need not stop because the patient asks him to desist. The right to revoke a consent is not affected by the fact that consent was given for a consideration. Consent to an act necessarily includes consent to all its natural consequences.

Section 91, I.P.C., explained.

Section 91 lays down that the exception in Sections 87, 88 and 89 does not extend to acts which are offences independently of any harm which they may cause or be intended to cause or be known to be likely to cause to the person giving the consent or on whose behalf the consent is given. The principle is clear, consent may wipe off an injury to the person consenting, but if the gravemen of the offence is not the injury to the consenting party but something else, the consent can have no effect on the offence. You may refer to illustration appended to the section. The causing of a miscarriage is not an injury to the woman alone. The child *a ventre sa mere* is clothed with legal rights for certain purposes and the causing of a miscarriage is an offence against the life of the child. The mother's consent therefore would not avail. Similarly as I have pointed out in the beginning of this lecture, most public offences are also offences against individuals, they being a part of the general public. In such offences the consent of the individual is of no avail. Unnatural offences, offence of bigamy may be cited as examples. It is needless to repeat that where an offence is purely a public offence no question of consent arises. There are various offences which are classed as offences against the public in one country, but are not so classed in another. For instance, incest is by itself no offence in India, but it is so in England by Statute. So that an incestuous connection with consent is no offence in India but would be an offence in England notwithstanding any consent.

There may be cases where it is not possible to get the consent of a person to an act intended for his benefit, but the circumstances are such where it can be inferred that if the man could he would have consented. Take, for instance, the case of a person who has met with an accident and is taken to hospital in an unconscious state. He cannot give consent to a very necessary surgical operation, but the consent may be assumed. **Implied consent.**

Section 92 accordingly provides that where a harm is caused in good faith to a person without that person's consent, where circumstances are such that it is impossible for that person to signify consent, or if that person is incapable of giving consent (being an infant or a lunatic), and if there is no guardian or other person from whom consent can be obtained in proper time, any harm caused to such a person for his benefit is justified under certain conditions which are the same as those applying under Section 89 to a person who acts with the consent of a guardian of a minor or lunatic with this slight difference, that under this section even the causing of simple hurt is prohibited for any purpose other than the prevention of death or hurt. I am not sure that an express condition to this effect was necessary. The expected benefit must in all such cases outweigh the harm to be **Section 92, I P.C., explained.**

inflicted, otherwise there is no benefit to the sufferers by such an act.

Section 93, I.P.C., explained.

Section 93 presents no difficulty. It lays down that no communication made in good faith is an offence by reason of any harm to the person to whom it is made if it is made for the benefit of that person. The illustration makes the meaning clear. A surgeon in good faith communicates to a patient his opinion that he cannot live. The patient dies in consequence of the shock. The surgeon has committed no offence, though he knew it to be likely that the communication might cause the patient's death. He might have thought it necessary to warn the patient that his end was near, so that he might make his will, for instance.

COMPULSION.

Section 94. Compulsion.

I have told you in the beginning of these lectures that a voluntary act is necessary to constitute a crime. An involuntary act is no offence. But this is subject to important limitations. The voluntary nature of an act may be affected either by the act being done under threat of injury or other kind of mental compulsion or under actual physical compulsion in which case the man acts without a will and is nothing more than an instrument in the hands of others. "An act done by me against my will is not my act," is a well-known maxim of law. But where an act is not voluntary, not because another uses his limbs for the commission of a crime and the man so used is a mere passive instrument, but because of mental compulsion, the doctrine has to be applied within certain limits. To illustrate what I mean—*A* catches hold of *B* and takes possession of all the money in his pocket, and says 'I would not return you the money unless you pick the pocket of *C*.' *B* picks the pocket of *C* in order to get back his money. Here undoubtedly there is mental compulsion, but not the kind of mental compulsion which the law considers to be a sufficient excuse for a crime. Section 94 of the Indian Penal Code deals with cases of compulsion. Shortly the effect of the section is that no amount of compulsion, by which is meant mental compulsion, *i.e.*, compulsion arising out of threat of injury can under any circumstances excuse the causing of death or the causing of any offence against the State punishable with death. To this extent the restriction is absolute. The law says in effect "if you have a choice between your death and the death of another person, you must choose the former." No amount of mental compulsion, no pressure of necessity, however great, can alter the situation. In *Rex* v. *Dudley* (14 Q. B. D. 273) a number of persons found themselves at sea in a boat without provisions to support life and after passing seven days without food and five days without water, the youngest of them a poor boy was chosen. He was killed and the survivors ate the flesh of the boy. They were held guilty of murder. This is an extreme case but is a good illustration of the principle. As was observed by Lord Coleridge who tried the case—"In this case the weakest, the youngest, the most unresisting was chosen. Was it more necessary to kill him than one of the grown men? The answer must

Mental compulsion and necessity. *Rex* v *Dudley*.

be 'No.' It is not suggested that in this particular case the deeds were devilish; but it is quite plain that such a principle once admitted might be made the legal cloak for unbridled passion and atrocious crime. There is no safe path for Judges to tread, but to ascertain the law to the best of their ability and declare it according to their judgment; and, if in any case the law appears to be too severe on individuals, to leave it to the Sovereign to exercise the prerogative of mercy which the Constitution has entrusted to the hands fittest to dispense it." The law enunciated in this case is the law that is laid down in the Indian Penal Code. But any other offence short of murder and offences against the State punishable with death, will be excused, if the threat under which the act is committed is one which reasonably causes the apprehension of instant death, provided, however, "the person doing the act did not of his own accord or from a reasonable apprehension of harm to himself short of instant death, place himself in the situation by which he became the subject of such constraint."

From the language of the section and the explanations given it appears that compulsion arising from mere necessity is not meant to be included. A man on the point of death by starvation may not plead his necessity as an excuse for theft.

The Indian cases on the applicability of this section are very few. In a case of perjury (10 W. R. 81) the defence of torture by the police for the purpose of falsely incriminating a certain person for murder was rejected, because "the accused were under no compulsion to make the statements which they did and which would have the effect of sending an innocent man to the gallows."

In Maganlal's case (14 Bom. 115) it was held that " the witnesses, who in order to avoid pecuniary injury or personal molestation had offered or given bribes to a public servant were abettors of the offence of taking an illegal gratification, and their evidence should be treated as that of accomplices." In *Devji Govindji* (20 Bom. 215) it was held that " a policeman is no more justified in torturing a man to death, simply because he had been ordered to do so by his superior, than a robber can justify his act on the plea that he had to obey his fellow confederates." It follows therefore that the principle established by the Indian cases is that " no man from a fear of consequences to himself short of apprehension of immediate death arising from threat of injury has a right to make himself a party to committing mischief on mankind." (See also Killykyatara (1912), M. W. N. 1108, 19 I. C. 207).

" Necessity knows no law " is a very common saying. The doctrine of compulsion may in some cases be the doctrine of necessity only. But there are various degrees of necessity and the degree of necessity that may on principle be recognised as a valid excuse for crimes of all descriptions, is the necessity to save one's life when it is in *immediate* danger, but as I have said the Indian Penal Code does not recognise necessity as a source of compulsion.

It has been said that what is unavoidable should not be an offence. The principle is right but the whole question is what is avoidable and what is not. Like "irresistible impulse," in cases of insanity, unavoidable necessity is often used to denote not the necessity that could not be avoided but merely the necessity that was not avoided.

The English law on the subject of compulsion is dealt with in Arts. 32 and 33 of Stephen's Digest. It would appear that under the English law not only the apprehension of immediate death, but also the apprehension of immediate grievous hurt saves a person from punishment. Art. 33 deals with a different class of compulsion, *viz.*, compulsion, the result of imperious necessity. The learned author strongly criticises the judgment of Lord Coleridge in *R.* v. *Dudley*, to which I have already referred. He is not prepared to accept as correct that any case can impose on a man a duty not to live, but to die and he thinks that the learned Judge based a legal principle upon a questionable moral and theological foundation. He can discover no principle in the judgment, which depends entirely on its peculiar fact. The boy was deliberately put to death with a knife in order that the body might be used as food. The learned author gives three examples to which it would be manifestly unjust to apply the law as laid down by Lord Coleridge. (1) Two shipwrecked men find themselves on a plank which can only support one of them. The stronger man pushes away the other. Here the successful man does no direct bodily hurt to the other. He leaves him the chance of getting another plank. (2) Several men are roped together on the Alps. They slip and the weight of the whole party is thrown on one, who cuts the rope in order to save himself.

Rex. v. *Dudley*, criticised.

Here the question is not that whether some shall die but whether one shall live. (3) The captain of a ship runs down a boat, as the only means of avoiding shipwreck. A surgeon kills a child in the act of birth, as the only way to save the mother. A boat being too full of passengers to float some are thrown overboard. Such cases, says the learned author, are best decided as they arise. The last case is not important as it is fully met by the provisions of Section 81 of the Indian Penal Code, and although when a person is placed in circumstances such as are referred to in illustrations (1) and (2) the threat of law will not operate to prevent a crime and on principle, it is useless to multiply the number of offences unnecessarily, but yet sometimes it is not useless even in matters of legal obligation to insist on a high ideal, though not likely to be attained. In illustration (1) suppose the man found himself in the same plank with a little girl who is helpless and who cannot swim, can it be said on the face of numerous examples of men who in cases of shipwreck, have refused to save their lives at the expense of women and children, that the ideal is too high even for the noblest of the human race ?

There will be no doubt in cases like these the clemency of the sovereign would be exercised to prevent any real hardship.

Besides, as the learned author himself recognises, the case of Dudley is different from the three cases, he brings forward as examples. In the first two cases there is no intention to kill but to save oneself at the *risk* of others, and the criticism is only directed against the very general terms in which the law was enunciated. If the statement of law in Art. 33 of the Digest is correct the law in England, recognising the validity of necessity as a source of compulsion, is on a footing more favourable to the accused than the Indian law.

English & Indian law compared.

There are also other points in regard to which the English law is less stringent. You may notice that an offence under Section 121 (waging war) is one of the offences against the State for which death is the penalty, and therefore a person guilty of an offence under that section cannot plead compulsion as a defence under the Indian Penal Code under any circumstances. Whereas under the English law such a defence is available. *R.* v. *Macnaghten* (18 St. Tr. 391).

Another point of difference which I may notice is that English law proceeds on the assumption that a *femme covert* is completely under the influence of her husband, and if she does anything in his presence she must be held to act under such compulsion as to save her from any liability for crimes committed by her. Indian women are treated as being under no such compulsion, and I am not sorry that this is so. But even under the English law the immunity does not extend to cases of extreme gravity, such as murder and treason. The insular habits of the English people where every man's house is said to be his castle makes all the difference in the relation of husband and wife in the two countries.

Acts causing slight harm.

Section 95, I.P.C. Trifles.

No reasonable man complains of mere trifles. No man can pass through a crowded thoroughfare without treading on somebody's toes or without clashing against some body and no reasonable man would complain of such small annoyances. "*De minimis non curat lex*" is an old doctrine of Roman law. The provision is unnecessary for ordinary men, but there are eccentric people all over the world, and it is to guard against eccentricities that a formal provision of law of this kind is needed.

LECTURE XI

POSSESSION IN CRIMINAL LAW.

In the last four lectures I have dealt with the provisions of the chapter of General Exceptions in the Code except those which relate to the right of private defence of person and property. The right to defend property is the right to defend possession of property and not the mere right to possession. It is therefore necessary before proceeding further to explain to you what possession means. Criminal Law does not, as a rule, concern itself with complicated questions of title, though Civil Law, being remedial in its nature, takes full account of it, and attaches more importance to title than to possession. It is the policy of Criminal Law to protect possession howsoever it may have been obtained, except where it is obtained by an act which constitutes an offence by itself, and goes so far that it punishes even the rightful owner if not in possession, who tries to obtain possession by illegal means. The definition of offences against property shows that the gist of such offences is the deprivation of *possession*. The justification for attaching so much importance to possession and so little to question of title is the necessity for prompt action and for preventing breaches of the peace.

Preliminary.

Theoretically, it is not the province of the Criminal Law to protect private rights as such. That is a function that is assigned to the Civil Courts, but in cases of movable property possession often is the only evidence of title, and if the prompt remedy obtainable in the Criminal Courts, is not extended to the protection of possession in such cases, and such matters are left to the tardy process of adjudication by Civil Courts, the result would often be the disappearance of the thing itself and of all evidence of title, thus leading to general insecurity in the enjoyment of property and consequent alarm to society at large. It is somewhat different with immovable property which being of a permanent character, has a long history to support the title of the rightful owner. Criminal Law, therefore, provides to a greater extent for the protection of possession of movables and even protects the mere right to possession against dishonest conversion (Sections 403 and 408). In cases of immovable property Criminal Law attaches little importance to the mere right of possession which is left to the Civil Courts and protects possession only, and even that for the purpose of preventing in vast majority of cases breaches of the peace and to prevent insult, annoyance and intimidation to the person in possession, as such acts are from their very nature likely to lead to disturbances of the public peace. Whereas in the case of movable property the gist of the offence is the deprivation of possession, in the case of immovable property the mere deprivation of possession or attempt at such deprivation is not sufficient to constitute an offence.

The provisions of the Code relating to possession of property fall into two classes. First, and by far the most important are those that are intended to punish, and thereby to prevent disturbances of possession. Then there are those special cases in which it is not the object of the law to protect possession, but punishment is provided for being merely in possession of certain things. Being in possession, is not an act, but a mere legal status. I have already told you that this departure from the ordinary principle that a crime must be an act or an omission, is justified either as a matter of caution to prevent future attempts or preparations to commit particular offences of a serious character or to punish an antecedent criminal act which possession in such cases implies. To the first class belongs a very large number of offences against property, such as theft, robbery, dacoity and offences involving trespass on immovable property. To the second class belong cases of possession of instruments for counterfeiting coins (Section 235), Government stamps (Section 256), trade marks (Section 485), currency notes (Section 489D) and possession of counterfeit coins (Sections 242, 243, 252, 253), of Government stamps (Section 259), of false weights and measures (Section 266), of obscene books (Section 293), counterfeit seals (Section 473), false currency notes (Section 489 C), etc. These and connected offences, you will observe, occupy a large part of the Code. There are also various special acts such as the Arms Act, the Opium Act, the Excise Act which deal with similar matters.

Offences relating to possession of immovable property are not so numerous as those relating to goods, and therefore, in Criminal Law more importance attaches to the latter than to the former, though the order is reversed when we come to civil law. The question of possession of immovable property generally arises in connection with offences relating to trespass on land (Section 441). It arises though indirectly in connection with land riots, the prevalence of which is a normal condition of life in Bengal, in which often the common object charged is 'to enforce possession of land.' It also arises in connection with the various preventive measures under the Criminal Procedure Code regarding disputes concerning immovable property, and in connection with questions of restitution dealt with at the end of that Code.

This enumeration is far from being exhaustive, but is sufficient to indicate the importance of the subject. Naturally this difference in the object of the legislature in the two classes of cases referred to above leads to different considerations in fixing upon the meaning to be attached to the word 'possession' for these two wholly divergent purposes. The conditions necessary to constitute possession in the two cases are therefore not always the same.

Possession not explained in the Code.

"Possession" is not defined in the Code. Any definition, however carefully guarded, could not possibly be exhaustive of the various phases of the question, and a definition that was incomplete or arbitrary would have been worse than useless. In ninety-nine cases out of a hundred possession as understood by the lawyer is not different from possession as understood by the man in the street. In the one case that may present any difficulty, the question has to be considered in the light of commonsense and the requirement of justice. An artificial definition, it may be apprehended, might have unnecessarily confused the issue in the ninety-nine cases which present no difficulty, and might have in the one case of difficulty rendered the line harsh and inlastic. "We believe it to be impossible," say the Law Commissioners in their Report, "to mark with precision by any words, the circumstances which constitute possession. It is easy to put cases about which no doubt whatever exists. and about which the language of the lawyers and of the multitude would be the same. It will hardly be doubted, for example, that a gentleman's watch lying on a table in his room, is in his possession, though it is not in his hand, and though he may not know whether it is on his writing-table or on his dressing table. As little will it be doubted that a watch which a gentleman lost a year ago on journey, and which he never heard of since, is not in his possession. It will not be doubted that when a person gives a dinner, his silver forks, while in the hands of his guests, are still in his possession, and it will be as little doubted that his silver forks are not in his possession when he has deposited them with a pawn-broker as a pledge. But between these extreme cases lie many cases in which it is difficult to pronounce with confidence, either that property is or that it is not in a person's possession." The Law Commissioners add that they leave the question to the understanding of mankind in general. but they do not for reasons that are not convincing throw light on those cases of doubt and difficulty which the intelligence of the layman is not sufficient to solve without

Unsatisfactory state of the law.

the aid of the lawyer. The ordinary man understands actual physical possession, and he also has some elementary idea of possession falling short of actual physical control. He understands that his watch in his pocket is in his possession, but does he understand whether he is still in possession when he has dropped it into the Ganges? He understands that so long as his watch is in the custody of his servant it is in his possession, but does he understand who is in possession when it is in the course of transit? It is clear that the law recognises not only *de facto* possession, but also constructive or legal possession which latter it is often difficult to distinguish from the mere right to possession.

The situation has been aggravated by the fact that the word "possession" must be given different meanings in different connections, otherwise grave hardships and injustice would follow which could not have been in the contemplation of the legislature.

To illustrate my meaning, *A* is and he knows he is, in possession of the house which he is actually occupying, but does he know that he is not in possession of the same house even when he is occupying it if *B* had the possession the day before, and *A* had gained access into the house by deceiving the servant in charge? It has been held that *B* has the right in such a case of turning *A* out with force in defence of his so-called possession.

In these cases the real question is not whether possession in the common acceptation of the term is with A or *B* though we put in it that form, but the real question is whether as a matter of policy it is not desirable to ignore the wrongful though actual possession of the trespasser, and proceed on the footing that though the *de facto* possession of *B* was lost, by a legal fiction he still continues in possession and is entitled to defend it by force. The question of policy was a question for the legislature, but instead of expressly enunciating that policy which would have been the more straightforward course they have left it to those charged with the administration of justice to give such an extended meaning to the term 'possession' as would make the law consonant with justice and requirements of society, and yet it is claimed that possession as used in the Code is not different from possession as understood by the man in the street. It is this policy of the legislature that is responsible for the introduction of the doctrine of constructive possession in criminal law with all the difficulties and complexities attendant on it. These difficulties could have been avoided if a fixed meaning had been assigned to the word "possession."

The same difficulty arises in construing other Acts of the legislature.

Take another case—*A* has a ring in one of his secret drawers; even without his knowledge of its existence, he is in possession, but if instead of a ring it were a piece of contraband opium he could not be held guilty of being in possession within the meaning of the Opium Act without proof of knowledge of its existence.

Possession explained

Though 'possession' is not defined, we get a glimpse of the underlying idea from the illustrations some of which are not always very illumining. I may here observe parenthetically that the scheme of explaining statutes by illustrations was novel, and in the words of Sir Lawrence Peel " many are useless, offering light in light day ; some darken whilst they attempt to give light ; some do not throw the light where the darkness prevails ; some are *ignes fatui* to mislead ; some are trivial and bordering even on the ludicrous, and a very few are open to more serious objections." Most of these illustrations will be found under the definition of theft in Section 378. These may be checked by a reference to illustrations to Sections 403 and 408. You may take it that if a case is covered by the illustrations to Section 403 or Section 405, in that case the person against whom the offence is committed is not in possession. Cases of criminal misappropriation are those in which the person in possession has lost his possession unintentionally or by an act of removal not amounting to an offence and this is followed by dishonest misappropriation or conversion ; and cases of criminal breach of trust are those in which possession is intentionally delivered to another who abuses the trust by similar misappropriation or conversion. In both the cases the owner is not in possession, but if he were, the case would be one of theft and not of criminal breach of trust or of criminal misappropriation.

It is worthy of notice that although the definition of theft has been explained by many illustrations which throw light on the conception of the possession of movable property under the Code, no such illustrations are to be found under the definition of criminal trespass which would have thrown light on the conception of possession of immovable property. The explanation may be found in the relative unimportance of the question to which I have already referred. The question of possession in regard to immovable property, though less important, is however much more difficult and complex than that regarding movable property.

Left unfettered by any rigid definition we are free in the investigation of the question to consider it in the light of common sense and try to avoid on the one hand any interpretation that would result in the condonation of acts that ought to be punished, or would on the other hand bring within the meshes of the criminal law acts the punishment of which would shock the conscience of an ordinary man. Having regard to the nebulous state of the law it would be satisfactory to analyse our ideas and formulate them, and then test them by reference to concrete cases and in the light of judicial decisions.

In Stephen's Digest "possession" of movables is thus explained :—" A movable thing is said to be in the possession of a person when he is so situated with respect to it, that he has the power to deal with it as owner to the exclusion of all other persons, and *when the circumstances are such that he may be presumed to intend to do so in the case of need.*" The qualifications mentioned in the words which I have *italicised* may be open to doubt, but to this I shall revert later. You will, in connection with this definition, bear in mind that the conception of possession of movables upon which the Criminal Laws of England are founded is materially different from that of the

Indian Penal Code. One reason is, that larceny under the English law is a more comprehensive term than theft of the Indian Penal Code. Cases falling within the definition of criminal misappropriation in the Code are within the definition of larceny by an extension of the meaning of the word "possession" and by insisting on the condition that possession in order to be legal must also be rightful. This difference in the conception of possession between the English common law and the Indian Penal Code will fully appear from a study of a few typicial English decisions on which are based some of Sir Fitzjames Stephen's illustrations, whereby he tries to elucidate the meaning of possession as defined by him.

Larceny and Theft.

In a case in which a Bureau was delivered for repairs to a carpenter the latter discovered money in a secret drawer, the existence of which the owner was not aware and then converted it to his own use; the question arose whether upon the facts stated there was felonious taking. Lord Eldon found the question so difficult that he did not trust himself to say anything until he had seen all the cases and consulted several of the Judges. Afterwards in delivering judgment the Lord Chancellor observed:—"To constitute felony there must of necessity be a felonious taking. Breach of Trust will not do. But from all the cases in *Hawkins* there is no doubt, this Bureau being delivered to the Defendant for no other purpose than repair, if he broke open any part, which it was not necessary to touch for the purpose of repair, but with an intention to take and appropriate to his own use what he should find, that is a felonious taking within the principle of all the modern cases; as not being warranted by the purpose, for which it was delivered. If a Pocket Book containing Bank Notes was left in the Pocket of a Coat sent to be amended, and the tailor took the Pocket Book, there is not the least doubt, that is a Felony. So, if the Pocket Book was left in a Hackney Coach, if ten people were in the Coach in the course of the day, and the Coachman did not know to which of them it belonged, he acquires it by finding it certainly, but not being trusted with it for the purpose of opening it; that is a Felony according to the modern Cases. There is a vast number of other Cases. Those with whom I have conversed upon this point, who are of very high authority, have no doubt upon it." *Cartwright* v. *Green* (VIII Ves. 405).

The same view was taken in *Merry* v. *Green* (1841, 7 M. & W. 623) of which the facts were shortly these: A person purchased, at a public auction, a Bureau in which he afterwards discovered in a secret drawer, a purse containing money, which he appropriated to his own use. At the time of the sale no person knew that the Bureau contained anything whatever: Tindal C.J. in his summing up told the Jury that as the property had been delivered to the plaintiff as the purchaser, in his opinion there was no felonious taking, but on a rule obtained to set aside the verdict it was held that if the buyer had express notice that the Bureau alone, and not its contents, if any, was sold to him; or if he had no reason to believe that anything more than the Bureau itself was sold, the abstraction of the money was a felonious taking, and he was guilty of larceny in appropriating it to his own use. This was a case of some doubt, but there was no doubt that so long as the Bureau was in possession of the owner, he was in possession of the purse although he was not aware of its existence. The doubt which the Lord Chief Justice felt was whether when the Bureau was delivered to the purchaser such delivery had not the effect of putting the buyer in possession of the purse also. Having regard to the definition of Criminal Misappropriation the question, if it had arisen in India, would have been dealt with differently.

Baron Parke in delivering the judgment of the Court said :—

"It was contended that there was a delivery of the Secretary, and the money in it, to the plaintiff as his own property, which gave him a lawful possession, and that his subsequent misappropriation did not constitute a felony. But it seems to us, that though there was a delivery of the *Secretary*, and a lawful property in it thereby vested in the plaintiff there was no delivery as to give a lawful possession of the *purse and money*. The vendor had no intention to deliver it, nor the vendee to receive it ; both were ingorant of its existence : and when the plaintiff discovered that there was a secret drawer containing the purse and money, it was a simple case of finding, and the law applicable to all cases of finding applies to this.

The old rule, that " if one lose his goods and another find them though he convert them *animo furandi* to his own use, it is no larceny," has undergone in more recent times some limitations: one is, that if the finder knows who the owner of the lost chattel is, or if, from any mark upon it, or the circumstances under which it is found, the owner could be reasonably ascertained, then the fraudulent conversion, *animo furandi*, constitututes a larceny. The learned Judge then quoted with approval the decision of Lord Eldon to which I have already referred. This case also if it had arisen under the Indian Penal Code would have been dealt with under Section 403, and on the footing that the true owner had lost his possession.

In *R.* v. *Thompson* (1862, L. & C. 225) a stranger had placed himself near a lady who wanted to purchase a ticket and was entrusted by her with money for that purpose The prisoner received the sove:eign but instead of applying for a ticket attempted to run away. The learned Judges all agreed that this was a case of larceny. Wightman J. said: "The true doctrine is that, if the owner delivers a chattel to another for a temporary purpose, and himself continues present the whole time, that other has only the custody of the chattel, and not the possession of it, and, if he converts it to his own use, may be convicted of larceny at common law." Under the Penal Code the offence would have been one of cheating. It would be difficult to hold that even after delivery of the money the owner continued *in possession*.

Thus the English cases on the question of possession are not safe guides for determining possession under the Penal Code and the absence of any light from the Code itself and the dubious light thrown by the English decisions make the study of the subject a difficult one. We will be on safe ground if in the consideration of the question, we attach to the word "Possession," the sense in which it is commonly understood and give it such extension of meaning as is necessary to make the existing law effective for securing peaceful enjoyment of property.

With these preliminary remarks I shall proceed to examine our ideas of possession. I have told you that possession of movable property differs in some respects from the possession of immovable property. It would, therefore, be convenient to deal with the possession of movables first. Idea of possession analysed.

When we speak of possession we have in mind a thing to be possessed, a person in possession and a particular time to which possession is referable. In some cases, though not always within the range of vision, appears another person who contests that possession. Where we have not to count with this last factor the matter becomes really simple. Movables.

The essential idea of possession is control, actual or potential. When it is actual physical control no doubt or difficulty arises. A watch which is in my pocket or a horse which I am riding are both in my posses-ion. The idea is most elementary and requires no discussion, but even the layman's view of possession is not confined to this elementary idea but extends beyond this, and comprises the equally elementary idea that even where the actual physical control does not exist if a person is so situated in regard to a thing that he can obtain actual physical control of it, he is in possession. No one doubts that the money in his chest, the watch in his box, the furniture in his house or the horse in his stable are in his possession. It is equally clear that mere permissive use or occupation is not possession. A guest sitting by me at the dinner-table is not in possession of the chair or of the knives and forks he is using or of the plates out of which he is eating. He has only the custody of the things for the time being and nothing more. So also the servants in charge of the goods. Mere custody is not possession.

So far the cases present no difficulty and the question would appear to be purely a question of fact, but difficulty arises in determining in cases of more complex nature whether the facts proved regarding the relation between a given possessor and a given thing suffice to establish the control necessary to establish possession. The power of control varies in degree and the question of difficulty that arises is, where actual physical control is wanting, whether the extent of a person's power of control is such in a particular case as to enable us to attribute possession to him or whether the impediment in the way of the exercise of the power is such as to negative such possession, and where there is another party claiming similar possession who has the better or more effective control.

The power of control is not the mere physical power, but it is also the legal power which is greater than the mere physical power backed as it is by the power of State, and control is established in the person having the legal right so long as complete physical control has not passed to another. A child is playing in a park. He has put down his toy and is standing at some distance from it. A powerful ruffian is close by and has the intention to assume control. The latter is undoubtedly in a better position to control, but suppose there is a stanger standing by more powerful than the ruffian, who in a struggle between the child and the ruffian would naturally take up the side of the child, you will have no difficulty in saying who has the better control. This third party who is stronger than the ruffian can and will, if necessary, overpower him to secure the control of the child. This third party, though he may not be always physically present, represents the power of the State, be it in the shape of the policeman or the magistrate, and the question of control between the child and the ruffian cannot be decided without considering what side this third party will take. Thus the question of right and legal possession become inseparable from the consideration of the question.

Any impediment, however great, not arising from any adverse claim set up by another as a rule, does not matter at any rate so long as there is the power to exclude others from obtaining the control, nor is this power to control at will affected by distance or by the time necessary to obtain it.

A person living in London may have a house in Calcutta in which he has left his furniture and has locked the gate; neither the distance nor the time affect the question of his possession.

I drop my ring into a tank which belongs to me. It may not be possible to find the ring at all by ordinary efforts, but as I have the power of exclusion, possession is with me in spite of all the difficulties of control, but if the tank belongs to another and he prevents me from going into it, then the possession of the ring is no longer with me but it has passed to the owner of the tank. If, however, I drop my ring into the Ganges and am looking for it, I am in possession, but when I have abandoned the idea of recovering it and have come back from the spot, I cease to be in possession.

The power of control is very often dependent on the legal right to control and exclude others, and a person who has the legal right is deemed to have the control so long as the control has not passed to some one else or the person having the right to control has not abandoned the idea of such control. Such abandonment may be presumed from circumstances. If I lose a ring in the streets of Calcutta not knowing where I have dropped it, I cannot say I am in possession of the ring. But if I drop a rupee and hearing the noise as it falls turn round to pick it up and another picks it up and runs away, he is guilty of theft.

A is the owner of a horse which has strayed from the stable and is grazing at some distance from *A's* house, *A* is still in possession. But if it has been lost in the Himalayas and cannot be recovered with ordinary efforts or if *A* has given up the idea of recovering it and has acquiesced in the loss of possession, he is no longer in possession. Under such circumstances it cannot be said that

A has either the ability to control the animal or ability to exclude others from taking possession of it.

The question of abandonment is a question of intention, but intention is not an essential idea in all cases of possession. For instance, to establish the power of control, it is not necessary that the person who has the power should be aware of the existence of the thing with reference to which the power is claimed. Such ignorance excludes the operation of intention. This may be illustrated by the case of *Elwes* v. *Brigg Gas Co.* (33 Ch. D. 562). That was a case in which a free-holder gave a lease reserving mines, minerals and water-courses. The lessee's servants in excavating for foundations discovered a pre-historic boat or rather a 'dug-out' canoe which had been under the earth for many centuries. The canoe was removed. It was held that the free-holder had the prior right to possession and had not divested himself of it by granting the possession and use of the soil for a special purpose. If the free-holder had been in possession of the land here could be no doubt that he was also in actual possession of the canoe, notwithstanding the fact that he was not aware of its existence. Take another instance of the same kind. A person is in possession of a tank. There may be pearls in that tank of which he is not be aware, he is in possession of the pearls: and any one removing them from the tank will be guilty of theft. In cases of this kind the power to control is established by the power of exclusion. The owner of the tank has the right and therefore the power to exclude others from entering it. In the same way if something is washed on my land by the sea, possession vests in me, and this would be so even if the title in the thing so washed is established in some one else. If a strong wind blows and cast iron sheets from my neighbour's shed into my land, and I remove or appropriate them, that would be criminal misappropriation but not theft.

Right of exclusion.

The right of exclusion generally arises from the ownership of land or buildings, but there may be cases where the owner by his own conduct may have waived the right, and in such a case possession cannot be established by mere ownership of the house or land. In *Bridges* v. *Hawkesworth* (21 L. J. Q. B. 75) a parcel of Bank-notes was left in a shop by a customer. Another customer picked it up before the owner of the shop knew anything about it. The finder made over the parcel to the shop-keeeper for the purpose of ascertaining the true owner, but the true owner could not be found. Three years later when all hopes of discovering the real owner had been abandoned the finder asked the shop-keeper for return of the notes but he refused. It was held that the finder was entitled to recover. In this case the title of the finder depended entirely on his possession, and that question depended on whether the possession of the parcel was with the shop-keeper before it was picked up, and it was held that the notes never were in custody of the shop-keeper nor within the protection of his house before they were found, as they would have been, had they been intentionally deposited there. The general proposition is supposed to be, that things left in any part of a building pass at once into the legal possession of the occupier, but the Court found neither authority nor reason for any such rule. I venture to think the rule of law is unexceptional, but the rule could not be applied to that case, because the owner by allowing customers to enter the shop without any restriction waived the right of exclusion on which the general proposition is based. A distinction has been made between cases of this kind and cases where the owner had deliberately deposited a thing in a part of the shop and had forgotten to take it back. It has been held that in such a case possession and a qualified right to possession is acquired by the shop-keeper and the first person who picks it up is not a real finder. Cases of this kind have been treated as cases of bailment without a contract. (Pollock and Wright, p. 39).

The general right of the finder to any article which has been lost as against all the world except the true owner was established in the case of *Armory* v. *Delamire*. His possession establishes his title except against the real owner.

Animals

Different considerations arise in cases of living animals. My horse is in my possession not only so long as it is in my stable but continues in my possession even when it has entered the compound of my neighbour or when it is grazing in my neighbour's field; and this possession continues so long as I have not abandoned the idea of bringing it back. The presumption is that all tame animals have what is called the *animus revertendi*, but when this cannot be attributed, possession does not continue. For instance, the fish in my tank is out of my possession as soon as it has left the tank, and so also a wild animal that I have captured, as soon as it has gone out of my control and has lapsed into a state of nature. In the case of wild animals the right of property is established by capture. Mere pursuit is not enough. If I shoot a bird and it falls into my neighbour's compound and he takes possession of it, he is guilty neither of theft nor of criminal misappropriation. His title is established by his possession as I had no possession at any time.

Physical possession must be exclusive.

Physical possession must be exclusive or it is nothing. If I throw away a piece of cloth outside my house and two persons catch it by the two ends and struggle for it, possession is not established in either until one of them has got it exclusively, and before he has done so and so long as the struggle goes on if a third party snatches it away, he cannot be guilty of theft.

Title deeds.

The possession of means whereby control can be obtained is sometimes equivalent to possession. This is undoubtedly so for the purpose of the possession which law would protect. For instance, the possession of railway receipts whereby delivery can be obtained may amount to actual possession, and so also the possession of the keys of a godown in which goods have been locked up. When I have locked up my box and having kept the key with me sent it for repairs or sent it to a pawnbroker without intending to pawn the contents, the box is no doubt in the possession of the bailee, but contents of the box are in my possession so long as the key is with me. The question of any large extension of the doctrine of construc-

Railway receipt.

tive possession in criminal cases is not free from difficulty, and such extension becomes the more objectionable when the question arises for determination not for the purpose of protecting possession but for purposes of punishing it. The decisions of the Calcutta High Court on this point are somewhat conflicting. In the case of *Kasi Nath Bania* v. *The Emperor* (9 C. W. N. 719) Henderson and Geidt JJ. held that where a railway receipt for a parcel of opium was found locked up in accused's box under circumstances which show that he was aware of the contents of the parcel, the possession of the receipt amounted to a possession of the opium within the meaning of Section 9 of the Opium Act. It was observed that though the accused was not in actual or physical possession, it was in his potential possession. In the case of *Ashruf Ali* v. *The King-Emperor* (14 C. W. N. 233) the correctness of this decision was doubted and Jenkins C.J. observed that if unfettered by authority he would have been disposed to hold that there was no possession. In the still later case of *Kali Charan Mookerjee* v. *King-Emperor* (18 C. W. N. 309), Mukerjee and Beachcroft JJ. observed that the doctrine of constructive possession must be very cautiously applied, specially in the department of criminal jurisprudence. The same question came up for consideration in the case of *Fong Kun (Khun) Chinaman* v. *King-Emperor* (23 C. W. N. 671) but not decided. If it be held that the possession of a railway receipt is possession of the goods, it would be necessary to avoid hardships to qualify the doctrine by insisting that the possessor of the receipt must be aware that the receipt in his possession is in respect of a particular article. This would unnecessarily complicate the question of possession which ordinarily does not involve such knowledge. This question was discussed in *Queen* v. *Hill* (1 Den C. C. R. 453 1849) in which a different view was taken. In that case the facts were these: *A* and *B* stole some fowls. *A* sent them by coach in a hamper without a direction to *Birmingham* stating that a person would call there for them. *C*, wife of *A*, called, and on the hamper being shown to her claimed it. It was not delivered to her, and she was apprehended. It was held that on these facts she was wrongly convicted of feloniously receiving. "Whoever," said the learned Judges, "had possession of the fowls at the coach office, when the prisoner claimed to receive them, never parted with the possession, and the prisoner was immediately taken into custody. The prisoner by claiming to receive the fowls, which never were actually, or potentially in her possession, never in fact or law received them, therefore the conviction was wrong."

Besides cases in which one person takes actual physical control of a thing belonging to another by force or fraud, there are various ways by which possession legally passes from one person to another. It passes by a voluntary act of the party in possession and sometimes by coercive legal process. The former is called delivery of possession. Delivery of possession may be effected by the possessor actually handing over the goods to another person, but very often possession passes by any

Delivery of possession.

act showing an intention to part with possession. In such cases the delivery of indices of title, such as railway receipts, etc., or the delivery of the key by which the transferee can obtain control over the goods is sufficient to put an end to the possession of the one and establish the possession of the other.

Goods in transit.

I think in all such cases it would simplify matters if it be held that when goods are in transit through common carriers, possession vests with the common carriers, and the consignee does not come into possession until the goods are actually delivered to him.

The possession by a person's wife, clerk or servant, is his possession when such possession is held on his account. This is laid down in Section 27 of the Code. The section is not exhaustive of all cases in which one has the custody and another has the possession. The case will not be different if custody instead of being with the servant or wife is with the son or any other dependent member of a family.

Custody and Possession.

The distinction in English law between custody and possession is not expressly recognised in the Indian Penal Code. In a note appended to his Digest, Sir James Stephen, after explaining what possession means, points out that the custody of a servant or person in a similar position does not exclude the possession by another, but differs from it in the presumable intention of the custodian to act under the orders of the possessor with reference to the thing possessed, and to give it up to him if he requires it. Although the distinction between custody and possession is not expressly made in the Code, the difference between the two has been recognised in Section 27, to which I have already referred. The distinction is also indicated in the following illustrations to Section 378 :—

(*d*) *A* being *Z's* servant, and entrusted by *Z* with the care of *Z's* plate, dishonestly runs away with the plate, without *Z's* consent. *A* has committed theft.

(*e*) *Z*, going on a journey, entrusts his plate to *A*, the keeper of a warehouse, till *Z* shall return, *A* carries the plate to a goldsmith and sells it. Here the plate was not in *Z's* possession. It could not, therefore, be taken out Z's possession and *A* has not committed theft, though he may have committed criminal breach of trust.

Servant and Bailee. The possession of a servant is different from the possession of a bailee inasmuch as the servant is bound at the will and pleasure of his master to make over to him any article which the master may have entrusted, whereas a bailee is not so bound, and this makes the distinction between the two cases illustrated above. When one has pledged his ring with a pawnbroker it cannot be said that he is still in possession. The distinction lies in the obvious difference in the degree of control that the owner has over property in possession of a servant and of a bailee. The possession of both is qualified possession. One is more precarious than the other. Whereas in the case of a servant, wife or any other dependent the control is so precarious that it may be terminated at the will of the owner at any time, it is different with a bailee. Therefore, where possession, is qualified and subject to conditions, and it is not wholly within the will of the owner to resume control at his will, the law attributes possession not to the owner but to the bailee. Whether it was necessary to retain the distinction between custody and possession is doubtful. Perhaps criminal breach of trust sounds more respectable, but the degree of criminality is much the same, and there is little to choose between one who commits theft and another who is guilty of criminal breach of trust. However, the distinction has been made and we must keep that in mind.

A "bailment" is defined in Section 148 of the Contract Act as the "delivery of goods by one person to another for some purpose, upon a contract that they shall, when the purpose is accomplished be returned or otherwise disposed of according to the discretions of the person delivering them." I have already pointed out that in exceptional cases there may be a bailment without a contract.

Possession of immovable property.

The principles governing possession of immovable property are not different from those that apply to possession of movables. The elementary ideas are the same—power of control and exclusion. From the very nature of things there is less room for actual physical control in the case of the former specially where large tracts are concerned, and there is therefore in those cases greater necessity for the application of the doctrine of constructive possession, and yet it may not be necessary in applying the doctrine to criminal cases to extend it very far, for there is in cases of property of this class little or no danger in leaving the remedy to the Civil Courts. But still it would obviously be

Constructive possession.

very inconvenient to leave all cases of this nature to the Civil Courts. If a man has a house in which he lives and some one during his temporary absence occupies it, it would lead to serious inconvenience and hold out a premium to people of a particular class to cause disturbances of the peace if Criminal Courts decline to deal with them. There can be little doubt that the dread of punishment is a more effective check on wrongs than the dread of having to make reparation. But where a dispute relates to a plot of agricultural land for instance with no crops on it the necessity for the interference of Criminal Courts is not so clear. In such cases the civil remedy which includes mesne profits should ordinarily be ample, and as a rule in such cases if a plea of *bona fides* is established there is no conviction. The policy of the Code may be gathered from the fact that a trespass on immovable property to be indictable must be with the intention of committing an offence or causing insult, annoyance or intimidation to the party in possession.

Waste land.

If a person has an extensive piece of waste land over which he is exercising no actual acts of possession, a trespass on such land would not necessarily indicate such an intention, whereas such an intention would naturally be attributed to cases of trespass on land or buildings in actual occupation of another at the time of the trespass. Where trespass is committed on land with crops or on jungle land containing valuable trees,

Cultivated land.

the circumstances may be such as to give rise to the inference that there was an intention to commit an offence, and the trespass would presumably be a criminal trespass.

In order to establish possession over immovable property proof of actual physical occupation at a particular moment is seldom available except where the property is a house or building or land forming the compound of a house. The question of constructive possession was fully discussed in the Full Bench case of the Calcutta High Court in *Mahomed Ali Khan* v. *Khaja Aldul Gunny* (9 Cal. 744), and I make no apology in reproducing some observations contained in the judgment of the learned Judge :

Possession not necessarily actual user.

"But possession is not necessarily the same thing as actual user. The nature of the possession to be looked for, and the evidence of its continuance, must depend upon the character and condition of the land in dispute. Land is often either permanently or temporarily incapable of actual enjoyment in any of the customary modes as by residence or tillage or receipts of a settled rent. It may be incapable of any beneficial use, as in the case of land covered with sand by an inundation ; it may produce some profit, bu trifling in amount, and only of occasional occurrence as is often the case with jungle land. In such cases it would be unreasonable to look for the same evidence of possession as in the case of a house or a cultivated field. All that can be required is that the plaintiff should show such acts of ownership as are natural under the existing condition of the land, and in such cases, when he has done this, his possession is presumed to continue as long as the state of the land remains unchanged, unless he is shown to have been dispossessed.

Submerged land.

"Lands again may by natural causes be placed wholly out of reach of their owner, as in the case of diluvion by a river. In such a case, if the plaintiff shows his possession down to the time of the diluvion, his possession is presumed to continue as long as the lands continue to be submerged. *Kally Churn Sahoo* v. *Secretary of State for India* (I. L. R., 6 Cal. 725); *Mono Mohun Ghose* v. *Mothura Mohun Roy* (I. L. R., 7 Cal. 225).

"When lands which have been in such a condition as to be incapable of enjoyment in the ordinary modes are reclaimed and brought under cultivation, the change is in many instances gradual and difficult of observation while in progress. Diluviated land may take years to reform. Jungle land is often brought under cultivation furtively by squatters clearing a patch here and a patch there at irregular intervals of time. So that it may be a matter of extreme difficulty to prove as to any piece of land, the exact date at which its condition became altered. And as the plaintiff who has complied with the conditions we have indicated, is in the absence of dispossession presumed to continue in possession as long as the state of the land remains unchanged, it is essential to inquire on whom the burden of proof of the date of the change lies.

"The true rule appears to us to be this: That where land has been shown to have been in a condition unfitting it for actual enjoyment in the usual modes at such a time, and under such circumstances that that state naturally would, and probably did, continue till within twelve years before suit, it may properly be presumed that it did so continue, and that the plaintiff's possession continued also, until the contrary is shown. This presumption seems to us to be reasonable in itself, and in accordance with the legal principles now embodied in Section 114 of the Evidence Act."

A similar view was taken by the Privy Council in the case of *Secretary of State* v. *Krishnomoni* (29 Cal. 518), in which their Lordships held that when land in the possession of a trespasser diluviates, the moment it does so the possession of the trespasser ceases and the possession is restored to the rightful owner.

These and other cases show how far the doctrine of constructive possession has been carried in civil law. In criminal law, although we cannot wholly ignore such possession, you will be convinced that it is not necessary to go the whole length of that doctrine. A dividing line has to be found. The relative situation of the possessor and the thing possessed and the reasonableness of the inference that the trespass was likely to cause annoyance, insult or intimidation determines this line when it arises in connection with the excuse of the right of private defence of property.

India is an agricultural country and in dealing with the question of possession regarding agricultural lands the test generally adopted, and I may say quite rightly, is who grew the crops, or if the question arises at a time when there are no crops on the land, then the question is asked who grew the last crop or ploughed the land. In large number of cases of mischief (Section 426) for cutting and removing paddy the same question arises daily for the consideration of

Courts in Bengal and dealt with in the same way.

Joint owners.

Among joint owners of immovable property possession of one is possession of the other. A co-sharer is in actual physical possession for himself to the extent of his share only and has possession of the rest for the other co-sharers; but this is so only so long as he has not signified his intention to hold to the exclusion of the other sharers. It often happens that a co-sharer for the more useful enjoyment of his property holds exclusive possession of a part of the joint property. In such a case if the other co-owner disturbs his possession he is guilty of trespass, but so long as such exclusive possession is not asserted and acquiesced in possession will be deemed to be the possession of all the owners.

Possession of part.

Possession of a part often amounts to a possession of the whole, but this is more a question of fact than of law. As observed by Lord Blackburn in *Lord Advocate* v. *Lord Blantyre* (L. R. 4 Ap. Cas. 770—791). "Every act shown to have been done on any part of that tract by the barons or their agents which was not lawful, unless the barons were owners of that spot on which it was done, is evidence that they were in possession as owners of that spot on which it was done. No one such act is conclusive, and the weight of each act as evidence depends on the circumstances; one very important circumstance as to the weight being, whether the act was such and so done that those who were interested in disputing the ownership would be aware of it. And all that tends to prove possession as owners of parts of the tract tends to prove ownership of the whole tract; provided there is such a common character of locality as would raise a reasonable inference that if the barons possessed one part as owners they possessed the whole, the weight depending on the nature of the tract, what kind of possession could be had of it, and what the kind of possession proved was." But as pointed out by Macpherson and Banerjee JJ. in *Mohini Mohun Roy* v. *Promoda Nath Roy* (24 Cal. 256) "the rule operates with full force only in favour of the rightful owner and should be applied with caution and reservation if at all in favour of a wrong-doer for the reason among others that the right to the whole which makes the possession of a part equivalent to the possession of the whole, and forms the connecting link between the whole and the part in the one case is wanting in the other." The application of the doctrine is, however, largely dependent on the nature of the property, its situation and the intention with which only the part is possessed, and the opportunity which the possession of the part gives to the possessor of such part to obtain control over the whole. If, for instance, *A* has a piece of waste land on three sides of which are the lands of *B*, and *A's* only means of access is on one side and that side is occupied by *B* which has the effect of blocking *A's* passage into the land that would amount to complete ouster of *A*; but on the other hand if there is a piece of waste land belonging to *A* between the lands of *A* and *B*, and *B* encroaches on a portion of the waste land adjacent to his own land, in such a case it cannot be inferred that *B's* intention was to assert possession of the whole, and even if it were, such an intention could have no effect inasmuch as the possession of the part did not render less effective the power of control which *A* had in respect of the rest of the land. As observed by Bramwell L.J. in *Coverdale* v. *Charlton* (4 Q. B. D. 104 ; 4 Ap. Cas. 798). "It is difficult to say that there is a *de facto* possession when there is no possession except of those parts of the land which are in actual possession and there is an interference with the enjoyment of the parts which are not in actual possession. If there were an enclosed field and a man had turned his cattle into it, and had locked the gate, he might well claim to have a *de facto* possession ; if there were an unenclosed common of a mile in length, and he turned (out) one horse on one end of the common, he could not be said to have a *de facto* possession of the whole length of the common."

The possession of the rightful owner is not affected by casual or secret acts of trespass as was observed by their Lordships of the Judicial Committee in *Radhamoni Debi* v. *The Collector of Khulna* (I. L. R., 27 Cal. 943) "in order to prove title to land by adverse possession it is not sufficient to show that some acts of possession have been done for the possession required, must be adequate in continuity, in publicity and in extent, to show that it is possession adverse to the competitor."

For a fuller study of the subject I would refer you to Pollock and Wright's Essay on Possession. Much of what I have said in the course of the discussion may not receive support from reported decisions or recognised text books. As observed by Lord Loreburn in *Glasgow Corporation* v.

Lorimer (L.R., A.C. 1911, p. 209) "Decided cases are chiefly valuable when they establish a principle, where they do not establish a principle but merely record the application of a principle to a particular set of facts they may be instructive as to the point of view from which the Judge regards the facts, but they are of little importance from any other point of view." And I have purposely avoided overloading the subject by referring to them too often. My object has been to place before you the various aspects of the question to enable you intelligently to examine it in all its bearings, and I shall be quite content if I have to any extent succeeded in my efforts.

LECTURE XII.

Right of Private Defence.

Preliminary. I now come to deal with the provisions of the Indian Penal Code relating to the right of private defence of person and property. The extreme frequency of riots in India, specially in Bengal, has kept the subject prominently before the Courts with the result that it is rich in reported decisions and almost every aspect of the law has received judicial notice. It would not be possible within the scope of my lectures to deal adequately with the case-law that has gathered round the subject, and all that I propose to do is to discuss its main features and consider a few of the more important decisions bearing on it. The right is recognised in every system of law and the extent of the right varies in inverse ratio to the capacity of the State to protect the life and property of the subject. The reason is obvious. This duty is primarily the duty of the State. But no State, no matter how large its resources, can afford to depute a policeman to dog the steps of every *budmash* in the country or to be present at every riot or affray. This necessary limitation on the resources of the State has given to the subject *pro tanto* the right to take the law into his own hands and to provide for his own safety. The right of private defence must, therefore, be greater in extent among the turbulent population of the Frontier Provinces than in the rest of India, and even greater in the interior of Bengal than in the town of Calcutta, where you get a policeman to come to your help at every turn of the road.

As observed by Holloway J. in a Madras case "the natural tendency of the law of all civilized States is to restrict within constantly narrowing limits the right of self-help, and it is certain that no other principle can be safely applied to a country (like this)."

The peculiar policy of the Law Commissioners apparently dictated by their experience of Bengal is thus stated in their report—

"It may be thought that we have allowed too great a latitude to the exercise of this right; and we are ourselves of opinion that if we had been framing laws for a bold and high spirited people, accustomed to take the law into their own hand, and to go beyond the line of moderation in repelling injury, it would have been fit to provide additional restrictions. In this country the danger is on the other side. The people are too little disposed to help themselves. The patience with which they submit to the cruel depredations of gang robbers and to trespass and mischief committed in the most outrageous manner by bands of ruffians, is one of the most remarkable, and at the same time, one of the most discouraging symptoms which the state of society in India presents to us. Under these circumstances we are desirous rather to rouse and encourage a manly spirit among the people than to multiply restrictions on the exercise of the right of self-defence. We are of opinion that all the evil which is likely to arise from the abuse of that right is far less serious than the evil which would arise from the execution of one person for overstepping what might appear to the courts to be the exact line of moderation in resisting a body of dacoits."

From what I have said it follows that there is no right of private defence where there is time to have recourse to the protection of the public authorities. The right is a right of defence both of person and property, not necessarily of one's own person and property, but also of the person and property of others. In this respect the English law was at one time narrower. According to that law, it would appear, that a man was justified in using force against an assailant or wrong-doer in the following cases: first, in defence of himself; secondly, in defence of his immediate kindred. (*Reg.* v. *Rose*, 15 Cox 540.) The later tendency has, however, been to widen the circle by including in it besides the first two classes any one else under a person's immediate protection (Foster 274). The circle is a gradually expanding one. But some restriction perhaps still exists in England. In America the law is that whatever one may do for himself he may do for another.

As to the right of private defence of property the value of property of all kinds depends on the security with which it can be enjoyed. In primitive days when there was no settled Government and Society had not properly organised itself, when might was right, the only law was—

> "That they should take who have the power,
> And they should keep who can."

With a settled Government and a vigilant police, property has gained in value and to the same extent the temptation to deprive others of their possession has become greater. The highly complicated machinery of the Indian Courts, the proverbial law's delays, the advantage which the law confers on a person in possession, in other words the advantage which a defendant always has over the plaintiff in a civil suit, all these furnish the strongest possible incentive to disturbances of public peace by attempts to obtain forcible possession.

Limits of the right.

The first thing to remember is that the right of private defence can under no circumstances justify anything which strictly is no defence but an offence. Therefore if, whilst defending yourself, you put your enemy to flight and then pursue him and inflict an injury on him, you are no longer on the defensive and cannot claim the right. However it may sometimes happen that an attack is the most effective way of making a defence. An attack in such a case is justifiable.

In the same way you cannot claim the right of private defence if you have yourself courted the attack. Nor can such a right be claimed by a person who deliberately joins in a riot and finds himself attacked and his life in danger. The law was laid down by Sir John Edge C.J. in an unreported case (*Queen* v. *Rupa*, in 20 All. 459) in the following terms :—" When a body of men are determined to vindicate their rights or supposed rights by unlawful force, and when they engage in a fight with men, who, on the other hand, are equally determined to vindicate by unlawful force their rights or supposed rights, no question of self-defence arises.

Neither side is trying to protect itself, but each side is trying to get the better of the other." This view was quoted with approval by Kershaw C.J. and Knox J. in *Queen Empress* v. *Prag Dutt* (20 All. 459). *See* also 7 W. R. Cr. 34. I have said that you cannot invoke the right of private defence against an attack that you have yourself courted. This, however, does not mean that there is any duty upon a man to protect himself by flight. "This is so far true that an assailed party cannot, unless driven to the wall, take his assailant's life. But as an elementary proposition it is not true that if I can evade an attack by flight, then I must fly to evade it. The fundamental principle is that right is not required to yield to wrong." (Wharton, Section 99).

"A person lawfully defending himself or his habitation is not bound to retreat or to give way to the aggressor before killing; but if the aggressor is captured or is retreating without offering resistance and is then killed, the person killing him is guilty of murder." (Halsbury IX, p. 587). The law is the same in India—" The learned Judge suggests that the first accused could have escaped further injury by resorting to less violence or running away. But this is placing a greater restriction on the right of private defence than the law requires." (*Alingal* v. *Emperor* 28 Mad. 454). "But a man," says Mayne, "is not bound to modulate his defence step by step, according to the attack, before there is reason to believe the attack is over. He is not obliged to retreat but may pursue his adversary till he finds himself out of danger, and if in the conflict between them he happens to kill, such killing is justifiable."

The law relating to the right of private defence is dealt with in Sections 96—106. Section 96 lays down the general proposition that nothing is an offence which is done in the exercise of the right of private defence. The other sections define the limits within which the right can be exercised, the persons against whom it can be exercised and the extent of injury that can be inflicted justifiably upon the person against whom the right avails.

Right of private defence.

Summary of the law.

Every person has the right to defend (*i*) his own body and the body of any other person against any offence affecting the human body; (*ii*) the property movable or immovable of himself or of any other person against theft, robbery, mischief, or criminal trespass or attempts to commit any of these offences. Section 97.

Section 97.

Dacoity is only an aggravated form of robbery and is therefore not expressly mentioned, but it was necessary to mention robbery as besides theft it includes extortion.

If an act is otherwise an offence the right of private defence arises against the author of the act, even though he is not punishable by reason of his personal incapacity to commit a crime or because he acts without the necessary *mens rea*. For instance, if a lunatic attacks you or runs away with your purse, or if a sane and adult person runs away with your purse believing that it is his own, your right of private defence is not affected thereby (Section 98).

Section 98.

Section 99 deals with a variety of questions, all of which are by no means connected and might have been conveniently split up into two or more sections. I shall take the different matters separately. First as regards the right of private defence against public servants, it follows from the provisions of Section 97 and independently of the
Section 99. provisions of Section 99, that so long as a public servant acts legally in the exercise of his official powers, there is no right of private defence for the simple reason that his act is not an offence. If his acts are wholly illegal, he is in the same position as any private individual and is not entitled to any special protection. The provisions of the 1st clause of Section 99 are intended to extend the protection to those acts of a public servant which are not strictly justifiable by law and yet not wholly unauthorised, if done in good faith under colour of his office, provided the act does not reasonably cause apprehension of death or grievous hurt.

The protection afforded to a public servant also extends to those who act under the direction of such public servant.

A person, however, is not deprived of the right of private defence against a public servant or against those acting under his direction, unless such person knows that the person against whom he is exercising the right is a public servant or is acting under the direction of a public servant. Explanations (1) and (2).

The law, however, does not require a person to submit to any act of a public servant which is not strictly legal if such act gives rise to an apprehension of death or of grievous hurt.

The rest of the section deals with two wholly distinct matters. It is first laid down that there is no right of private defence in cases in which there is time to have recourse to the protection of the public authorities. As I have already told you that the right of private defence is a right which the State hands over to the individual, because the State is not always able to give its protection in proper time, and it follows from this that where such timely help can be obtained no one should take the law into his own hands.

The next provision is that the right in no case extends to the infliction of more harm than it is necessary to inflict for the purpose of defence.

Sections 100, 101, 103 and 104 may be taken together. These relate to the extent of injury that may be inflicted on an assailant in the exercise of the right. Wherever the right exists it extends to the causing of any injury short of death necessary for the purpose of defence, but in certain special cases even the causing of death is justified. These special cases are— Sections 100, 101, 103 and 104.

(1) assaults which reasonably cause apprehension of death or grievous hurt or of rape or unnatural offence, kidnapping or abduction or wrongful confinement in particular circumstances ;

(2) robbery, house-breaking by night, mischief by fire to any building, tent or vessel used for purposes of dwelling or custody of property;

(3) theft, mischief or house-trespass under such circumstances as may reasonably cause the apprehension that

death or grievous hurt would be the consequences if the right of private defence is not exercised.

The first relates to the defence of person and (2) and (3) to defence of property.

Sections 102 and 105.

Sections 102 and 105 fix the time when the right commences and the time during which it continues. Section 102 provides that the right of private defence of the body commences as soon as a reasonable apprehension of danger to the body arises, even though the offence may not have been committed and continues as long as such apprehension continues. According to Section 105 the right of defence of property commences when a reasonable apprehension of danger to the property commences. Its continuance depends on the nature of the offence. In cases of theft it continues till the offender has effected his retreat with the property or either the assistance of public authorities is obtained, or the property has been recovered. In cases of robbery it continues as long as the offender causes or attempts to cause to any person death or hurt or wrongful restraint, or as long as the fear of instant death, hurt or of instant personal restraint continues. In cases of criminal trespass or mischief the right continues as long as the offender continues in the commission of criminal trespass or mischief.

In cases of house-breaking by night it continues as long as the house-trespass which has been begun by such house-breaking continues.

Section 106.

Section 106 lays down that where an assault causes apprehension of death the person so threatened may take the risk of doing any harm to an innocent person. The illustration shows the meaning.

A is attacked by a mob who attempt to murder him. He cannot effectually exercise his right of private defence without firing on the mob and he cannot fire without risk of harming young children who are mingled with the mob. *A* commits no offence if, by so firing, he harms any of the children.

The above is a summary of the law as is contained in the Code.

Before discussing the more controversial questions that have arisen in connection with the right of private defence, I should like to make a few observations on the law generally.

Defence of possession not of right.

An important question for consideration is what is meant by the words "the property of himself or of any other person." Does it mean property rightfully belonging to a person or property which is in his possession? There can be little doubt that it means the latter, for without possession no trespass on any movable property can amount to theft, robbery or mischief, and no trespass on immovable property could amount to criminal trespass. In a case in which a person had seized a cow with the object of impounding it and was attacked by the owner, Mr. Justice Seton-Karr held that the person who had seized the cow had the right to defend his possession under Section 101 of the Indian Penal Code. Here, there was only possession but no right of property. The cow belonged to the assailants and the person who seized the cow had nothing but possession to defend.

In this particular case the decision might have been equally based on the right of defence of person.

Where the rightful owner is not in possession but tries to obtain possession by illegal means be may, under certain circumstances, be guilty of the offences enumerated in Section 97, and even the wrongdoer in possession in such a case has the right to defend his possession against the rightful owner.

Burden of proof.

The right of private defence is a plea of avoidance and the burden of proof is on the person who sets up the right (Section 105, Evidence Act). But this does not mean that he must adduce evidence in support of the plea. He may if he chooses elicit facts upon cross examination of the witnesses for the prosecution to make good his defence. The right need not be specifically pleaded, but if it arises it must receive judicial notice—*Queen* v. *Sohan* (2 W. R. Cr. 59).

How pleaded

A somewhat different view was taken in *Jamsheer Sirdar* v. *Queen-Empress* (1 C. L. R. 62). It was observed: " It is obvious that, under the provisions of the Evidence Act, Section 105, an answer setting up the right of private defence, must be supported by evidence giving a full and true account of the transaction from which the charge against an accused person arises. No accused person can at the same time deny committing an act and justify it. The law does not admit of justification by putting forward hypothetical cases; it must be by proof of the aotual facts."

In *Queen-Empress* v. *Timmal* (21 All. 122), it was laid down that an accused person who at his trial has not pleaded the right of private defence, but has raised other pleas inconsistent with such a defence, cannot in appeal set up a case, founded upon the evidence taken at his trial, that he acted in the exercise of the right of private defence, neither is the Court competent to raise such a plea on behalf of the appellant.

But in the more recent cases both in Calcutta and Allahabad the decision in *Queen* v. *Sohan* has been followed. In the Full Bench case *King-Emperor* v. *Upendra Nath Dass* (19 C. W. N. 654), Jenkins C.J. in delivering the judgment of the Court observed : "This burden can be discharged by the evidence of witnesses for the prosecution as well as by evidence for the defence on such a plea being set up ; and the accused are clearly entitled to claim an acquittal if, on the evidence for the prosecution, it is shown that they have committed no offence."

See also *Emperor* v. *Wajid Hossain* (32 All. 451).

Duty to retreat before killing.

I have already said that there is no obligation on a man to escape from danger instead of defending himself, but here a reflection arises in connection with the provisions of Section 98 whether a modification of the principle would not have been wiser. If a mad man attacks you, would it not be more reasonable to insist that if you knew the man was mad and had a chance of escape that you should avail yourself of it. It would have done no harm, for in such a case no one would accuse you of cowardice. However the question is one for the legislature, and, I have no doubt, this is the course which the ordinary man would adopt when attacked by a lunatic instead of killing him.

This duty to retreat and thereby avoid killing an assailant is not a new idea that I am putting forward before you for the first time.

In America it has in some cases been held that it is a question for the jury whether from the evidence the slayer had, apparent to his comprehension as a reasonable man, the means at hand to avoid killing the deceased without incurring imminent danger of losing his own life or of suffering great bodily harm.

The law in England, however, on this point is the same as in India and has been thus stated in Halsbury's Laws of England: "A person lawfully defending himself or his habitation is not bound to retreat or to give way to the aggressor before killing him; he is even entitled to follow him and to endeavour to capture him; but if the aggressor is captured or is retreating without offering resistance and is then killed, the person killing him is guilty of murder."

Sections 97 and 99 have given rise to much controversy and perhaps no portion of the Code has more often been considered judicially than these two sections.

Land riots in Bengal.

In Bengal land riots are matters of daily occurrence and the *chur* lands in Eastern Bengal are the most fruitful sources of riots attended with murder and other grave offences. The most typical cases are these:

A typical case.

A has a plot of land on which he has grown his crops. Before the time of harvesting has come

B attended with a number of *lathials* takes advantage of *A's* absence, enters the land and begins to cut the crops to establish his possession; sometimes it is a plot of land on which at the time of occurrence there are no crops, and *B* goes to plough up the land or finding the land already ploughed and sown he uproots the seedlings for fresh sowing to create evidence of possession. *A* hears of the trespass, collects men, and when he comes to the land he finds a number of persons there prepared to resist *A's* entry. This leads to a riot in which either *A* or *B* gets the worst of it. Sometimes it is the case of a *chur* which is just becoming fit for cultivation when the people of a neighbouring village, having no right, take it into their heads to go and squat there. In the course of the night old huts from the village are removed to the *chur* and erected there. To make their possession sacrosanct they introduce their women folk into those huts. The next morning the people of another village who rightly claim the *chur* as accretion to the land of their village coming to know of it, rush to the *chur* with a number of *lathials*, burn the huts or take possession of them, and then claim to have erected the huts themselves. Men from both sides are found wounded and sometimes killed. Both parties are prosecuted and placed on their trial for offences under Section 147 or 148 with the addition of graver offences of grievous hurt or murder sometimes independently and sometimes by operation of Section 149, in which the common object alleged is to enforce a right or a supposed right. Both parties defend the charge by saying that they were already in possession and therefore, could not be said to have the common object of enforcing a right which means securing such right by means of force, and they claim the protection of the right of private defence of property. It often happens that the party really in possession heard of the encroachment or of the intention to encroach an hour or two before or may be the previous evening, that the Police Station is very close, so that the persons in possession, if they chose, instead of turning out in force to eject the trespassers, might have gone to the Thana and asked for Police interference.

Questions.

On these facts four different questions often arise :—

(*i*) When the owner in possession found the trespassers already in occupation, had he still a possession to defend ?

(*ii*) Was he a member of an unlawful assembly having an unlawful common object or in other words was it the object of the assembly to enforce a right or supposed right ?

(*iii*) Was he bound to apply for the protection of the public authorities ?

(*iv*) Was the apprehension of danger continuing when the right was exercised ?

(*v*) Was the apprehension sufficiently grave to justify the amount of injury caused ?

When is possession lost.

On the first question the authorities are not clear, but the principle has been definitely laid down in several English cases. In *Browne* v. *Dawson* (1840) (12 A. & E. 624) the facts were shortly these :—Plaintiff, a school master, was in possession of a room in a school house. On the 29th of June he was dismissed and the premises were peaceably taken possession of by the trustees of the school and locked up by them. On the 30th the plaintiff returned and re-entered by force. On the 4th of July he was required by notice to depart; and persisting in remaining there he was ejected on the 11th for which an action was brought. Lord Denman C.J., in delivering the judgment of the Court, said: "A mere trespasser cannot, by the very act of trespass, immediately and without acquiescence, give himself what the law understands by possession, against the person whom he ejects, and drive him to produce his title, if he can without delay re-instate himself in former possession. Here by the acquiescence of the plaintiff, the defendants had become peaceably and lawfully possessed as against him, he had re-entered by a trespass: if they had immediately sued him for that trespass, he certainly could not have made out a plea denying their possession. What he could not have done on the 1st July he could as little have done on the 11th, for his tortiously being on the spot was never acquiesced in for a moment; and there was no delay in disputing it. But, if he could not have denied their possession in the action supposed, it follows clearly that they might deny this in the present action; for both parties could not be in possession."

In a later case of *Scott* v. *Mathew Browne & Co. Ltd.* (1884), (51 L. T. 746), Mr. Justice Key quoted this decision with approval and commenting on the decision in *Beddall* v. *Maitland* (1881), (17 Ch. D. 174, 188), in which it was said that when a man is in possession he may use force to keep out a trespasser, but when a trespasser has gained possession the rightful owner cannot use force to put him out, but must appeal to the law for assistance, the learned Judge observed : "Can a man come into my house when I am out, and then say that he claims to be there, and I cannot use force to turn him out? I cannot think that the law would admit of any one taking such a position."

In *Collins* v. *Thomas* (1859), (1 F. & F. 416), it was held that a person having no possessory title to premises, but fraudulently pretending to have such title, and so allowed by the servant of the true owner to enter, does not thereby acquire possession, but may be forcibly expelled by him on discovery of the fraud ; and if in such a case assaults are committed in consequence, the question for the jury will be, whether there has been an excess of violence. A subsequent attempt by force to re-enter and so causing an affray, was an indictable offence, for which the party might be given in charge.

What amounts to acquiescence in such cases cannot be answered merely with reference to the period during which the trespasser has been suffered to remain in occupation. In *Queen* v. *Sachee* alias *Sachee Boler* (7 W. R. 112) fifteen days' possession, in *Moher Sheikh* v. *Queen-Empress* (21 Cal. 392) four or five days' possession and in *Jairam's* case possession for a few hours was held sufficient, whereas in the case of *Chandulla Sheikh* (18 C. W. N. 275) fourteen hours' possession was held insufficient. That question must depend on various circumstances, but there can be little doubt that if the rightful owner goes to the law for his remedy he loses the right of ejecting the trespasser by force.

If the right of defence of property is once recognised in cases of this kind in India, the Indian Courts will not be bound by the limitation regarding the amount of force laid down in those cases. The Indian cases have not gone generally the whole length of the principle stated above, though they have sometimes gone very near it, as will appear from the cases which I propose to discuss under the fourth head. In dealing with the English cases I have quoted, a distinction may reasonably be drawn between cases of wrongful entry into a house and similar entry into waste or culturable land. On this basis the somewhat narrow view of possession taken in Jairam's case (35 Cal. 103) may perhaps be defended. I shall consider this case hereafter. Browne's case was however quoted with approval in *Chandulla Sheikh* v. *The King-Emperor* (18 C. W. N. 275).

The question when a trespass puts an end to the possession of the rightful owner has been often discussed in connection with the interpretation of Section 141 of the Indian Penal Code, which defines the common objects which render an assembly unlawful. In cases where the common object of the assembly was stated to be "to enforce a right or supposed right," the question has been discussed whether such an intention could be attributed to a person who was in possession immediately before the riot and to those who came to his help.

Enforce a right.

This brings us to the consideration of the second question, which though not having a direct bearing on the question of self-defence is intimately connected with it. In the case of *Queen-Empress* v. *Mitto Singh* (3 W. R. Cr. 41), Mr. Justice Campbell, discussing the provisions of Section 141 with special reference to the words, to enforce a right or supposed right, observed: "I think the latter provision applies to an active enforcement of a right not in possession, and not to the defence of a right in possession."

In the case of *Pachkauri* v. *Queen-Empress* (24 Cal. 686) Ghose and Gordon JJ. took the same view: "It seems to us that if the party of the accused were rightfully in possession of the land on the date in question, and if they found it necessary to protect themselves from aggression on the part of the complainant's party, they were justified in taking such precautions as they thought were required. and we think that in doing so they could not rightly be held to be members of an unlawful assembly."

In the more recent case of *Silajit Mahto* v. *Emperor* (36 Cal. 865) Jenkins C.J. and Mukerjee J. said: "Upon the facts which have been established, the common object here was not to enforce any right or supposed right. It was rather to maintain undisturbed the actual enjoyment of a right. If so, no question of unlawful assembly arises." The same view was taken in *Ramnandan Prosad* v. *The Emperor* (17 C. W. N. 1132.)

The decisions on this point have been uniform so far as the principle is concerned, and if there has been any difference of opinion, it has been in respect of the application of the principle to the facts or a particular case.

In the case of *Emperor* v. *Ambica Lal* (35 Cal. 443) where the complainant's party consisting of 12 or 13 persons went with *kodali* to a *bund* erected on the land of the master of the accused, in order to cut it, as it obstructed the flow of water from their lands and destroyed their crops, and the accused hearing of this at once assembled to the number of 50 or 60, and at the time the accused arrived at the scene the complainant's party had either finished the cutting or ceased to do so, and the accused attacked the complainant's party and chased them and killed one man who was not connected with the cutting in any way. Rampini and Sharfuddin JJ. said: "Then it is obvious that the accused's party was from the beginning an unlawful assembly. They went up armed with *lathies* intending to enforce their right at all hazards. Even if it be admitted for argument's sake to have been a lawful assembly at first, it became an unlawful assembly the moment the complainant's party stopped cutting the opening in the *bund* and the accused chased and beat the complainant's party and killed Chatar Dass." If the *bund* was on the land of the accused's maliks and the complainant's party attempted to cut it, the accused were certainly justified in preventing mischief being done to that property. It was another matter altogether if they attacked the complainant's party after they had ceased cutting the *bund* and chased them and killed one of them. Till that moment the assembly cannot be said to have been an unlawful one. Other decisions may be quoted bearing on the question, but it would serve no useful purpose to multiply them.

Protection of public authorities.

On the third question different views have been taken having regard to the different facts and circumstances of a case. The necessity to have recourse to the public authorities for protection cannot be for the mere purpose of regaining or recovering possession of the property, but for the purpose of preventing the trespass on such property, otherwise the restriction will practically take away the right of private defence altogether, as one can always have recourse to the Civil or Criminal Courts for recovering possession from a trespasser. Upon this point Wharton says: "It has been said that the right does not exist when the party attacked had an opportunity of calling on the public authorities to intervene. This, however, is not universally true. As there are few attacks which the injured party could not have more or less clearly expected, it would be incumbent on him, if the position here contested is sound, to call on the Government for protection in every case, or else to lose the right. But to call on the Government for aid is only necessary when such aid can be promptly and effectively given. There are many cases of suspicion also, in which a prudent man would decline to call in Governmental aid, feeling that the case is not sufficiently strong to justify so extreme a remedy. As a rule, therefore, we cannot say that self-defence cannot be resorted to, when the party asserting the right could have protected himself by calling in the Government.

* * * * *

There is no pebble in our way which we could not remove by action of law. But there is no pebble on the high way as to which an action of law would not be absurd. We kick it out of the way. Just as we exert the right of self-defence in innumerable other cases in which going to law would be equally absurd. And we may in like manner forcibly remove an intruder from a house or a railway car without stopping to call in a Magistrate or tear from a wall an insulting libel, or push back from a highway an overhanging bough. If so, we may defend life and limb, though the attack is one we may have so far anticipated as to have been able to call in official aid in advance." (Wharton I ss. 97 a.)

In *Birjoo Singh* v. *Khub Lall* and others (19 W. R. Cr. 66) Couch C.J. said: "The Magistrate seems to have considered that it was the duty of the Rajapur people to offer no opposition whatever to the cutting of the *bund*, that they were to go away to seek the Magistrate, who might be at a great distance and to obtain an order from him, and if they failed in that they were to be left to a civil suit to recover compensation for the injury to their crops from persons whom it might be difficult to identify as those who actually committed the mischief, and from whom, if identified, it might not be possible to recover the amount of the compensation. I think that is a view which cannot be supported."

In this case it does not appear that the information which the accused obtained was either definite enough upon which he was bound to act or was received in good time to enable him to go to the authorities to prevent the trespass.

In *Narsingh Pattabhai* (14 Bom. 441) it was laid down that the apprehension which justifies a recourse to the authorities ought to be based on some information of a definite kind as to the time and place of the danger actually threatened. The accused No. 1 received information, one evening, that the complainants intended to go on his land on the following day and uproot the *jarasi* seed sown in it. At about 3 o'clock next morning he was informed that the complainants had entered on his land and were ploughing up the seed. Thereupon he at once proceeded to the spot, followed by the other accused and remonstrated with the complainant. It was held that the accused were not bound to act on the information received on the previous evening and seek the protection of the public authorities as they had no reason to apprehend a night attack on their property. In dealing with the Law Birdwood J. said: "The right of private defence of property commences when a reasonable apprehension of danger to the property commences. Before such apprehension the owner of the property is not called upon to apply for protection to the public authorities. The apprehension which justifies a recourse to the authorities ought generally to be based on some information of a definite kind, as to the time and place of danger actually threatened."

In Pachkauri's case to which I have already referred, although it appeared that the party of the accused had become aware that the complainant's party wanted to take forcible possession of the land, the accused were held to be justified in collecting a large number of men and going to plough the land, and in taking necessary precaution to protect their possession when the complainant's party attacked them.

On the other hand if definite information, such as a reasonable man can act upon is received in time to enable the party to have recourse to the protection of public authorities and he abstains from so doing, he loses the right of private defence.

In the case of *Queen* v. *Moizuddin* (11 W. R. Cr. 41) the finding of the Sessions Judge was as follows :—" I am unable to say that they are to blame for arming themselves or preparing themselves for the possible contingency of a fight in defence of their property. There is not sufficient evidence to show that there was a certainty of their being attacked on the morning of the 4th June last, and they were aware of it, otherwise it would have been their duty to have had recourse to the protection of the police." Markby J. said : " I would observe, however, that had the Sessions Judge found that Moizuddin (who had struck the fatal blow) and his companions had neglected to take the precautions which the law has pointed out to persons who apprehended a breach of the peace, I should have said the plea of self-defence failed altogether."

A similar view was taken in *Queen* v. *Jeolall* (7 W. R. Cr. 34), in which it was found that both parties knew what was likely to happen for both turned out in force, and the learned Judges observed: "There was a Police Station within easy distance, to which they could have applied for assistance if they had a claim to it, and in any case the Civil Courts were open to them to recover damages from Jeebun for a breach of his contract."

The following observations in the case of *Queen* v. *Mana Singh* (7 W. R. 103) may lead to a misconception unless read in the light of the facts found: "There was time," said the learned Judges, "to have had recourse to the protection of the public authorities; indeed, if they had not gone to the disputed land, there would have been no riot at all."

In the case of Baijanath Dhanuk (36 Cal. 296) when the accused went armed with swords, spears and *lathies* where labourers of the opposite party were reaping some *masuri* crops and attacked them, it was held that the right of private defence existed though it was exceeded, one man being killed.

In the case of *Jairam Mahton* v. *Emperor* (35 Cal. 103) it was held that no man has the right to take the law into his own hands for the protection of his person or property if there is a reasonable opportunity of redress by recourse to the public authorities.

That was a case in which the accused were not in actual possession before, but on the basis of a title acquired from the landlord entered the land by force and attempted to plough the land when they were attacked by the complainant's party who had been in possession for a long time before the occurrence. The Court held that under the circumstances the accused being actually in possession had the right to defend their possession, but as they must have anticipated that their action was likely lead to a riot, the Court (Mitra and Caspersz JJ.) observed: "If a person has the right to possession and was in law constructively in possession, but was not in actual occupation just before the occurrence, he may ordinarily have recourse to the proper authorities for the prevention of any wrong to him, and he should not be allowed to plead the right of private defence of property." It may be doubted if in this case the accused had any possession to defend.

A different view was taken in the case of *Kabiruddin* v. *Emperor* (35 Cal. 368) in which Sharfuddin J. observed: "It is contended on behalf of the appellants that they, having arrived on the spot first, had the right to remain there, and if disturbed in that right they were entitled to set up the plea of the right of private defence. I cannot accept the above proposition as such an enunciation of law would be dangerous to the peace of the country. It would justify a regular race between two factions as to who should arrive first." "The right of private defence would become a force," said Sharfuddin and Cox JJ. in *Chandulla Sheikh* v. *The King-Emperor* (18 C. W. N. 275), "if it depended on a race between two factions, to see who should arrive first." The principle laid down in Browne's case was followed.

As regards the fourth question, it is obvious that when the apprehension of danger is over the right is at an end (Section 105). The danger may disappear in more ways than one. The attacking party may take to flight at the sight of a superior force or may retire having accomplished its purpose. In either case an attack on the retiring party would not be defence but offence.

Continuance of the right.

In the case of *Emperor* v. *Ambika Lall* already referred to, it was said that the assembly became an unlawful assembly the moment the complainant's party stopped cutting the opening in the *bund*, and the accused chased and beat the complainant's party and killed Chater Dass.

When it ceases.

Where an old woman caught stealing was given severe blows which caused her death, it was held by a majority of the Judges that the case was one of murder (5 W. R. Cr. 33). The ground no doubt was that the danger to property if any had disappeared when the woman was caught, after which no right of private defence could be claimed.

Where a person wilfully killed another who was endeavouring to escape after detection in the act of house-breaking by night for the purpose of committing theft, it was held that the case was one of murder, and that there was no right of private defence (5 W. R. Cr. 73).

Where *A* trespassed into the land of *B* whose servants seized and confined *A* till the following day, it was held that the action could not be justified by any right of private defence (13 W. R. Cr. 64).

When the first four questions are answered in favour of the accused the right of private defence is established and then the fifth question arises for consideration, namely, whether the apprehension of danger was sufficiently grave to justify the amount of injury caused.

In the case of *Ganouri Lal* v. *Queen Empress* (16 Cal. 206) the whole question relating to the right of private defence was discussed. The facts were that some of the complainant's servants went upon accused's land for repairing or erecting a *bund.* The accused collected *lathies* and injured five persons. It was held by Pigot and Macpherson JJ., that the accused were rightly convicted of rioting—as complainant's act amounted to a civil trespass, and there was no immediate or pressing necessity of a kind, showing that there was no time to have recourse to the protection of public authorities. This in effect was a case in which the right of private defence was considered to have been exceeded. If only sufficient force were used to eject the complainant's party without causing them any serious injury the plea of the right of private defence would, I am sure, have prevailed. It has been thought that this case has the effect of unduly narrowing the right. **Excessive exercise of the right.**

Whether more harm has been inflicted than was necessary for the purpose of defence is purely a question of fact. In the following cases it was held that the right was not exceeded :— **Right not exceeded.**

(*a*) When a person finding a thief enter his house at night held him by his face down and the latter died of suffocation (3 W. R. Cr. 12).

(b) Where the accused struck a blow with a *lathi* causing death when he was attacked with a spear (11 W. R. Cr. 41).

(c) Where accused gave a blow with *lathi* to a thief stealing crops which were frequently stolen (12 W. R. Cr. 15).

(d) Where accused in resisting a sudden attack upon them for cutting their crops inflicted a wound with a bamboo from the effects of which the man died (14 W. R. Cr. 69).

(e) Where a number of men attacked a kutchery in which there were cash and other properties of the zemindar, and one of the servants shot dead one of the assailants (22 W. R. Cr. 51).

(f) Where the deceased struck a blow on the accused which felled him to the ground and the accused inflicted a blow on the head of the deceased fracturing his skull and causing death (13 C. W. N. 1180).

Right exceeded

In the following cases it was held that the right of private defence had been exceeded :—

(a) Where a thief was caught at night with half his body and his head inside the wall of a house and was struck with a pole five times on the neck. It was held that more harm was done than was necessary. The accused were convicted of culpable homicide not amounting to murder (6 W. R. 50).

(*b*) Where accused wanted to construct a path through joint land belonging to himself and the deceased, and was stopped by the deceased which led to exchange of hot and violent words and the deceased wrested the *kodali* from the hands of the accused who having recovered it struck a violent blow driving the *kodali* right through the skull into the brain which resulted in death 18 days after, it was held that although the prisoner was justified in meeting force by force, he caused more injury than was necessary (6 W. R. Cr. 89).

(*c*) Where deceased attempted to commit house-breaking by night, was subjected to gross maltreatment and strangled by the accused when he was fully in their power and helpless, it was held that there was no right of private defence (14 W. R. Cr. 68).

(*d*) Where a gun was fired from a distance of five and twenty yards when there could not be any imminent danger to the party of the accused, the act was held not justified (17 W. R. Cr. 46).

(*e*) Where a Head Constable unlawfully arrested one of a party of gipsies, and all of them turned out, some four or five being armed with sticks and stones and advanced in a threatening manner towards the Head Constable and were fired with a gun and one of the gipsies was killed, and it appeared that the crowd would have retired if the gipsy who was arrested had been released, it was held that the right of private defence had been exceeded (3 All. 253).

(*f*) Where *A* caused crops to be sown on land, as to the enjoyment of which there was a dispute between her and *B*. Persons having proceeded to reap the crop on behalf of *B*, the servants of *A* went to the place with a police officer and some armed constables. The police officer ordered the reapers to leave off and disperse, but they did not do so, whereupon he ordered one of the constables to fire and he fired into the air. Some of the reapers remained and assumed a defiant attitude. The police officer without attempting to make any arrests and without warning the reapers that, if they did not desist, they would be fired at, gave orders to shoot and one of the constables fired and mortally wounded one of the reapers. It was held that there was no right of private defence as the police officer did not act with good faith (21 Mad. 249).

(*g*) Where the accused three of whom were armed with a sword, *garasa* (scythe) and a *lohanda* (iron stick) respectively and the rest with *lathies*, went in a large body to the disputed land, where the labourers of the opposite party were reaping the crops, attacked them, fatally wounded one and severely injured another, it was held that the accused who ordered the attack and those who used the sword, *garasa* and *lohanda* had exceeded the right of private defence, and so also the others who continued in the unlawful assembly thereafter and aided and abetted the former (36 Cal. 296).

Where the right is exceeded and the injury caused is not justified, the person causing such injury is in the same position as if he had no right of private defence at all.

In cases of murder, however, an excessive exercise of the right reduces the offence to culpable homicide not amounting to murder (Section 300, Exception 2).

A careful study of the important decisions of the various High Courts on the question of the right of private defence, would show that though sometimes they appear to be conflicting, they are fairly in agreement on all essential questions of principle, the difference being generally due to the answer given, in view of the circumstances of each case, to the four questions which I have discussed. For instance, some Courts have held upon particular facts of the case before them that the information that an attack was contemplated was sufficiently definite, and that there was ample time to seek the protection of the authorities. In other cases a different inference has been drawn. In some cases it has been inferred that the danger to property was sufficiently grave to justify the use of force, and that the injury caused was not more than what was necessary. A contrary view has been taken in some other cases. But these differences are differences in respect of inferences of facts drawn by Judges in particular cases. So far as the law is concerned there has been on the whole very little difference of opinion.

The five questions which I have discussed in connection with typical cases of land riots that arise so often in Bengal will serve to elucidate the principles which govern all cases relating to the right of private defence whether they arise upon attempts to commit criminal trespass on land or upon attempts to commit theft, robbery and other offences of the same kind in respect of movable property. The essential principles are the same in all.

The only other question of any difficulty that remains to be considered is the right of private defence against public servants when they purport to act in their official capacity.

Right against public servants.

Section 97, as you have seen, gives the right of private defence only against *offences* affecting the human body or certain *offences* against property. Therefore no right of private defence arises against any act done by a public servant in execution of his duties as such public servant even without the special provisions of Section 99, which are intended to protect only those acts of a public servant which, though not wholly illegal, are not strictly legal. There are cases where a public servant does something which the law does not authorise him to do, or does an act authorised by law without fulfilling the conditions upon which alone the law gives him such authority, or cases where by mistake he exercises his authority against the wrong person. In such cases if the act is one which is wholly unauthorised, a public servant is in the same position as a private individual. Where, however, he acts in good faith and under the colour of his office and the act is one not wholly unauthorised and yet not strictly legal, then he can claim the protection of the first clause of Section 99 unless the act reasonably causes the apprehension of death or of grievous hurt, in which case the person against whom the authority is sought to be exercised is not required to submit to anything which is not strictly legal.

That a public servant should enjoy some amount of immunity, even where he exceeds his authority, is obvious. It would be disastrous if an officer of a court could be assaulted with immunity, because he omitted certain non-essential formalities and his procedure was not quite regular. It will be equally disastrous, if a public servant were allowed recklessly to exercise his authority without proper care and caution, and in defiance of those provisions of the law which are intended to safe-guard the liberty of the subject. In a large number of cases the dividing line is not easy to discover. There are very few reported decisions on the subject in which any definite principle has been laid down for our guidance.

From this point of view the most important case in Bengal is that of *Bisu Halder* v. *The Emperor* (11 C. W. N. 836), where on the complaint of one

G that his wife was wrongfully confined by his father-in-law, a warrant was issued under Section 96, Cr. P. C., which is wholly inapplicable to cases of wrongful confinement. The Police attempting to execute this warrant at the house of the father-in-law was obstructed by him; it was held that the warrant being wholly illegal, Section 99 could not apply. Stephen and Coxe JJ. said: "The question then arises whether the resistance offered in this case comes within the terms contemplated by the first paragraph of Section 99 of the Code, the effect of which would be to deprive the petitioners of a right of private defence he would otherwise have, and this depends on the further question whether the conduct of the Police was not something more than 'not strictly justifiable by law' according to the words of the section, there being no question of their acting in good faith under colour of office. We think the provision of this section does not extend to the case. In Mr. Mayne's Commentary on Criminal Law, Section 225, it is stated that the words 'not strictly justifiable by law' seem to point to cases where there is an excess of jurisdiction, as distinct from a complete absence of jurisdiction, to cases where the official has done wrongly what he might have done rightly, not to cases where the act could not possibly have been done rightly. This seems to us to be a sound exposition of the law and to express exactly what has happened in this case and therefore Section 99 does not apply."

General principle.

This decision may be taken as an authoritative exposition of the principle applicable to cases of this kind. The difficulty, however, arises in determining in particular cases whether the act falls within the one class or the other ; or in other words whether the act is wholly and clearly unjustifiable or whether it was a mere irregularity not affecting the merits of the case.

The following are some of the more important cases in which the acts of public servants were held to be wholly illegal and without jurisdiction and as such not entitled to protection :—

Acts wholly illegal.

(a) Where a peon was under orders of a Forest Settlement Officer impressing carts for the use of the latter and was resisted. *In re the petition of Rakhmaji* (9 Bom. 538).

(b) Where a surveyor attempted to divide a joint property the subject of a Civil Court decree being deputed for the purpose by the Collector of the District—*Queen-Empress* v. *Tulsiram* (13 Bom. 168). Birdwood and Parsons JJ. observed: "The protection which extends to acts not strictly justifiable in law, does not extend to an act which is altogether illegal."

(c) Where a police constable entered upon the premises of a person of suspicious character, and knocked at his door to ascertain if he was there—*Dorasamy Pillai* v. *Emperor* (27 Mad 52).

In the last case Bhashyam Ayyanger J. said: "The constable in entering upon the accused's dwelling house and knocking at his door at midnight with the intention of finding out whether the accused, who is regarded as a suspected character by the police, was in his house, was technically guilty of housetrespass under Section 442 of the Indian Penal Code. The course adopted by the constable was certainly one which would cause annoyance to the inmates of the house, and is also insulting to the accused and under Section 104 the accused was justified in voluntarily causing to the complainant the slight harm he inflicted on him and the constable cannot be regarded under Section 99, Indian Penal Code, as acting in good faith."

(*d*) Where a vaccinator attempted forcibly to vaccinate a child against the wishes of its father and was assaulted. *Bahal* v. *Emperor* (28 All. 481). *See* also *Mangobind Muchi* v. *Empress* (3 C. W. N. 627).

(*e*) Where a constable went to search for purposes mentioned in Section 165, Cr. P. Code, without any written authority, *Idu Mondal* v. *Emperor* (6 C. L. J. 753).

(*f*) Where a police officer conducting a search outside his jurisdiction, with a constable who had jurisdiction, but who had no order from his own Sub-Inspector, was assaulted, it was held that no offence under Section 353 I. P. C. had been committed (13 A. L. J. 691).

(*g*) Where a *surveille* on a domiciliary visit being paid to him by a police officer, refused to allow his thumb impression to be taken and on the officer attempting to take it, produced a *lathi* saying he would not allow the impression to be taken and if any one asked for it he would break his head, it was held that Section 99 of the Penal Code applied to the case. *Birbal Khalifa* v. *Emperor* (30 Cal. 97).

(*h*) Where an excise Sub-Inspector attempted to search the house of a person on information of his being in possession of Gujrat Ganja which not being an excisable article the action of the excise officer in entering and searching the house of the petitioner was without legal authority, it was held that Section 99 of the Indian Penal Code could not protect the excise officer in such a case and an assault on him under the circumstances was no offence. Jagarnath Mandhata (1 C. W. N. 233).

Regarding the legality of warrants of arrests, attachment, etc., the law in England is thus stated—"Arrest on a warrant for misdemeanour is not legal unless it is effected by or in the presence of the person named or designed thereon, and he has the warrant with him for production if necessary." (Russell 737). In a case in which a warrant was given to a constable to arrest *P*, which the constable gave to his son, who went in pursuit of *P*, the constable himself remaining behind at about a quarter of a mile and *P* gave a wound with a knife which, it appeared, he did not hold for resisting

Irregular warrants.

English law.

illegal violence, Parke B. said: "The arrest was illegal as the father was too far off to be assisting in it; and there is no evidence that the prisoner had prepared the knife beforehand to resist illegal violence. If a person receives illegal violence, and he resists that violence with anything he happens to have in his hand, and death ensues, that would be manslaughter." (*R.* v. *Patience*, 7 C. & P. 775). But in order that the officer executing a warrant may claim protection for his act, it is necessary that the process should be legal. "It must not be defective in the frame of it, or bad on the face of it, and must issue in the ordinary course of justice from a Court or Magistrate having jurisdiction in the case" (Russell 738), but it is not necessary to show the validity of the proceeding prior to the grant of the warrant.

Then, again, the protection does not extend to an officer who arrests a person who is intended to be arrested, but whose name is not correctly stated in the warrant. Thus in a case where a Justice issued his warrant directing a constable to arrest *J. H.*, charged with stealing a mare, the constable arrested *R. H.*, who was the party against whom the warrant had been issued and who had been intended to be arrested and who had been supposed to be *J. H.*, his name being really *R. H.*, *J. H.* being his father's name, and the constable was resisted, Coltman J. told the jury that the law would not justify the constable's act, the warrant being against *J.* and not against *R.*, although *R.* was the party intended to be taken." (*Hoye* v. *Bush*, 1 M. & Gr. 775) (Russell, Vol. II, 739-40).

In another case in which the Christian name of the person intended to be taken was omitted without assigning any reason for the omission, the warrant was hold to be bad (*R.* v. *Hood*, 1 Mood. 281) (Russell 740).

The law in England seems to be stricter in favour of the subject.

There are cases in which a warrant is wholly *ultra vires*, not being issued by any authority competent to issue such warrant, or as is more often the case, issued in the exercise of a power which does not exist in the particular case, or is so defective in form or the manner of its execution so reckless or improper as to render the proceeding wholly illegal. On the other hand, there are cases in which a warrant is issued by an authority competent to issue such warrant, but is only slightly defective in form or the manner of its execution is to a certain extent irregular, so that it could not be said that either the warrant or the procedure in execution was in strict conformity with law. The execution of a warrant falling within the first class is a wholly unauthorised act to which the law affords no protection. It is only to cases of the second kind that the law gives protection to the public officer concerned, provided he acts in good faith and without malice, and the mistake or omission does not unduly restrict the liberty of the subject. In all cases of irregularity the question of protection depends on the degree of irregularity. Illegal warrant.

In *Queen-Empress* v. *Jogendra Nath Mukerjee* (24 Cal. 320) where a District Magistrate issued a warrant for the arrest and production of a witness for the purpose of giving evidence to an investigation held by the police, and in attempting to execute such warrant the police arrested the wrong person, and were assaulted in the attempt, it was held by Ghose and Gordon JJ., that there being no provision in the Code of Criminal Procedure whereby a Magistrate could issue a summons or warrant for the arrest of a person to be brought before a police officer to give evidence in an investigation before him, the warrant was illegal, and hence the conviction under Sections 143 and 186 could not be upheld. But generally irregular acts of public servants in connection with the execution of warrants have been held to be protected.

The following are some of the cases in which this principle has been adopted :—

Warrants not strictly legal protected.

(*a*) Where a warrant issued for the arrest of a debtor under the provisions of Section 251 of Civil Procedure Code was initialled and not signed, as it should have been done under the law, and the officer executing the same was forcibly resisted—*Queen-Empress* v. *Janki Prasad* (8 All. 293). It was said by Oldfield J. that the act of the accused did not cease to be an offence on the ground that the act was done in the exercise of the right of private defence, as there is no such right under Section 99 of the Indian Penal Code against an act done or attempted to be done by a public servant acting in good faith under colour of his office, though the act may not be strictly justifiable by law.

(*b*) Where a man was arrested by some police officers without having the warrant with them and without the warrant being duly endorsed to them and the man arrested was rescued by the accused who caused hurt to two constables—*Queen-Empress* v. *Dalip* (18 All. 246). In this case the Court whilst holding that the arrest was illegal was of opinion that the accused could not claim the right of private defence, inasmuch as they were acting in good faith and under the colour of their office.

(*c*) Where a Sub-Inspector of Salt and Abkari attempted, without a search warrant, to enter a house in search of property, the illicit possession of which is an offence under the Madras Abkari Act, and was obstructed and resisted where it was not shown that the officer was acting otherwise than in good faith and without malice—*Queen-Empress* v. *Pukot Kotu* (19 Mad. 349).

(*d*) Where a warrant of distress had been issued for the attachment of the property of defaulters who had failed to pay a house tax, and the officer executing the warrant attached a bucket, a spade belonging to the defaulting potter, although the attachment of such properties was illegal. *Queen-Empress* v. *Poomalai Udayan* (21 Mad. 296). Subramania Ayyar and Davies JJ. in considering whether the circumstances justified the resistance said: "We clearly think that it did not, as the act, however irregular or illegal it may have been, was the act of a public servant acting in good faith under the colour of his office, and against such an act the accused had no right of self-defence under Section 99 of the Indian Penal Code, inasmuch as there was no apprehension of death or of grievous hurt." The remarks in this case are somewhat broader than the words of the Section would seem to justify.

(*e*) Where a proclamation had been issued for the attachment of the property of certain absconding persons, and during the attachment an objection was raised that the property attached did not belong to the absconders, and the accused assuming a threatening attitude prevented the police officer from attaching the property—*Bhai Lal Chowdhury* v. *Emperor* (29 Cal. 417). Prinsep and Stephen JJ. said: "We may add with reference to the facts found in the case that even supposing that the property attached was not the property of the absconders, the rightful owner had no right of private defence of his property, inasmuch as the evidence shows that the police officer was acting in good faith under colour of his office, and even supposing that the order of attachment might not have beer properly made, that would in itself be no sufficient ground. The law, as expressed in Section 99, Explanation 2 of the Indian Penal Code, is clear on this point."

(*f*) Where an order was made to the police purporting to be under Section 145 of the Criminal Procedure Code directing them to take charge of some crops in dispute, and the police went to the spot where the crop was stored and proposed to guard it, and the accused and some men of their party put them into confinement—*Bhola Mahto* v. *Emperor* (9 C. W. N. 125).

It was observed that although the order may not have been strictly lawful, the action of the accused was violently aggressive and not merely self-protection.

Good faith

The question as to what constitutes good faith was raised in the case of *Bhawoo Jivaji* v. *Mulji Dayal* (12 Bom. 377). There the accused, a police constable, was on duty one morning and about 7 A.M., he saw the complainant carrying under his arm three pieces of cloth. Suspecting that the cloth was stolen property, he went up to the complainant and questioned him, and getting an answer which he considered to be unsatisfactory he took hold of one of the pieces to examine it more closely. The complainant objected and there was a scuffle between them, and the accused arrested the complainant. Birdwood and Farran JJ. said : " If he had an honest suspicion, as we think he had, even though the same facts might not have raised any suspicion in the mind of a police officer of higher grade, still he acted, we think, with due care putting in questions, the answers to which might clear away his suspicion. The putting of questions under these circumstances was in itself an indication of good faith as defined in Section 52, Indian Penal Code...........He himself, as we think, believed that he was legally justified in detaining the cloth ; and though he was entirely mistaken as to the character of the complainant, we think that his belief as to his legal right was a *bona fide* belief and that he is protected by Section 79, Indian Penal Code. If he acted with due care and attention, such as ought to be expected from a constable in his position, in the circumstances in which he was placed, then he acted in good faith ; and even though his act might not have been strictly justifiable by law that is, even though there might not have been a complete basis of fact to justify a reasonable suspicion that the cloth was stolen property—still the complainant had no right of private defence, as the accused was a public servant acting under colour of his office, and his act was not one which caused the apprehension of death or of grievous hurt."

There are numerous cases in which convictions under section 186 have been set aside by reason of slight defects in the warrants or irregularity in the procedure, but the considerations that arise in dealing with cases under that section are materially different and do not help in the interpretation of section 99. Decisions under section 353 have however a more direct bearing on the provisions of section 99 relating to public servants. Section 186 and 353 Distinguished.

CHAPTER XIII.

THE TRIAL.

In my previous lectures I have discussed the principles relating to the substantive law of crimes. In my introductory lecture, I have explained to you what crimes are and how they differ from civil injuries. I have told you that a crime must be an act or an omission and that an omission to be punishable must be one in breach of a legal duty, I have explained what those omissions are, what is meant by an act that an act or omission must be that of a rational human being capable of distinguishing right from wrong, and that the criminal act must be the outcome of an evil intent. Incidentally I have discussed the question of the liability of corporations for crimes. I have tried at some length to explain to you what evil intent means, and in Lecture III, I have discussed the question of inchoate crimes, and have told you that ordinarily a mere intention or even a preparation to commit a criminal act is not punishable, and that among inchoate acts what is punishable is an attempt, which in the technical sense in which it is used in criminal law is something representing a stage after preparation. I have dealt at some length upon the difference between attempts and preparations. I have also explained to you in this connection the meaning of abetments and conspiracies to commit crimes. I have devoted the whole of the fifth lecture to an explanation of *mens rea* as a necessary ingredient in crimes, and have discussed the circumstances in which *mens rea* may be imputed to a person charged with a criminal act. I have then attempted to explain in some detail the meaning of the various terms used in the Indian Penal Code to denote the *mens rea* for various classes of offence defined in the Code.

In Lectures VII, VIII and IX, I have dealt with the provisions of Chapter IV of the Code which may be said generally to deal with matters which negative *mens rea* or in other words with the conditions of non-imputability. In connection with the Chapter of General Exceptions I have dealt with the following matters :—

(1) Mistakes of law and fact. Sections 76 and 79.

(2) Exemption from liability of judicial officers and those acting under their orders. Sections 77-78.

(3) Accident. Section 80.

(4) Harm caused to prevent greater harm. Section 81.

(5) Mental incapacity—
Infancy—Sections 82 and 83.
Insanity—Section 84.
Drunkenness—Sections 85 and 86.

(6) Consent. Sections 87, 88, 89, 90, 91 & 92.

(7) Compulsion. Section 94.

(8) Acts causing slight harm. Section 95.

(9) Right of private defence. Sections 96-104.

As the last question is one of great importance I have dealt with this separately in Lecture XII, and have for a better understanding of the subject devoted a lecture explaining the meaning of possession in criminal law.

In these twelve lectures all the important questions of principle have come under consideration.

When the principles governing the Law of Crimes are understood the next thing to consider is the method of trial.

In India there is no division of crimes between treasons, felonies and misdemeanours. There is only a division between Summons cases and Warrant cases. A warrant case is the case of an offence punishable with death, transportation or imprisonment for a term exceeding six months (Section 4 clause *w*). All other cases are Summons cases.

The Complaint.

There are some cases in which the party injured must himself complain otherwise the court cannot take cognizance in the case. These are offences relating to contracts of service, those relating to marriage or defamation. There are certain other offences of a political character in which the sanction of the Local Government is necessary for initiating criminal proceedings. Then there are certain other offences relating to proceedings in courts of Justice or which concern public servants which cannot be entertained by a Magistrate without the sanction of the Court or without the complaint of the public servant concerned (Section 195). In the last mentioned cases Civil and Revenue Courts are also authorised to send offenders for trial to the nearest Magistrate at their own instance.

Subject to these provisions of the Code a Magistrate can take cognizance of an offence in one of the three ways mentioned in section 190 of the Criminal Procedure Code, *i.e.*—

(*a*) Upon a complaint

(*b*) Upon a police report.

(*c*) Upon information from any person other than a police officer or upon the Magistrate's own information.

In a case instituted upon complaint the Court first examines the complainant and then makes any further inquiry that it thinks necessary, and then either dismisses the complaint or issues process against the accused. When the accused appears if the case is one triable exclusively by the Court of Sessions, the Magistrate holds an inquiry and if a *prima facie* case is made out he commits the case for trial to the Court of Sessions and the accused is tried there, generally, with the aid of a Jury, and in a few Districts with the aid of Assessors.

The procedure in the trial of summons and warrant cases is slightly different. In a summons case the Magistrate is not bound to frame a charge but it is sometimes done and the accused is asked as soon as he appears if he is guilty and if he admits his guilt he is convicted and sentenced forthwith; but if he does not admit then evidence is taken on behalf of the prosecution and also such evidence as the accused may choose to adduce. The Magistrate then, as a rule, examines the accused without administering an oath to him after which he either acquits or convicts and passes sentence. In cases instituted on complaint if on the day fixed or on any adjourned date of hearing the complainant is absent, the accused is acquitted. In cases of frivolous and vexatious charges

Principle of oath to accused.

instituted on complaint or on information to a police officer or to a Magistrate, the Magistrate may on acquitting the accused direct the payment of compensation to him. This power is common to both Summons and Warrant cases.

The procedure in warrant cases is somewhat different. Being of a more serious character the accused is entitled to know the precise charge that he has to meet. So long as he does not know, he can not be called upon to enter on his defence, and obviously the precise nature of the charge can not be indicated until the Magistrate knows what the evidence is. The result therefore is that whereas in a summons case the accused is asked to plead at the very beginning, he is not asked to do so in a warrant case. When he appears the evidence for the prosecution is first recorded. The Magistrate then examines the accused, the object of such examination being to give the accused an opportunity of explaining away any circumstance that may appear against him in the evidence. The Magistrate may then if he has not already discharged the accused, discharge him, if in his opinion there is not sufficient evidence for framing a charge against him; but if the evidence is sufficient the Magistrate frames a charge. If he thinks the case against the accused is not established he may at any stage discharge him, but if he comes to that conclusion after the charge is framed he acquits the accused. An order of discharge may be set aside by a superior Court but an order of acquittal can only be set aside by the High Court.

Accused as a witness.

The charge must contain the following particulars:— The Charge.

(*a*) The offence with which the accused is charged is to be described by name, if any, and by the Section of the Code under which it falls.

(*b*) Particulars as to time and place of the offence alleged, the person against whom or the thing in respect of which it was committed and such other matters as may be sufficient to enable the accused to know the precise charge which he has to meet.

If the charge is defective, a conviction based upon such a charge may be set aside by a court of appeal or revision if the defect did in fact mislead the accused and has occasioned a failure of justice. But before judgment is pronounced the charge may always be altered or amended. When a charge is framed the accused then enters upon his defence. He is asked to say whether he is guilty or has a defence to make. He is not bound to answer any questions. It is his privilege to stand mute if he chooses. Even if he pleads guilty the law, in its tenderness towards an accused person, leaves it to the discretion of the Magistrate to convict the accused upon his own plea or not to do so. If the accused refuses to plead or does not plead or claims to be tried, he is asked whether he wishes to cross examine the witnesses for the prosecution. He has this right even if he has cross examined the witnesses before charge, and the only ground upon which this right can be refused, is that it is made for the purpose vexation or delay. Accused then, if he chooses, calls evidence in his defence and in doing so is entitled to all reasonable assistance of the court. If the Magistrate finds the accused not guilty, he acquits the accused, but if he finds him guilty he convicts and sentences him.

Discharge.

An order of discharge is no bar to a fresh trial on the same facts. In a warrant case the absence of the complainant does not put an end to the trial except where the offence is compoundable, in which case it is in the discretion of the Magistrate to discharge the accused at any time before the charge is framed. What offences are compoundable are stated in section 345 of the Criminal Procedure Code. In a summons case there is no distinction between a discharge and an acquittal.

Nolle Prosequi.

It is the right of the Crown at any stage of a trial but before judgment is pronounced, to enter a *nolle prosequi*. Section 333 gives the power to the Advocate-General in cases tried before the High Court. In other cases the Public prosecutor performs a similar function, (Section 494).

There are certain offences which are triable summarily as provided for in Chapter XXII of the Criminal Procedure Code.

In cases triable by the High Court or the Court of Sessions there is an enquiry by a Magistrate preliminary to commitment. When committed the accused is tried either with the aid of assessors or with the aid of a Jury. The Judge is not bound to accept the opinion of assessors, but he can not convict or acquit an accused against the opinion of a Jury or a majority of the Jurors as the case may be. If he differs he refers the case to the High Court.

He is not in any case bound to accept the verdict. But in cases tried by the High Court the Judge is bound to accept the unanimous verdict of the Jury or the opinion of the majority when divided in the proportion of 6 : 3. Jury.

The Crown as well as the accused have the absolute right of challenging a certain number of Jurymen in trials before the High Court, but for the Mufassil this can only be done on good cause shown. In a trial by Jury when the evidence is closed the case is argued on behalf of the prosecution and defence. If the accused adduces no evidence he has the last word. When the arguments are over the Judge charges the Jury, summing up the evidence for the prosecution and defence and laying down the law.

The Judge is required in a Jury trial to record only the heads of charge to the Jury. Judges of the High Court are not bound to make any such record. The Jury is bound by the directions of the Judge regarding all questions of law, but as to facts they are the sole Judges. The Judge decides all questions of law including questions as to admissibility of documents, their construction and other matters mentioned in Section 298 Criminal Procedure Code.

An appeal lies to the High Court from a conviction in Sessions Cases both on questions of law and fact, but in the case of trial by a Jury an appeal lies only on questions of law. A question of sentence is a question of law. The local Government has Sec. 418.

the right of appeal even in cases tried by a Jury and the appeal lies both on questions of law and fact. The accused has the right of appeal in some cases but not in all (Chap. XXXI). A sentence of death can not be carried into execution without confirmation by the High Court whether the accused appeals or not. The matter always comes upon a reference under section 307 and even when the trial is by Jury, the High Court has to consider the case both on law and facts.

Evidence.

This is a very general summary of the procedure at the trial. The evidence in criminal cases must as a rule, be recorded in the presence of the accused. Evidence recorded by one Magistrate cannot be used by another if the accused insists on a trial *de novo* (Sec. 350).

The question of evidence in criminal cases requires special consideration. Although the provisions of the Evidence Act, where there is no indication to the contrary, apply both to evidence in civil and criminal cases, there is a marked difference between the two regarding the method of its treatment. First, as regards the quantum of evidence, whereas a mere preponderance of probability due regard being had to the burden of proof, is a sufficient basis of decision, in criminal cases a much higher degree of assurance is required. There is first the general presumption of innocence which has to be rebutted in every case. This is not an artificial rule of law, but is founded on the undoubted fact established by universal experience that the human mind is naturally averse to crimes and that the graver the offence the greater is the aversion. The most confirmed pickpocket may not hesitate to commit an act of theft, but however depraved he may be, he would still retain an aversion to kill a child for the sake of its ornaments. Naturally the degree of evidence required to convince the mind must vary in proportion to the gravity of the offence charged. The graver the crime, the clearer and the plainer ought to be the proof of it. This seems to be common sense. It is a princiciple upon which we act in the ordinary concerns of our life. We take greater care and insist on greater satisfaction when we purchase a horse than we do when purchasing a sheep and very much more care when purchasing a piece of valuable land. Theoretic objections have however been raised to the application of the principle by an eminent Judge, who said—

"......Nothing will depend upon the comparative magnitude of the offence ; for be the alleged crime great or small, every man standing in the situation in which the prisoner is placed, is entitled to have the charge against him clearly and satisfactorily proved." *R.* v. *Ings.* 33 St. Tr. 1135.

The next point for consideration is the infinitely greater misery and suffering which the sentence of a criminal Court entails than the decree of a Civil Court. In the former often a man's life is at stake whereas in the latter it is only his property. These considerations have given rise to the well known maxim of law that it is better that ten guilty men should escape than that one innocent man should suffer (Per Holyroyd J. in *Sara Hobson's* Case).

Onus of Proof.

The principles enunciated above have greatly influenced the rules relating to the onus of proof and degree of certainty required for a conviction in criminal cases. It has been laid down repeatedly and has never been questioned, that though in civil cases a mere preponderance of evidence would suffice that is not enough for criminal cases. Probability may constitute sufficient ground for a verdict and if the matter is doubtful the Jury may found their verdict upon that which appears the most probable. Willes J. in *Cooper* v. *Slade* (6 H. L. C. 77).

'What is necessary in such cases' said Baron Parke in *R.* v. *Sterne* (Sum. Ass. 1843 M. S.) 'is such moral certainly as convinces the mind of the tribunal as reasonable men beyond all doubt.'

The same principle has been enunciated in various cases in India.

Sir Elijah Impey C. J. in charging the Jury in *Nanda Coomar's* case observed:—"You will consider on which side the weight of evidence lies, always remembering that in criminal and more especially in Capital cases you must not weigh the evidence in a golden scale; there ought to be a great difference of weight in the opposite scale before you find the prisoner guilty."

In *Reg.* v. *Madhab Chandra* (21 W. R. cr. 13) better known as the Mohunt of Tarakeswar's case. "It seems to me" said Birch J. "that the only distinction, if any, which can be drawn between civil and criminal cases as to the amount of proof requisite is this. In ordinary Civil Cases a Judge of fact must find for the party in whose favour there is a preponderance of proof, although the evidence be not entirely free from doubt. In criminal cases no weight of preponderant evidence is sufficient short of that which excludes all reasonable doubt. The party accused is entitled to the benefit of the legal presumption in favour of innocence, and in doubtful cases that may suffice to turn the scale in his favour, the burden of proof is undoubtedly upon the prosecutor ; if upon such proof as he adduces there is reasonable doubt remaining, the accused is entitled to the benefit of it."

The doubt however is not the doubt of a timid and vacillating mind, but an honest and conscientious doubt. In no country, much less in India, does a court of justice meet a case where the evidence makes an inference of guilt absolutely certain and the law does not require that degree of certainty but reasonable certainty is all that is necessary—such certainty upon which one would act in his own grave and important concerns. L. C. Baron Pollock in *Reg.* v. *Manning.*

The prisoner being put on his trial for a criminal offence it is for the prosecution to make out a distinct case against him ; not for the prisoner in the first instance to justify himself and show that he had just and lawful grounds. The prosecution must establish everything essential for the establishment of the charges and the inculpating facts must be shown to be inconsistent with the hypothesis of innocence.

Where for instance it was established that a criminal act was committed either by A or B in the absence of definite proof that any one of them in particular was responsible for the act, the benefit of the doubt would be given to both and both would be acquitted. (*Nibaran Chandra Roy* v. *King-Emperor*, 11 C. W. N. 1085).

It is also a rule of law dictated by considerations such as those I have already stated that a penal statute must be strictly construed. In *R.* v. *Bond* (1 B. & Ald. 390 at 392) Abbot J. said "It would be extremely wrong that a man should, by a long train of conclusions be reasoned into a penalty when the express words of the Act of Parliament do not authorise it."

Willes J. said in *Britt.* v. *Robinson* (L. R. 5 C. and P. 503 at 513) "That criminal enactments are not to be extended by construction and that when an offence against the law is alleged and when the court has to consider whether the alleged offence falls within the language of a criminal Statute, the court must be satisfied not only that the spirit of the legislative enactment has been violated but also that the language used by the legislature includes the offence in question and makes it criminal." These cases were referred to and the principle underlying them was applied by Pontifex and Field JJ. in the case of *Empress* v. *Kola Lalang* (8 Cal. 214).

As regards guilty knowledge that is often incapable of direct proof and has to be inferred from surrounding circumstances, the presumption being that every man knows the consequences of his own act. The first thing to establish is that an offence has been committed or in other words that the *corpus delicti* has been proved. It is then and then alone that the question whether the offence was committed by a particular person at all arises; *e.g.*, in a case of theft it must be shown that some thing has been stolen ; or in a case of murder that some person has been killed. "This" says Stephen in his Introduction to the Indian Evidence Act "is the foundation of the well-known rule that the *corpus delicti* should not in general in criminal cases be inferred from other facts, but should be proved independently." As observed by Norman J. in *Queen* v. *Ahmed Ally* (11 W. R. cr. 27). "Every criminal charge involves two things : *first*, that a crime has been committed ; and *secondly*, that the accused is the author of it. It is almost a universal rule that crime is not to be presumed "*Diligenter cavendum est judice supplaecam pricipite antequam crimine constiterit.*" If a criminal fact is ascertained,—an actual *corpus delicti* established presumptive proof is admissible to fix the crime, remembering at the same time that criminal intent or knowledge is not necessarily imputable to every body who acts against the law. "Has the Crown proved substantively that he had a guilty knowledge ? The Sessions Judge says that every man must be presumed to know the law. So he must in a certain sense. But it does not follow that criminal intent or knowledge is necessarily to be imputed to every man who acts contrary to the law" (Per Macpherson J. in *Queen* v. *Nobokisto Ghose*, 8 W. R. cr. 87 at 92).

It is a settled rule that it is unsafe to convict on the uncorroborated testimony of an accomplice, it is not a rule of law, but only a rule of practice, which is said to have 'all the reverence of law, evolved out of a long course of judicial experience. An accomplice is a guilty associate in a crime. Accomplices.

The same principle applies to a person, who knows ot a crime being intended or committed, but takes no steps to prevent it or to disclose it. The corroboration must be by independent evidence, connecting the accused with the crime. One accomplice cannot be corroborated by another. As I have said this is a rule of practice only so that if a Jury convict upon the uncorroborated testimony of an accomplice the conviction is not against law and cannot be set aside on appeal. But if the judge fails to caution the Jury that would amount to a misdirection.

Confession. A confession made by an accused person if caused by any inducement, threat or promise, proceeding from a person in authority is wholly inadmissible. Confessions to be admissible must be voluntary. A confession is not defined in the Evidence Act, but the definition suggested by Sir James Stephen, the author of the Act, is this "A confession is an admission made at any time by a person charged with a crime, stating or suggesting the inference that he committed the crime." A confession made to a Police Officer cannot be proved as against a person accused of any offence, and no confession made by a person whilst he is in the custody of a police officer is admissible, unless it is made in the immediate presence of a Magistrate. But when any fact is deposed to as discovered in consequence of information received from a person accused of any offence, in the custody of a police officer, so much of such information, whether it amounts to a confession or not as relates distinctly to the fact thereby discovered, may be proved.

The confession of an accused even when voluntary is only evidence against him, not evidence against others, even when on trial with the accused unless the confession is such that the accused thereby implicates himself to the same extent as he implicates the others. Where he tries to minimise his own share in the criminal act, the confession cannot be considered against the co-accused. The same rule applies to a statement made by an accused in the course of his examination at the trial. It is common experience that accused persons often retract a confession after having made it, and courts generally refuse to place any reliance upon such retracted confession except against the person making it. The accused can never be examined on oath nor can he be cross-examined. Even the Court cannot compel him to answer any questions.

The rule is different in France, but in England the law has been altered by the Criminal Evidence Act 1898 and the accused is a competent though not a compellable witness. There is a suggestion to introduce a similar rule of law in this country.

That an accused person is of good character is relevant, but unless such evidence has been given in a case, the fact that he has a bad character is irrelevant.

Autrefois acquit.

There is nothing exactly of the nature of the doctrine of *Res-Judicata* applicable to Criminal Cases. But there is the principle of *autrefois acquit*, which forbids any person being put to jeopardy for the same act twice over. There are limitations to this rule which will be found in Sec. 403 of the Cr. P. Code.

Sentence.

Lastly of the question of sentence. In all systems of modern law a wide latitude is given to the courts in this matter. It is one of the most unsatisfactory features of the law as introducing a large element of uncertainty in the administration of criminal justice. Attempts to standardise sentences have hitherto met with little success. In the Indian Penal Code the only instance of a fixed sentence is to be found in section 302, (murder). In cases of murder there are only two alternative sentences which a court is competent to pass, namely, a sentence of death or transportation for life.

Under Section 401 the Governor-General in Council or the Local Government is authorised conditionally or unconditionally to suspend the execution of any sentence passed by any court or remit the whole or part of any such sentence.

ERRATA.

Page 14 line 18 *after wondered insert at.*
,, 17 ,, 28 *for set read sit.*
,, 24 ,, 17 ,, annonymous *read* anonymous.
,, 35 ,, 11 ,, naccuracy ,, inaccuracy.
,, 38 ,, 19 ,, omissoins ,, omissions.
,, 38 ,, 22 ,, tary *read* tory.
,, 118 ,, 2 ,, et ,, let.
,, 162 (marginal note) *for* causa *read* causal.
,, 175 line 15 *for* well being ,, well-being.
,, 185 ,, 26 ,, stupified ,, stupefied.
,, 187 ,, 26 ,, moralt urpitude *read* moral turpitude.
,, 196 ,, 3 ,, offen *read* often.
,, 215 ,, 22 ,, grevious *read* grievous.
,, 222 ,, 6 ,, Rex ,, Lex.
,, 224 ,, 10 ,, lier ,, liar.
,, 265 ,, 26 ,, person and unin—*read* person unin—
,, 300 ,, 23 ,, medicals fficer ,, medical officer.

INDEX.

A